Buying and Selling
Private Companies
and Businesses

D1352286

Buying and Selling Private Companies and Businesses

Humphrey Wine
LL B, ATII, Solicitor

Third Edition

London
Butterworths
1986

United Kingdom	Butterworth & Co (Publishers) Ltd, 88 Kingsway, LONDON WC2B 6AB and 4 Hill Street, EDINBURGH EH2 3JZ
Australia	Butterworths Pty Ltd, SYDNEY, MELBOURNE, BRISBANE, ADELAIDE, PERTH, CANBERRA and HOBART
Canada	Butterworths Canada Ltd, TORONTO and VANCOUVER
Ireland	Butterworth (Ireland) Ltd, DUBLIN
Malaysia	Malayan Law Journal Sdn Bhd, KUALA LUMPUR
New Zealand	Butterworths of New Zealand Ltd, WELLINGTON and AUCKLAND
Puerto Rico	Equity de Puerto Rico, Inc, HATO REY
Singapore	Malayan Law Journal Pte Ltd, SINGAPORE
USA	Butterworth Legal Publishers, AUSTIN, Texas; BOSTON, Massachusetts; CLEARWATER, Florida (D & S Publishers); ORFORD, New Hampshire (Equity Publishing); ST PAUL, Minnesota; and SEATTLE, Washington

British Library Cataloguing in Publication Data

Wine, Humphrey
  Buying and selling private companies and
  businesses. — 3rd ed.
  1. Private companies — Registration and transfer
  —England
  I. Title
  344.206'6626   KD2115

ISBN 0 406 42418 7

First edition	1980
Second edition	1983
Third edition	1986

Made and printed in Great Britain by
Butler & Tanner Limited, Frome and London

Preface

In this third edition alterations and additions have been made to the text to take account of (inter alia) the passing of the Companies Act 1985 and related Regulations; a new 'Yellow Book' which includes the statutory requirements imposed by The Stock Exchange (Listing) Regulations 1984; and the Stock Exchange's booklet on the Unlisted Securities Market. I have also added brief sections in the text on the relevant provision of the Restrictive Practices Act 1976 and the Competition Act 1980. Tax legislation passed since the last edition was written has necessitated amendment in particular to those sections of the book respectively concerned with stamp duty and capital gains tax 'retirement relief'. Since the book went to press a number of changes in tax legislation have been proposed in the 1986 Budget. In particular, relief from stamp duty on takeovers, schemes of reconstruction and demergers will be withdrawn from 25 March 1986. Subject to certain conditions, company reconstructions involving no change of ownership will remain exempt.

Unfortunately my forecast in the preface of the last edition regarding the Transfer of Undertakings (Protection of Employment) Regulations 1981 that 'certain matters of interpretation will be in doubt' has proved correct. The continuing appearance of learned critiques on the 1981 Regulations, and on cases decided thereunder, bears witness to the continuing uncertainty of the law in this area.

It cannot be stressed too much that this book should be treated as a point of departure rather than as a final destination.

Accordingly, the warning footnote concerning use of the precedents which appeared in previous editions, has been printed in bold. Vendors and purchasers who read this book should of course not proceed on any transaction without appropriate professional advice.

I wish to thank Patrick Harrex and Bob Murgatroyd of Spicer and Pegler for reading the manuscript and for their comments on it. They have been most generous of their time. Peter J. Scott, Solicitor, has over the years read and commented on the manuscripts of all three editions of this book—special thanks go to him for both his time and his patience. As always, this book could not have been written, nor revisions to it made, without the encouragement of my wife. It is, she says, the perfect excuse for my opting out of household chores. I agree with her.

The law is stated as at 1 December 1985.

Humphrey Wine,
London SW14.

Contents

Abbreviations

The following abbreviations are used in this book:

1948 Act	The Companies Act 1948
1980 Act	The Companies Act 1980
1981 Act	The Companies Act 1981
1985 Act	The Companies Act 1985
ICTA 1970	Income and Corporation Taxes Act 1970
CGTA 1979	Capital Gains Tax Act 1979
FA	Finance Act
EPCA	Employment Protection (Consolidation) Act 1978
1981 Regulations	Transfer of Undertakings (Protection of Employment) Regulations 1981

Table of Statutes

Table of Cases

1 Introduction

There are two principal methods of acquiring a commercial enterprise. The first is to acquire the assets (and possibly liabilities), which make up that enterprise. The collection of assets and liabilities making up a commercial enterprise is for the purposes of this book subsequently referred to as a business. The second, which applies only if the enterprise is being conducted by a company, is to acquire control of the company through the acquisition of its shares.

The two methods of acquiring an enterprise are fundamentally different in their legal effect, even if the commercial effect may prove similar. In the case of the acquisition of a business the purchaser acquires a collection of tangibles and intangibles which will be incorporated directly into the purchaser's balance sheet. Where, however, a company is acquired, the company's underlying assets and liabilities will continue to belong to the company and the only items appearing in the purchaser's balance sheet will be the shares in the company at their acquisition cost. All the rights of and against the company being acquired will continue to be enforceable by or against that company with no direct effect on the purchaser, except on the value of its investment.

Sometimes there is no choice in the method to be used for purchasing the enterprise, because, for example, it is conducted by an individual or partnership or because, although conducted by a company, it is one of a number of enterprises run by the company. Where there is a choice, the purchaser will often prefer to acquire assets (with or without liabilities) rather than shares because (i) the documentation and investigation is simpler; (ii) the assets and, more particularly, the liabilities being acquired are more certain; (iii) no capital allowances are available on the acquisition of shares whereas (given the presence of other qualifying circumstances) they are available on the acquisition of plant and machinery; (iv) on a share purchase that part of the consideration which reflects the value of the company's trading stock will not be deductible from the purchaser's profits for tax purposes. On the other hand, the vendor will usually prefer to realise a capital gain on the sale of the shares rather than have the gain within its company and the consequent problems of avoiding excessive fiscal penalties on getting it out. This will be the case especially where the vendor has unrelieved capital losses.

The companies expressed to be bought or sold in this book are (i) unquoted, (ii) limited by shares and incorporated under the Companies Act 1985[1] and (iii) private. A company is a private company unless, being limited by shares or limited by guarantee and having a share capital, its memorandum states that it is to be a public company, and unless it has on or after 22 December 1980 complied with the provisions of the 1985 Act or of former Companies Acts as to registration or re-registration as a public company[2]. This means, for example, that every company incorporated as private under the Companies Act 1948 and which was private on 22 December 1980 will remain private in the absence of some positive act by it to re-register as public. Because, for some years to come, practitioners will have to deal with many companies incorporated under the Companies Act 1948[3], it is worth stating that a company was private on 22 December 1980 if on that date it was a private company as defined by the Companies Act 1948, section 28, that is a company which by its articles of association:

(a) restricted the right to transfer its shares, and

(b) limited the number of its members to 50 excluding employees and certain ex-employees, and

---

[1] Companies Act 1985, s. 1(3).

[2] There are many companies in existence incorporated under the 1929 Companies Act to which reference should then be made.

[3] Companies Consolidation (Consequential Provisions) Act 1985, s. 31(8); Companies Act 1985, s. 746.

(c) prohibited any invitation to the public to subscribe to any shares or debentures of the company.

Such restriction, limitation and prohibition were contained in Part II of Table A of the 1948 Act so that any company the articles of which are expressed to adopt Part II is private, and the 1985 Act does not affect the application of Table A of the Companies Act 1948 to any company existing immediately before 1 July 1985, the commencement date of the 1985 Act[4]. Companies incorporated after 21 December 1980 will not have incorporated Part II of Table A of the 1948 Act since Part II was then repealed for such companies, but there was no statutory necessity for them to do so in order to be private. A private company, whenever incorporated and whether containing the prohibition in its articles or not, is prohibited from offering shares or debentures to the public. Because contravention of the prohibition constitutes a criminal offence, it is nevertheless advisable to incorporate the prohibition into a company's articles as a reminder.

However the enterprise is to be acquired, the question remains how best to do it. Perhaps because these transactions are not everyday concerns for most solicitors, and do not have as long a history as do transactions in land, they are free of many of the usual practices of conveyancing. It is advisable for the preparation of the draft contract for the purchase and sale of shares to be undertaken by the purchaser's solicitor because of the extensive warranties required of the vendor, but the practice is not universal. The tendency is for solicitors for whose client's protection the agreement is framed to prepare the draft of that agreement. Thus X Limited may wish to buy a majority holding in AB Limited on the basis that A and B (on whose expertise AB Limited depends) will continue as full time service directors of AB Limited for some period, at the end of which A and B require X Limited to purchase their remaining shares. The purchaser's solicitors will probably draft the agreement for sale of shares and the service agreements of A and B with AB Limited. The vendors' solicitors will, however, wish to be responsible for the put option agreement and for the agreement protecting A and B's minority position pending their exercise of the option (in practice these will be amalgamated into a single document).

---

[4] Companies Act 1985, s. 81(1).

As regards the sale of businesses some solicitors try to mould standard sets of conveyancing conditions into an agreement for the sale of a business. The risk in this practice is in putting undue emphasis on that part of the business in question which consists of an interest in land, and in overlooking the other assets which make up the business. For that reason, the better practice is for the purchaser's solicitors to prepare the draft contract of sale incorporating by reference, but not using, one of the standard sets of printed conditions insofar as an interest in land is being transferred, and leaving space for the vendor's solicitors to include conditions as to title.

2 The Subject Matter of the Transaction

Accurate identification of the subject matter of the transaction is an essential prerequisite of an effective agreement for its purchase. An obvious enough statement perhaps, but answering the question: what are you buying? requires care. Indeed, because the purchase or sale of a concern often involves more than a transfer of ownership of assets, a better question may be: what position do you wish to achieve on completion? For the purpose of this book (except for the section on minority shareholders) it is assumed that the answer will be: complete control of the concern.

Achieving control of the concern requires control over its constituent assets. If these assets are owned by a company either the assets must be acquired from that company or control must be acquired over the company itself. The latter is achieved by obtaining control over the composition of its board of directors. If the assets are owned by an individual or a partnership the outright acquisition of the assets will usually be the appropriate method, but creating or expanding a partnership could provide an alternative where, say, both parties wish the seller to remain closely connected with the business. Assuming, however, that the assets are owned by a company and that the preferred method is control over the company's board of directors, it will be necessary to examine the constitution of the company.

A limited company is a separate legal person. Subject to certain statutory exceptions a company is solely responsible for its own acts. Its assets, as well as its liabilities, are its own and not those of the shareholders or directors. The general rule is that the management of the company's business is vested in its board of directors and that the control over the composition of the board of directors is vested in the holders of the majority of the issued shares of the company. It therefore becomes necessary to examine at an early stage the company's constitution as contained in its memorandum and articles of association to see whether it contains anything involving a departure from these rules. The memorandum and articles of association are the written agreements adopted by the first shareholders on the company's incorporation and lodged with the Registrar of Companies at that time. They are available for public inspection and any alteration to the memorandum and articles which the members of the company subsequently resolve to make must also be filed with the Registrar and thus be available for inspection. If, therefore, a company's file at Companies House is up-to-date there will be no difficulty in discovering its constitution.

The memorandum of most limited companies is straightforward. It contains the company's name; a statement that the liability of the members of the company is limited; the amount of the company's authorised share capital on incorporation; a statement as to the situation of its registered office; and the company's objects. The rules concerning transfer of shares, rights attaching to shares, election and resignation of directors and directors' powers are usually all contained in the articles of association (as altered by any special resolution adopted subsequent to incorporation). Since these are the rules governing effective control of the company, scrutiny of them is vital. For example the company's share capital may be divided into 100 'A' shares of £1 each and 900 'B' shares of £10 each. Only the 'A' shares carry a right to vote at general meetings of the company; furthermore the rights attaching to the 'B' shares both as regards dividends and on a winding-up are limited. It will be seen that, if the company has net assets of substance, the 'A' shares are the ones to buy.

Again, another company's share capital may be divided into 100 £1 'A' shares and 100 £1 'B' shares and 100 £1 'C' shares. The articles may provide that the holders of the majority of the 'A' shares have the right to appoint two directors (the 'A' directors), the holders of the majority of the 'B' shares have the right to appoint two directors ('B' directors) and so on with the 'C' shares. If the articles contain a requirement for unanimity on the board of directors on certain fundamental points of the company's management it will be seen that ownership of a simple majority of the company's issued shares will not of itself necessarily give total control of the company.

Such provisions in a company's articles, however, are the exception rather than the rule. Most private companies incorporated since the passing of the 1948 Act and before 1 July 1985 have largely adopted the model articles set out in Table 'A'[1] of that Act save for extending the directors' borrowing powers, and most companies to be incorporated after that date will presumably adopt in large part the new Table A as set out in the 1985 Regulations. Since section 303 of the 1985 Act, like the corresponding provision of the 1948 Act, provides for removal of a company's directors by a simple majority of votes cast at a general meeting of the members of the company (notwithstanding anything in the Articles to the contrary) and since Table 'A' (old and new versions) provides that each share (not each member) shall have the right to one vote, the rule for most companies is as stated above, namely that ownership of a majority of its issued shares will carry control over the management of its business. Control of management includes control over the disposal and utilisation of the company's assets, but 100 per cent of the value of the company can only be obtained by acquiring 100 per cent of the company's issued share capital and, in practice, many purchases of private companies are in respect of the whole issued share capital.

The answer to the question first posed, namely: what are you buying? is therefore not the company but all of its issued shares (or at least the majority of such of its shares as will give effective control over the composition of its board of directors). In practice, most sales of shares in private companies are made with the agreement of all shareholders and directors, and it is not necessary to invoke the majority shareholders' statutory power under section 303 of the 1985 Act to remove directors. Sometimes however there will be a director on the board who has no interest in the company's shares and whose services the purchaser does not wish to retain. In such a situation, if terms cannot be agreed, section 303 can be used by the new owners of the shares but

---

[1] Amended by Companes Act 1980, Sch. 3, para. 36 as regards companies registered after 21 December 1980.

removal of a director under this provision will not deprive him of any right to compensation for loss of office[2]. Questions concerning employees generally are dealt with in chapter 12.

Where the concern to be acquired is an unincorporated business the answer to the question: what are you buying? will consist of a list of the assets (and, if appropriate, liabilities) of the business.

The most recent accounts of the business will provide a starting point but in the absence of these a rough and ready check list of assets would be (a) premises; (b) goodwill and name; (c) motor vehicles, office machinery and other fixed assets; (d) stock-in-trade; (e) work in progress; (f) book debts; and (g) licences and know-how where appropriate. The position concerning unincorporated businesses is discussed in more detail in chapter 7.

Companies Act 1985, sections 151 to 158.

Having decided the subject matter of the transaction the purchaser will wish to examine methods of funding his purchase[3]. The relevant provisions concerning financial assistance by a company for acquisition of its own shares are contained in sections 151 to 158 of the 1985 Act.

Subject to an important exception for private companies (see below) section 151(1) of the 1985 Act makes it unlawful, where a person is acquiring or proposing to acquire shares in a company, for the company or any of its subsidiaries to give financial assistance directly or indirectly for the purpose of that acquisition before or at the same time as the acquisition takes place. Subsection (2) provides that where a person has acquired shares in a company and any liability has been incurred (by that or any other person) for the purpose of that acquisition, it is not lawful for the company or any of its subsidiaries to give financial assistance directly or indirectly for the purpose of reducing or discharging the liability so incurred.

'Financial assistance' is defined in section 152(1) and includes

---

[2] Companies Act 1985, s. 303(5).

[3] A person proposing to issue sterling securities to a value (by that issue and any other within a twelve-month period) of £3 million or more will require consent under the Control of Borrowing Order 1958 (SI 58/1208), amended by the Control of Borrowing (Amendment) (No. 2) Order 1985 (SI 85/1150).

financial assistance given by way of gift, loan, the giving of a guarantee, security or indemnity and any other financial assistance given by a company the net assets of which are thereby reduced to a material extent, or which has no net assets. The definition of 'financial assistance' would appear to permit the sale of assets by a purchaser to a target company and the utilisation of the proceeds of sale to finance the acquisition, so long as (i) the value of the assets in the company's books (having regard to all statutory accounting requirements) is not less than the price paid; (ii) the company has some net assets to begin with; and (iii) the company receives the assets on or before paying the price.

Even if the provision of financial assistance by the target company will not reduce its net assets to a material extent or at all (for example if its assets are charged to secure a loan to the new owner), it will be prohibited unless the company can be shown to be receiving consideration for such payment[4].

There are a number of exceptions to the prohibition. These include:

(1) the three exceptions formerly contained in section 54 of the 1948 Act and now in section 153(4) of the 1985 Act;

(2) assistance given in good faith in the interests of the company where the company's principal purpose is not to give the assistance for the purpose of any acquisition of its shares or of shares in its holding company; or the giving of assistance for that purpose which is but an incidental part of some larger purpose of the company. There is also an exception to the prohibition contained in section 151(2) so that, for example, a newly acquired subsidiary may give security to secure additional group borrowings for normal trading, so long as the subsidiary may benefit from the increased facilities; but not to repay borrowings and interest incurred by the holding company in acquiring its shares;

(3) any distribution of a company's assets by way of dividend lawfully made, the allotment of any bonus shares and the redemption or purchase of any shares made in accordance with sections 159 to 181 of the 1985 Act. A distribution will not be lawfully made unless it complies both with the

---

[4] Companies Act 1985, s. 152(1)(a)(i).

company's articles and with Part VIII of the 1985 Act. Any proposal to use a newly acquired subsidiary's pre-acquisition profits to repay the holding company's borrowings by payment of a dividend will also have to take account of the taxation consequences;

(4) private companies, for whom the prohibitions are relaxed, as discussed in the following paragraph.

Section 155 of the 1985 Act permits a private company to give financial assistance for the acquisition of its shares (or those of its holding company being a private company with no intermediate public company) if the provisions of that section and of sections 156 to 158 are complied with. Such assistance may, however, only be given if the company has net assets which are not thereby reduced, or to the extent that those assets are thereby reduced, if the financial assistance is provided out of distributable profits.

In order to take advantage of section 155, a company must comply with a number of formalities. These include:

(a) the making of a statutory declaration by the company's directors in Form No. 155(6)(a) as prescribed by the Companies (Forms) Regulations 1985, SI No. 854 (or Form No. 155(6)(b) where the financial assistance is for the acquisition of shares in the company's holding company). Among the matters to be sworn by the directors is a statement that the company 'will be able to pay it's (sic) debts as they fall due during the year immediately following' the date on which the financial assistance is proposed to be given. Where the financial assistance is being given by a target company, its directors prior to change of control will not wish to swear such a statement except in the (unlikely) event of their retaining control for the year following the assistance being given. For similar reasons auditors appointed by the old regime will be unwilling to give a report as next mentioned.

(b) there must be attached to the statutory declaration a report by the company's auditors in accordance with section 156(4);

(c) the provision of financial assistance must be approved by a special resolution of the company in general meeting, unless it is a wholly-owned subsidiary. Where the provision of assistance is for shares in a holding company, the holding company and any intermediate holding company, must also approve the provision of financial assistance by special resolution;

(d) the financial assistance must be given within the time limits provided in section 158, and may not be given where an application for the cancellation of any such special resolution is made under section 158(3) of the 1985 Act before the final determination of the application, unless the court otherwise orders. Such an application may be made by the holders of not less than 10 per cent in aggregate in nominal value of the company's issued share capital or any class thereof, or if the company is not limited by shares, by not less than 10 per cent of the company's members.

It should be noted that whether the company giving financial assistance is public or private, it will, in addition to fulfilling the statutory conditions, need to alter its articles if these incorporate regulation 10 of Table A of the 1948 Act, which regulation repeats the prohibitions on a company providing financial assistance for the purchase of its shares formerly contained in section 54 of that Act.

Other statutory provisions which will need to be considered at an early stage of the transaction are the following:

(1) Prevention of Fraud (Investments) Act 1958

Section 14 of the above Act makes it an offence for an unauthorised person to distribute a document which is a circular inter alia containing any invitation to dispose of, or to acquire, or subscribe for securities except with the consent of the Department of Trade. Authorised persons include recognised dealers in securities and members of the Stock Exchange. In practice, circular offer documents are not required where the number of offeree shareholders is small as will usually be the situation in the case of a private company. However, a letter of offer sent by the vendor or his solicitors to the majority shareholder and copied for convenience to other shareholders would strictly speaking be within the section.

If there is any doubt whether a proposed letter is within section 14, permission should be sought from the Department of

Trade. Specific permission will not, however, be necessary in respect of an offer document complying with the terms of any of the published General Permissions. The General Permission most likely to apply in the present context is General Permission No. 3 which applies to offers for private companies not covered by the City Code. The offer document must meet the conditions specified in the Permission which include conditions that the offer terms have been recommended by all the directors of the offeree company, that the offer is for all the equity or preference share capital or all the debentures of the target not already held by or on behalf of the offeror, and that the consideration is cash or securities in the offeror company, or both[5].

(2) Fair Trading Act 1973, Part V

Under the Fair Trading Act 1973, section 64 the Secretary of State may refer a merger to the Monopolies and Mergers Commission if it appears to him that it is, or may be, the fact that two or more enterprises, of which one at least is carried on in the United Kingdom by or under the control of a company incorporated in the United Kingdom have ceased to be distinct enterprises, and that either as a result of the merger a market share of one-quarter or more in any goods or services within the UK, or a substantial part of it, is created or augmented, or the value of assets taken over exceeds £30 million[6]. The value of assets taken over is to be determined in accordance with section 67. If the Commission concludes that a merger is against the public interest, the Secretary of State may prohibit the merger, or if it has taken place, require the assets to be divested.

(3) Restrictive Trade Practices Act 1976

An acquisition agreement may be registerable under the Restrictive Trade Practices Act 1976 if it contains any of certain restrictions accepted by at least two parties to the agreement, and at least two parties (who need not be the same as the parties accepting the restriction) carry on business within the UK. A restriction is defined to include a negative obligation, whether express or implied and whether absolute or not. The relevant restrictions

---

[5] New legislation is planned in this area as foreshadowed by a White Paper published by the Department of Trade on 29 January 1985.
[6] Merger References (Increase in Value of Assets) Order 1984.

include those in respect of the areas or places in or from which goods are to be supplied or acquired, or designated[7] services are to be made available or supplied. It seems therefore that acceptance of a non-competition covenant by two or more vendors in an acquisition agreement will make the agreement registerable. Failure to register will make the agreement void in respect of all restrictions accepted, and render it a breach of statutory duty for any party thereto carrying on business in the UK to give effect or to enforce the restrictions. Usually the requisite particulars should be submitted for registration to the Office of Fair Trading before the date on which any relevant restriction takes effect, and in any case within three months from when the agreement is made. Inclusion of a provision such as clause 14 of the specimen agreement in Appendix A is advisable.

An agreement, once registered, must be referred by the Director-General of Fair Trading to the Restrictive Practices Court who will order the parties not to apply the restrictions unless the Court is satisfied that any one or more of the circumstances specified in section 10 apply. The Director need not however so refer an agreement if it appears to the Department of Trade, on the Director's representation, that the restrictions are not of such significance as to require investigation by the Court: section 21(2). When, therefore, the agreement is submitted to the Office of Fair Trading it should be accompanied by a request that the Director General[8] makes representations under section 21(2). Whether he will do so depends on the circumstances of each case and an early informal approach to the Office of Fair Trading is therefore desirable.

(4) Competition Act 1980

This Act provides for investigation, and ultimately prohibition, of 'anti-competitive practices', that is a course of conduct which has, or is intended or likely to have, the effect of restricting, distorting or preventing competition in the UK or any part of it not being a course of conduct required or envisaged under an agreement registerable under Restrictive Trades Practices Act

---

[7] See The Restrictive Trade Practices (Services) Order 1976, SI 1976/98 and the Restrictive Trade Practices Act 1976.

[8] For procedure on furnishing details of an agreement to the OFT see the Registration of Restrictive Trading Agreements Regulations 1984, SI 1984/392.

1976. The 1980 Act applies to goods and services. Thus, any agreement under which one party only submits, for example, to a non-competition covenant is capable of investigation under the 1980 Act.

(5) Treaty of Rome, Articles 85 and 86

By Article 85 agreements between undertakings which may affect trade between member states of the EEC, and which have as their object or effect the prevention, restriction or distortion of competition within the EEC, are made void. Among other types of agreement, Article 85 refers in particular to those which limit or control production, markets, technical development, or investment and the Commission of the European Communities regard a vendor's non-competition covenant as potentially within the provision of the Article[9]. By a Notice of 19 December 1977 the Commission of the European Communities has expressed the opinion that agreements of 'minor importance' are outside the prohibition of Article 85, and that there is therefore no point in parties to them applying to the Commission for negative clearance. The Notice states that an agreement is of minor importance if (i) the products which are the subject of the agreement, and other products of the parties to the agreement and certain associates considered to be similar by consumers, do not represent in a substantial part of the EEC more than 5 per cent of the total market for such products, and (ii) the aggregate annual turnover of such parties and associates does not exceed 50 million units of account. The Notice is issued for guidance only and without prejudice to the interpretation of the European Court of Justice. Furthermore, in one case the Commission decided that where the market in a product in a member state was large but fragmented, a market share as small as 3 per cent might, if it exceeded that of most competitors, justify finding that restrictive practices relating to imports of the goods into a member state were capable of affecting the pattern of trade between member states contrary to Articles 85[10]. Where, therefore, there is doubt and the proposed agreement is not within any of

---

[9] Re Reuter/BASF AG, (EC Commission Decision 76/743) OJ L254, 17.9.76, p. 40 [1976] 2 CMLR D44.
[10] Case 100–103/80, *Musique Diffusion Française SA v EEC Commission* [1983] ECR1825, [1983] 3 CMLR 221.

the published exemptions, application for negative clearance should be made on Form A/B (obtainable from the Department of Trade and Industry).

Article 86 prohibits any abuse by one or more undertakings of a dominant position within the EEC, or in a substantial part of it, insofar as it may affect trade between member states. A dominant position has been stated as 'a position of economic strength enjoyed by an undertaking (or undertakings) which enables it (them) to prevent effective competition being maintained on the relevant market by giving it (them) the power to behave to an appreciable extent independently of its (their) competitors, customers and ultimately its consumers' (Case 27/76, *United Brands Co and United Brands Continentaal BV v EC Commission* [1978] ECR 207, [1978] 3 CMLR 83). A merger which eliminates or discourages competition may be within Article 86 (Case 6/72, *Europemballage Corpn and Continental Can Co Inc v EC Commission* [1973] ECR 215, [1973] CMLR 199). A dominant position may exist in a narrow market without reference to the size of the undertakings concerned, i.e. for new replacement tyres for heavy vehicles (*Bandengroothandel Frieschebrug BV v Netherlandsche Banden-Industrie Michelin NV* [1981] OJ L353/33, [1982] 1 CMLR 643). It is possible to apply to the Commission for negative clearance, although no form of application is prescribed. An agreement between competitors whereby one can exercise control or decisive influence over the affairs of the other may be regarded as an abuse of a dominant position by the EC Commission even where the acquisition is of a minority shareholding only (*Re agreements between Philip Morris Inc and Rembrandt Group Ltd* [1984] 2 CMLR 40).

(6) Companies Act 1985, section 130

Where a company issues shares at a premium whether for cash or otherwise, and does not thereby secure at least a 90 per cent equity holding in another company[11], a sum equal to the aggregate amount or value of the premiums on those shares must be transferred to a separate 'share premium account'. Amounts so transferred may be used only in paying up bonus issues and in

---

[11] Companies Act 1985, s 131. In the case of group reconstructions, reference should be made to Companies Act 1985, s. 132.

paying certain expenses, and may be reduced only with the consent of the court. Shares will be issued at a premium wherever the consideration for the shares issued exceeds the nominal value of those shares.

3 The Contract—Protecting the Vendor

A. GENERAL

Protection for a vendor of shares in relation to taxation is dealt with in a separate section of this chapter. This section is concerned with the methods by which a vendor may limit his liability arising from the warranties and indemnities normally required by a purchaser. These warranties are usually extensive. Taking into account sub-paragraphs, schedule 5 of the precedent agreement in Appendix A contains some 90 separate warranties relating to various aspects of the business of the company whose shares are being acquired—in addition to the indemnity contained in schedule 4. Dependent upon the circumstances of the company in question, a purchaser may wish to include warranties additional to those included in the precedent, the problem from his point of view being to pinpoint all the areas of the company's activity (or non-activity) which could increase losses or liabilities or reduce profits or assets. Since the company can do anything which its usually wide objects clauses permit it to do, the loss potential is substantial. For precisely opposite reasons the vendor will wish to limit his liability and it should be noted that a contract in so far as it relates to the creation or transfer of securities is outside the protection afforded to purchasers by sections 2 to 4 of the Unfair Contract Terms Act 1977 (Schedule 1, para 1(e)).

Warranties are also sometimes required by the purchaser of a business (as distinct from shares) but on a less extensive scale, since the warranties need relate only to the particular assets being acquired. Limitation of liability is accordingly relevant here also.

A vendor's liability may be tortious arising from misrepresentation, or contractual arising from a breach of warranty. The following is a rough and ready summary of the purchaser's remedies:

(1) If a purchaser can show that a misrepresentation of fact induced him to enter the contract, he may rescind the contract unless

   (a) he has subsequently taken some action affirming the contract i.e. selling of some of the shares he has bought or

   (b) the status quo ante cannot be restored or

   (c) rescission would prejudice an innocent third party.

The Court may however if it thinks fit award damages instead of rescission[1].

(2) If the misrepresentation is negligent within the meaning of the Misrepresentation Act 1967 or fraudulent[2] damages may be claimed equal to the difference between the price paid and the value of the shares received.

   Where however the sale contract provides that the purchaser is relying on no representations other than those incorporated as warranties into the contract, it is thought that a vendor's liability in tort for misrepresentation will be excluded and the purchaser's remedy will be a contractual one. This applies because such a term in the contract is (except in the case of fraudulent misrepresenation) likely to satisfy the requirement of reasonableness stated in the Unfair Contract Terms Act 1977, section 11(1) where both parties are businessmen or commercial concerns independently advised. If the requirement of reasonableness is not satisfied any term in the contract (including a contract for the transfer or

---

[1] Misrepresentation Act 1967, s. 2(2).

[2] It is an offence to induce or to attempt to induce a person to enter, or offer to enter into, an agreement for the acquisition or disposal of, or subscription for, securities by making any statement, promise or forecast which is known to be misleading, false or deceptive, or by any dishonest concealment of material facts, or by recklessly making (dishonestly or otherwise) a statement, promise or forecast which is misleading, false or deceptive; Prevention of Fraud (Investments) Act 1958, s. 13.

creation of securities) purporting to restrict liability for misrepresentation will be ineffective, and the onus is on the party claiming that the term satisfies the requirement to show that it does[3]. The practical effects of excluding tortious liability for misrepresentations are

(a) to limit the purchaser's remedies to damages except where there is a fundamental breach, or where a misrepresentation made prior to contract becomes a term of the contract when rescission is available subject to the matters mentioned in (1) above and

(b) to cause only the contractual measure of damages to be applicable (see (3) below) and

(c) to restrict the statutory limitation period to six years from the time of breach of contract rather than six years from its discovery.

(3) The remedy for breach of warranty is damages. The amount recoverable is equivalent to the loss which might at the date of the contract objectively have been expected to arise from the breach or, if greater, that which may reasonably be supposed to have been in the contemplation of the parties at the date of the contract as the probable result of the breach. This is not necessarily the same as the measure of damages in respect of a negligent or fraudulent misrepresentation (see (2) above).

(4) In any case where a party claims damages he must take reasonable steps to mitigate the loss. This is not a particularly onerous duty. For example, if a third party claim is made against the company, reasonable steps should be taken to examine the merits of the claim and, if necessary, to contest it. Were the company to permit judgment to be entered against it in default of appearance or a defence without such an examination, a vendor could reasonably complain of a failure to mitigate. In any event, in these circumstances an examination of the merits of a third party claim would be common sense, since, if the claim were unmerited, it

---

[3] Misrepresentation Act 1967, s. 3, as substituted by Unfair Contract Terms Act 1977, s. 8(1).

would be unlikely to constitute a breach of warranty by the purchaser.

(5) Although the usual remedy for a breach of warranty is damages, if the breach is fundamental the alternative remedy of rescission is available subject to the matters mentioned at (1) above. In another context the delivery of apples instead of pears would constitute a fundamental breach. Possibly an analogous situation would be the transfer of partly paid shares instead of fully paid shares, but other examples may be the invalidity of the company's principal patent, the illegality of the company's principal trading agreement or a compulsory purchase order on its place of business—assuming in each case that these events constitute a breach of warranty under the terms of the particular contract and that they go to the substratum of the company's business. The burden of proof on a plaintiff, to show that the breach is so fundamental that damages would be inadequate, is a heavy one.

(6) A vendor's liability under a deed of indemnity is governed by the terms of the deed itself which will be strictly construed against the person claiming under it. The vendor usually gives an indemnity in respect of the tax liabilities of the company whose shares are being sold and a typical deed of indemnity is incorporated in schedule 4 of the precedent contained in Appendix A.

Limitations on a vendor's liability may for convenience be classified under the following heads (in addition to restricting or excluding liability for misrepresentation which has been discussed above):

1. Limitation of amount.

2. Limitation of share of liability where there is more than one vendor.

3. Limitation in time.

4. Limitation by disclosure prior to contract.

1. Limitation of amount

A vendor may request that his aggregate liability under all warranties and indemnities given in the contract for sale shall not exceed the amount of the purchase price. Suppose for example that the whole issued share capital in the company is being sold on a net value basis for £10,000. The balance sheet is warranted showing total assets of £100,000 and total liabilities of £90,000. If bad debts prove to be £20,000 as opposed to say £2,000 as shown on the balance sheet or if the liabilities are greater than disclosed because a substantial undisclosed claim has been made against the company by a third party, a limitation on the vendor's liability would materially prejudice the purchaser unless the latter is willing to permit the company to go into liquidation. In the author's view this type of limitation on liability should if possible be avoided where shares in a company are valued on a net assets basis and the company is being bought as a going concern. Where, however, a purchaser has been allowed to carry out a full investigation into the company's financial and tax affairs prior to exchange of contracts, this and other limitations may be acceptable, and indeed may be insisted on by a vendor who would otherwise be underwriting the purchaser's investigation.

Clearly, where the cost of the shares being acquired is nominal, the main consideration paid by the purchaser being, for example, the assumption of certain of the company's liabilities, limiting the vendor's liability to the price as such is inappropriate.

In the absence of a limitation on the maximum damages payable the measure of damages for breach of warranty would in effect be such as to restore the balance sheet position of the company to what it would have been had the warranty been true, i.e. in the example give above to pay the excess of bad debts, or to meet the undisclosed liabilities, subject to the damages being reduced by the amount of tax the target would have paid had the warranty been true. If, however, the damages arise from a misrepresentation, the damages would equal the difference between the price paid and the value received. Since negative values do not appear to be recognised for this purpose, the vendor's liability for misrepresentation is effectively limited to the price paid. For this reason, any representation on which a purchaser is relying should be included as a term of the contract. If, as is usually the case, written enquiries are made and written replies received prior to the contract, these should, from the purchaser's point of view, be incorporated by reference.

Where the warranties include some relating to taxation matters, a breach could give rise both to a warranty claim by the purchaser and to a claim by the target company under the tax indemnity[4], which should therefore contain a provision for avoidance of a double payment. For capital gains tax purposes a payment under a warranty claim will create a downward adjustment in the price[5], so that where the vendor has a capital gains tax liability arising from the sale, he should, all else being equal, endeavour to include provision in the agreement whereby the warranty claim should be made in priority to the claim under the indemnity.

2. Limitation of share of liability

Where there is more than one selling shareholder, the liability for each under the contract of sale will usually be expressed to be joint and several. Thus, whatever rights of contribution each vendor may have against each of the others[6], the purchaser will be able to choose any one (or more) of them to sue for the total liability under the contract. This may be unfortunate for the 10 per cent shareholder who chooses to stay in the UK when the rest of his former co-shareholders emigrate to some remote jurisdiction, and joint and several liability is therefore often resisted by vendors. It is however precisely for this reason, i.e. wealthy potential defendants leaving the jurisdiction or dissipating their funds, that a purchaser should try to resist the inclusion of the provision whereby each vendor is, as between himself and the purchaser, responsible only for that percentage of the loss equal to the percentage of shares sold (or price received) by him.

The vendors should however provide in another agreement for rights of contribution between themselves where there is not total identity between the vendors and the persons who give the warranties, i.e. where vendors who are minority shareholders and who have not participated in the target company's management give no warranties, or some warranties only, or all or some

---

[4] See section B of this chapter below.

[5] CGTA 1979, s. 41. The tax treatment of a payment under a tax indemnity is not clear.

[6] The right of contribution as between two or more vendors under a contract entered into after 1978 is governed by the Civil Liability (Contribution) Act 1978; see also Limitation Act 1980, s. 10(1).

warranties qualified by words such as 'to the best of the vendors' knowledge information and belief'.

Another situation where a vendor may wish to limit his share of liability is where a company is owned, say, as to 55 per cent by individuals and as to 45 per cent by trustees of a discretionary trust. On a sale of the whole issued share capital the trustees will be unwilling to give any warranties whatsoever other than as to title to their shares—besides being minority shareholders and having presumably taken no active part in the management of the company, they will not wish to undertake a personal liability when the benefit of the deal is for the discretionary beneficiaries. There may therefore have to be two contemporaneous agreements, the first between the individuals and the purchasers incorporating the full warranties, and the second between the trustees and the purchaser warranting title only to the shares. It is probable that in this situation, if there is a breach of warranty by the individuals, then in the absence of some limitation to the contrary, they will be liable for the whole loss suffered by the purchaser and not just 55 per cent, because the greater percentage represents the damages which may reasonably be supposed to have been in the contemplation of the parties (that is the individuals and the purchaser) at the time of the contract as the probable result of a breach of warranty.

It is sometimes suggested that trustees should give full warranties, but that their liability should be limited to an amount equal to the value of the trust capital net of tax and charges on capital for the time being held by them, and that they should agree not to distribute capital to any beneficiary without that beneficiary first giving warranties to the purchaser pro tanto. Whether trustees can agree such a provision will depend upon their powers under the trust in question and it will in any event be inappropriate where, for example, a beneficiary will become absolutely entitled during the limitation period for claims, or where the trustees may otherwise become obliged to pay out capital, albeit having a discretion as between possible beneficiaries.

3. Limitation in time

The limitation period for beginning an action for breach of contract is generally six years from the date of the breach which, in the case of a breach of warranty, would normally be the contract date. The vendor could therefore face a claim some years after the sale of shares where, for example, an undisclosed liability matures years after completion of the sale. Since most vendors are unwilling to put funds aside to meet contingent claims, it is common for the agreement to stipulate that any claim for breach of warranty must be brought within some stipulated period which is less than the statutory limitation period. Claims under general warranties should become apparent on the audit next following completion. This suggests a time limit for claims, say, six months after the end of the target company's financial year current at completion. The usual six-year period is however often reserved in the case of tax warranties since in the ordinary case an assessment to tax may be made at any time up to six years after the end of the chargeable period to which the assessment relates[7].

To avoid a purchaser notifying a claim within the permitted period but then leaving it open, a vendor may wish the agreement to provide that notified claims will be waived unless proceedings are issued and served within, say, a year thereafter.

4. Limitation by disclosure prior to contract

Even if there are only two parties to the contract, the pre-contract negotiations for the sale of shares may be conducted by a multiplicity of individuals. If buyer and seller are companies, then possibly more than one director of each will be concerned in the negotiations. In addition there will be correspondence and verbal exchanges between the respective parties' solicitors and accountants. For this reason it may be desirable from the point of view of both parties to define those representations which form part of the contract and then to agree in the contract that no other representations shall count[8].

In addition it is usual to restrict the vendor's warranties so as to exclude liability for all matters disclosed in writing on or before exchange of contracts, but the vendors will usually be asked to warrant the accuracy of their disclosures. Prior to exchange the vendor's solicitors and accountants will go through

---

[7] Taxes Management Act 1970, s. 34(1).
[8] As to the effect of the Misrepresentation Act 1967 on such a term, see above.

each of the warranties with the vendor item by item noting whether the precise terms of any particular warranty can be met. For example, the company may from time to time have been late in filing returns at the Companies Registry; or there may be a quantity of seconds included in the company's stock in trade. Any such fact is incorporated into what is known as a disclosure letter[9]. The contract then provides that the vendor's liability under warranties shall not include liability for any matter disclosed in the disclosure letter.

Care needs to be taken in drafting the disclosure letter to ensure that a particular disclosure is effective for all the purposes for which it is made and general disclosures should not be used to cover specific matters. '... a party who wishes by disclosure to avoid a breach of warranty [is required] to give specific notice for the purpose of the agreement and a protection by disclosure will not normally be achieved by merely making known the means of knowledge which may or do enable the other party to work out certain facts and conclusions'[10]. Further, a disclosure may itself amount to a representation.

Negotiations between the vendor and purchaser concerning the various methods of limiting the vendor's liability may be assisted by the vendor agreeing to lodge a percentage of the purchase price with the purchaser (or preferably the purchaser's solicitors) as a primary fund with which to meet any claim for breach of warranty. Assuming that the amount of the deposit is adequate, there will be less reason for the purchaser to object to each of several vendors being responsible only for a specified percentage of any damages, and it may be felt that a time limitation is more acceptable if the purchaser has the security of funds available to meet a claim.

One other matter which it is convenient to consider within this section is how to deal with any outstanding guarantees or other security given by the vendor in connection with bank facilities which have been given to the target company. No vendor will wish to remain contingently liable for the debts of a company which he ceases to control and the sale agreement will need to provide for the purchaser to procure release of the guarantees on completion. Provided that an early approach is made

---

[9] A precedent disclosure letter is contained in Appendix C.
[10] *Levison v Farin* [1978] 2 All ER 1149 at 1157.

to the bank or other lender, it should be possible to agree and have available on completion whatever alternative security documentation may be required for the guarantee to be released. Similarly, the sale agreement may provide for any loans owing to the vendor by the company being acquired to be repaid on completion.

B. TAXATION[11]

Agreements for the sale of shares in limited companies are usually drafted by the purchaser's solicitors. Most such agreements contain an indemnity by the vendors in favour both of the purchaser and of the company being acquired in respect of any tax payable by, or disallowance of relief to, the company other than any provided for in annexed accounts or some other document such as a disclosure letter (see Appendix C).

'Tax' is usually widely defined to include every current form of impost, and including some which are defunct such as profits tax and betterment levy. Generally every effort is made to ensure that every conceivable undisclosed liability of the company not provided for is covered. Care needs to be taken to limit the period in respect of which the indemnity is to operate to accounting periods ending, events happening and transactions undertaken prior to completion.

Usually such an indemnity contains a covenant by the purchaser and the company being acquired to permit the vendor, at his own cost, to have the conduct of any negotiations or litigation with the Revenue in respect of any claim for tax which may be the subject of a claim under the indemnity. In addition the vendor may require the purchaser to give counter-indemnities in respect of certain potential tax liabilities of the vendor which may arise from the activities of the purchaser after completion, and to agree that the vendor's liability under the indemnity should not extend to tax liabilities which may arise as a result of such activities[12].

The more important of a vendor's potential tax liabilities which may arise from some act or omission of the purchaser are the following:

---

[11] See also p. 22 above.
[12] See also pp. 178–9 below.

(1) ICTA 1970, section 460 (transactions in securities)

Section 460 applies where, in any of the five circumstances mentioned in section 461 a person obtains, or is able to obtain, a tax advantage in consequence of a transaction (or transactions) in securities unless such transactions were carried out for bona fide commercial reasons or in the ordinary course of making or managing investments and none had as their, or one of their, main objects, to enable a tax advantage to be obtained.

An exhaustive account of each of the five circumstances set out in section 461 (some of which apply only where one of the parties is a dealer in securities) would be out of place. It is sufficient to look in outline at the two circumstances described in paragraphs C and D of section 461 since these have more widespread application[13].

Circumstance C applies wherever three conditions are satisfied:

(i) The consideration received on a sale of shares represents cash or other assets in the company available for distribution by way of dividend, or debtors, or trading stock. It will be seen that this condition will be satisfied on almost every sale of a company as a going concern.

(ii) The consideration receivable by the vendor is not taxable as income. Unless the vendor is a dealer in securities, this condition will usually be satisfied.

(iii) The consideration received by the vendor must be received in consequence of a transaction whereby any other person (e.g. the purchaser of the shares) subsequently receives, or has received, an abnormal amount by way of dividend[14]. This condition will be satisfied where, for example the purchaser of shares, using cash already in the company, or converting into cash debtors or trading stock in existence at the time of sale, subsequently declares a dividend which 'substantially exceeds a normal return on the price paid for

---

[13] See p. 102 below regarding circumstance E of s. 461.
[14] Circumstance C also applies where any other person subsequently becomes entitled, or has become entitled, to a deduction in computing profits or gains by reason of a fall in the value of the securities resulting from the payment of a dividend thereon or from any other dealing with any assets of a company. This is unlikely to apply except where the purchaser, or one or more of several purchasers, is a dealer in securities.

the securities': section 467(3)(b) ICTA. This could happen when a purchasing company borrows money to acquire a company as its wholly owned subsidiary and the subsidiary subsequently declares a dividend sufficient to enable its parent to pay off the loan[15]. Such event will be outside the control of the vendor who should therefore be advised to obtain the indemnity of the purchaser and his successors in title to the shares against the tax consequences of any such action.

It is sometimes said that if a vendor stipulates for such an indemnity he must have had section 460 in mind and therefore the transaction was not bona fide commercial and/or had as one of its main objectives the obtaining of a tax advantage. In reality, however, such a vendor is merely trying to protect himself against subsequent action of a purchaser over whom he has no control. In any event the intention of the indemnity is hopefully to encourage a purchaser not to declare an abnormal dividend in which case paragraph C will be of no application.

Paragraph D applies inter alia where in connection with the distribution of profits, or the transfer or realisation of assets, of a company to which the paragraph applies, the person in question so receives consideration that he does not pay or bear tax on it as income and the consideration represents either cash or other assets in the company available for distribution by way of dividend, or debtors, or trading stock. Paragraph D applies to all companies unless quoted and also not under the control of five or fewer persons. This paragraph was held to be applicable where an owner of shares in the purchaser company, who also owned the shares of the company being acquired, procured the former company to buy her shares in the latter. The cash received by the vendor from the purchasing company as consideration for shares might have been paid to her by way of dividend, and the tax advantage so obtained was counteracted by an assessment to income tax under section 460 on the grossed-up equivalent of the cash paid[16]. Thus, where the vendor is also a shareholder in the purchaser company, he cannot expect an indemnity in respect of liability under section 460.

ICTA 1970, section 464 provides a procedure for a person to

---

[15] But see *IRC v Garvin* [1981] 1 WLR 793, [1981] STC 344, HL.
[16] *Cleary v IRC* [1968] AC 766, [1967] 2 All ER 48, HL.

obtain Revenue clearance of a proposed transaction. Provided that particulars of the proposed transaction are supplied to the Revenue and these particulars are sufficient in the Revenue's opinion, it is bound to notify the applicant for clearance within 30 days of receipt of the particulars whether it considers section 460 to be applicable. Where a vendor of shares proposes to apply for Revenue clearance under section 464, the share sale agreement is often made conditional on such clearance being obtained[17].

(2) ICTA 1970, section 478 (transfer of assets abroad)

A sale of shares by a UK resident individual to a non-resident is a transfer of assets within section 478 which deems certain income of persons resident or domiciled out of the UK to be the income of individuals ordinarily resident there. The section does not however apply if the sale of shares is a bona fide commercial transaction not designed for the purpose of avoiding liability to taxation[18], and is only relevant in the context of a share sale if the purchaser is a non-resident settlement or company and the vendor might continue to enjoy indirectly the income flowing from the company whose shares are sold[19].

(3) ICTA 1970, section 483 (change in ownership of company: disallowance of trading losses)

The usual tax indemnity given by a vendor to a purchaser should be limited so as to exclude any liability for disallowance of relief to the company arising from a 'major change in the nature or conduct of a trade carried on' by it or after the sale of its shares.

The other limb of this section applies when at any time after the scale of the activities in a trade carried on by a company has become small or negligible and before any considerable revival of the trade there is a change in the ownership of the company.

---

[17] Application for clearance should be made to Inland Revenue Technical Division, Alexandra House, Kingsway, London WC2B 6TR.

[18] ICTA 1970, s. 478(3).

[19] Neither is FA 1981, s. 45 (transfer of assets abroad: liability of non-transferors) likely to be relevant in the usual case.

Here too the vendor will wish to exclude liability for disallowance of relief[20].

(4) ICTA 1970, section 488 (artificial transactions in land)

The section applies whenever (a) land or any property deriving its value from land, is acquired with the sole or main object of realising a gain from disposing of the land or (b) land is held as a trading stock or (c) land is developed with the sole or main object of realising a gain from disposing of the land when developed, and in any of these cases a gain of a capital nature is obtained from the disposal of the land. Where the section applies, the whole of the gain is taxed as the unearned income assessable under Case VI of Schedule D of the persons by whom the gain is realised[1].

Land is treated as disposed of if, by any one or more transactions, or by any arrangement or scheme, whether concerning the land or property deriving its value from the land, the property in the land, or control over the land, is effectually disposed of. It will be seen therefore that the disposal of a majority of the shares in a company holding land could give rise to a section 488 assessment on the vendor. There is however an exemption in the case of a disposal of shares in a company which holds land as trading stock, or a company which owns directly or indirectly 90 per cent or more of the ordinary share capital of another company which holds land as trading stock. In those cases, so long as all the land so held is disposed of in the normal course of its trade by the company which held it, and so as to procure that all opportunity of profit in respect of the land arises to that company, then any gain made by the vendor of the shares will not be assessed under section 488[2]. The vendor should therefore require the purchaser of such a company to covenant that all land held as trading stock will be disposed of in the normal course of trade by the company so as to procure that all opportunity of profit in respect of the land will arise to the company. There is a clearance procedure under section 488,

---

[20] See section C of chapter 4 for a discussion of the carry forward of trading losses from the purchaser's point of view.

[1] ICTA 1970, s. 488(3).

[2] ICTA 1970, s. 488(10).

but it is not available when the land in question is held as trading stock.

(5) Capital reconstruction at the time of sale

Where the consideration for the purchase is substantial and consists of cash (or where the exemption from transfer duty on amalgamation is not applicable on an exchange of shares) stamp duty will be payable on the share transfers at an ad valorem rate, presently one per cent. In the event of the purchaser wishing the vendor to co-operate in some scheme to reduce the duty payable, the vendor should, as a condition of agreeing, require the purchaser to indemnify him against any adverse tax consequences arising from the reconstruction. Under the former 'pref-trick' scheme for mitigating stamp duty (described in the previous edition of this book, pages 52-3) there were usually no adverse tax consequences, although each case required examination, particularly in relation to capital gains[3] and, where a close company was involved, capital transfer tax[4]. The 'pref-trick' no longer works following enactment of section 81, Finance Act 1985, but the requirement for an indemnity will continue should any replacement stamp duty mitigation scheme arise.

(6) Exchange of shares

Under the provisions of section 85 of CGTA 1979 a disposal of shares in exchange for other shares does not give rise to a taxable gain if the company issuing the shares (i.e. the purchasing company) holds or in consequence of the exchange will hold more than 25 per cent of the ordinary shares of the other company. The taxable gain will arise only when the substituted shares are disposed of. CGTA 1979, section 87(1) provides that this deferral of tax will not apply 'unless the exchange reconstruction or amalgamation in question is effected for bona fide commercial reasons and does not form part of a scheme or arrangement of which the main purpose or one of the main purposes is avoidance of liability to capital gains tax or corporation tax'.

---

[3] CGTA 1979, s. 25(2).
[4] Capital Transfer Tax Act 1984, s. 94.

The vendor will usually be well advised to seek Inland Revenue clearance under the procedure laid down in CGTA 1979, section 88. When the matter is too urgent to permit an application for clearance, the vendor should seek an indemnity from the purchasing company in the event of relief being disallowed to the vendor as a result of any action by the purchasing company. The relief is of course only a deferral of tax rather than its complete avoidance, so a purchasing company may well object to giving a blanket indemnity particularly if the vendor is able to cash the exchange shares immediately after the sale. Clearance should also be sought under ICTA 1970, section 464 where both companies are under the control of five or fewer persons and unquoted[5].

(7) Close company apportionments

The definition of a close company may be found in ICTA 1970, section 282 and other provisions of Chapter III of Part XI of that Act. Since the great majority of unquoted companies resident in the UK are close (excluding subsidiaries of non-close companies) it is not proposed to discuss the definition further.

In order to prevent the undue accumulation within a company of profits available for distribution as dividends, the Revenue may apportion the excess of a close company's relevant income over its actual distributions for any accounting period among the participators in the company[6]. For accounting periods ending after 26 March 1980 the trading income of a company which is a trading company, or a member of a trading group, will not form part of its relevant income, but investment income may be apportioned. The effect of an apportionment is, broadly speaking, that the company is treated as having distributed by way of dividend, and the participators as having so received in accordance with their interests in the company at the end of the accounting period, the amount apportioned. A participator who is an individual must pay tax at the higher rates on the amount apportioned to him[7].

---

[5] See pp. 28–9 above and p. 104 below.

[6] FA 1972, Sch. 16; and see ICTA 1970, s. 303, for the definition of 'participator' which includes a shareholder.

[7] FA 1972, Sch. 16, para. 5. An amount apportioned to a close company may be sub-apportioned to participators in that company, FA 1972, Sch. 16, para.

A vendor of shares will therefore be concerned to know the level of actual distribution made by a company for the accounting period preceding the sale. Once the sale has been completed he will have no way of controlling the level of distribution for that period so that, if no or too small a distribution is made, he could be faced with an assessment to higher rate tax on sums not actually received by him. Where the purchaser of shares is an individual or a close company, the purchaser will usually wish to distribute as little as possible. Where the purchaser is an open company, however, the declaration by the company being acquired of a dividend sufficiently high to avoid a shortfall need not have adverse tax consequences for the purchaser. In such circumstances it is desirable for a vendor to include a term in the share sale agreement that the purchaser will procure the company being acquired to declare a sufficient dividend for the accounting period in question.

Except for paragraph (6) above which applies where the acquiring company holds or obtains more than 25 per cent of the target company's ordinary shares, the above comments apply whenever the purchaser obtains control of the company being acquired whether as a 51 per cent or a 100 per cent subsidiary and whether or not the vendor retains any shares. Where the vendor does retain shares as a minority shareholder, there are additional tax considerations (see chapter 9).

1(4). In relation to accounting periods ending on or after 6 April 1984 no amount is to be apportioned to an individual unless it is at least £1000: FA 1984, s. 32.

4 The Contract—Protecting the Purchaser

Prior to exchange of contracts enquiries about the company or business to be transferred may be made from (i) the vendor and the vendor's professional advisers and (ii) third party sources. As regards the value of the replies to enquiries in the first category this depends upon the relevant terms of the contract or lack of them, i.e. paragraph 90, schedule 5 of the draft agreement in Appendix A and see generally chapter 3, section A. So far as the purchaser is concerned, if he is relying on a particular reply, he should be advised to incorporate it in the contract as a warranty by the vendor. Specimen pre-contract enquiries on the purchase of shares are contained in Appendix B, but they will require substantial additions and modifications to suit the circumstances.

Purchasers frequently instruct their accountants to conduct an investigation into the target company prior to exchange of contracts. Such an investigation should yield more detailed and up-to-date information than is available from the audited accounts, and should enable purchasers to form a view on profit and cash-flow forecasts.

Enquiries of third party sources are not conclusive in that they offer no formal protection if the information contained is inaccurate. The first source is the Companies Registry and a full search may be made against the company being acquired and its holding company if any, or in the case of a transfer of a business against the vendor company. A company search against the purchasing company may be appropriate where there is reason to doubt its ability to complete the contract, or where the contract is to provide for post completion payments to the vendor, if, for example, certain profit figures are achieved. Company searches will reveal all particulars filed by the company relating to its memorandum and articles, share capital, directors and secretary and registered office. However only the shareholders at the date at which the company's last annual return is made up are shown, so that this information is often out of date. If there has been any allotment of shares since that date, the return of allotments will show to whom they have been made. In addition charges registered against the company will be shown, but since a secured creditor has 21 days to register a charge in order to obtain priority against the company's other creditors, there can be no guarantee that a recently made charge is not about to be registered. There will also have been filed with the company's last annual return a set of audited accounts which, read together with the audited accounts for earlier accounting periods, may yield valuable historical information.

Information as to many companies' credit-worthiness may be obtained by reference to credit reference agencies. Because of the confidential and up-to-date nature of the information offered it may be desirable to obtain it even before commencing the negotiations.

However, in respect of financial years beginning after 14 June 1982, companies which qualify as small or medium-sized by reference to Companies Act 1985, section 248, may deliver modified accounts to the Registrar of Companies. For example, the directors of a small company need not deliver a profit and loss account. In future, therefore, statutory accounts on their own may prove an inadequate basis for financial warranties in the takeover of a company qualifying as small or medium-sized.

B. GENERAL

The draft form of contract for the sale of shares contained in Appendix A follows a format which is frequently adopted, namely scheduling to the main agreement (a) factual information which it is inconvenient to put in the recitals (b) the warranties (c) draft ancillary documents. All of these items could be included in the main body of the agreement but this would make both its drafting and its comprehension difficult. In addition because all the necessary information is not usually available when the first draft document is prepared, it is found easier in practice to insert information and to make amendments and additions when the document is broken up into a principal agreement and several schedules.

A contract for the sale of shares like any other contract can contain any terms which the parties care to agree. Subject to general rules relating to illegality, unreasonable restraint of trade, ultra vires etc., the terms will be enforceable. The normal form of contract is concerned principally with two matters namely (i) the events which are to happen on completion and (ii) the terms which are to continue to have effect after completion.

Terms governing completion

These will be found in Clause 5 of the draft agreement in Appendix A.

The draft assumes that the purchaser is buying the whole issued share capital of the company and is concerned with the vesting in the purchaser of effective control of the company to the exclusion of the vendor in return for payment of the price for the shares. The question of control has been discussed elsewhere in this book[1] but in summary, in the absence of special provisions in the company's memorandum or articles, the management of a company is in the hands of its board of directors, and the composition of the board of directors is in the hands of the majority shareholder. In addition certain matters, for example, altering the company's constitution can be exercised only on an affirmative resolution of the company's members in general meeting holding a specified percentage of the company's voting shares.

Some reference needs to be made to the mechanics of exercise of control. Section 22 of the 1985 Act, describes the members of the company as the subscribers of its memorandum on the registration of the company and every other person who agrees

---

[1] See Chapter 2.

to become a member and whose name is entered in the company's register of members. Thus until a transferee of shares is entered in the company's register, he is not entitled vis-à-vis the company to exercise any right attaching to his shareholding, although the transferor will be bound to exercise any such rights in accordance with directions given by the transferee. Furthermore whatever equities may exist between transferor and transferee section 360 of the 1985 Act provides that no notice of any trust, express, implied or constructive, shall be entered on the register, or be receivable by the registrar in the case of companies registered in England.

The transferee of shares cannot be registered in respect of those shares until a proper instrument of transfer has been delivered to the company and the transfer approved by the directors. A proper instrument of transfer is one that has been duly stamped with the appropriate amount of stamp duty. Since stamping invariably follows completion, it will be seen that even the transferees of the whole issued share capital of the company (of which there should be at least two)[2], will be unable immediately following completion to exercise control in their own right. For this reason the usual practice is for the outgoing shareholders to agree that on completion they will pass any resolution of the company required by the purchaser and further that they will procure the outgoing directors to pass any necessary resolutions of the board. It should be noted that the directors as such cannot bind themselves to vote since they have a fiduciary duty to the company.

The principal matters which the purchaser will require the outgoing directors to approve at the completion board meeting will be approval (subject to due stamping) of the transfer of shares to the purchaser or his nominees, the registration of the purchaser or his nominees under letters of allotment, the appointment of the purchaser's nominees as directors pursuant usually to Regulation 79, Table A of the 1985 Regulations ensuring that any maximum number of directors stipulated by the Articles is not exceeded, and the acceptance of the existing directors' resignations.

The resignations of the existing directors should be in writing and if they are to contain a waiver of claims against the

---

[2] Companies Act 1985, s. 24.

company they should be under seal since the directors as such receive no consideration for the waiver.

The contract will provide for these resignations (and for those of the secretary and possibly the auditors) to be handed over at completion, together with duly executed share transfers and the relative share certificates. In addition provision will be made for the company's books and records and documents of title to be handed to the purchaser on behalf of the company since the company will retain ownership throughout. The items which will be so handed over will include the statutory books and certificate of incorporation; the company seal; financial records; documents of title to the company's properties; cheque books and paying in books; insurance policies; counterpart service agreements and all other agreements. In addition it will be found convenient to provide for alteration of a company's bank mandate by resolution of the board on completion and, in appropriate cases, for the delivery of all technical drawings and specifications of a confidential nature. Finally, in connection with the preparation of completion minutes, it should be noted that if the company's articles contain pre-emption provisions, any transfer of its shares will require consent as specified in those provisions.

It is convenient at this point to discuss briefly directors' duties in relation to completion board resolutions. Before passing these and any other board resolutions each of the outgoing directors will need to consider his duties towards the company and its members. In summary a director must observe the utmost good faith towards the company, may not do anything which may give rise to a conflict of interest between the director's private interests and the duties of his office and may not make use of any information or opportunity obtained in his capacity as a director of the company. In the case of the smaller unquoted company where the directors are often the major shareholders, the opportunities for breach of these provisions are legion, but any act or omission of a director which is capable of ratification is permissible. Where a director has an interest which is declared, the company's articles may or may not permit him to be counted in the quorum and vote at a directors' meeting.

In addition section 309 of the 1985 Act provides that the matters to which the directors of a company are to have regard shall include the interests of the company's employees in general as well as the interests of its members. The duty imposed on the directors is however owed only to the company and is enforceable in the same way as any fiduciary duty owed to a company by its directors i.e. is enforceable by the company or, in certain circumstances, by members, but not by any employee as such.

Section 320 of the 1985 Act broadly speaking requires certain arrangements between a company and any of its directors to be first approved by a resolution of the company in general meeting. The arrangements are those for the acquisition by a director from the company of one or more non-cash assets of the requisite value, and for the acquisition by the company from a director of any such assets. Thus, the sale of shares to a company by one of its directors, or vice versa, will require the consent of the company's shareholders in general meeting if the assets are of the requisite value. A non-cash asset is of the requisite value if it is worth at least £1,000 and, subject to that, its value exceeds £50,000 or 10 per cent of the amount of the company's assets value as defined by section 320(2).

Except in certain circumstances an arrangement entered into by a company in contravention of section 320, and any transaction entered into in pursuance of the arrangement whether by the company or any other person, is voidable at the instance of the company. Additionally, the director concerned, and any other director of the company who authorised the arrangement or any transaction entered into in pursuance thereof, will, unless he shows that he took all reasonable steps to secure the company's compliance with the section, be liable to account to the company for any gain made by the arrangement or transaction directly or indirectly, and to indemnify the company for any loss or damage resulting therefrom.

A company can itself be a director, or can be a person connected with a director for the purposes of section 320. A purchaser of shares will therefore require a warranty that the company being acquired has neither entered into any arrangement in contravention of section 320, nor was connected (within the meaning of section 346 of the 1985 Act) with any person who has entered into such an arrangement at the time the arrangement was entered into.

In the exercise of the power and the discharge of the duties of his office in circumstances of any description a director of a company owes a duty to the company to exercise such care and diligence as could reasonably be expected of a reasonably prudent person in circumstances of that description and to exercise such skill as may reasonably be expected of a person of his knowledge and experience[3]. It is possible that there will be circumstances where this will provide the purchaser of shares with a remedy against former directors in addition to his remedy under the contractual warranties should the state of the company be worse than expected. A remedy against the directors would be available to the company and not to the purchaser as such[4]. The outgoing shareholders will often be identical to the outgoing directors in which case they may wish to restrict their liability to their contractual liability under the warranties. If so, the vendors will on completion require the purchaser to covenant to indemnify the outgoing directors against any action brought against them by the company following their resignation. Since, however, such an action may be brought by a liquidator following a liquidation caused by the very negligence in question, a purchaser should not readily accede to this request. It is suggested that company directors should consider insuring themselves against potential liabilities of this kind.

Post completion terms

On a conveyance of land, in the absence of agreement to the contrary, all terms of the contract of sale are deemed to be merged in the conveyance on completion. It is possible that the courts would apply this rule to the transfer of shares by analogy and it is therefore prudent to incorporate in the contract a term that insofar as any term shall not be performed at completion it shall remain in full force and effect. The main terms which will be outstanding at completion will be the vendor's warranties relating to the company, the shares of which he has sold. Any deed of indemnity or other document executed on completion

---

[3] *Re City Equitable Fire Insurance Co Ltd* [1925] Ch 407. In the case of non-executive directors, a higher standard of competence will be expected from those who are professionally qualified, at least in a relevant way: *Dorchester Finance Co Ltd v Stebbing* (1980) 1 Co Law 38.

[4] But company auditors have been held to owe a duty of care to potential purchasers in the preparation of a target company's accounts: *JEB Fasteners Ltd v Marks, Bloom & Co* (a firm) [1983] 1 All ER 583, where however the necessary element of causation was absent in the particular case.

will stand independently of the agreement for sale and will not therefore require any saving provisions.

A breach of warranty does not of itself entitle a purchaser to rescind, and it is therefore advisable for the agreement to provide for his entitlement to do so in the event of a breach being discovered prior to completion. Such a provision may be made subject to a de minimis proviso to avoid a purchaser having the opportunity to take unfair advantage of it.

As regards breaches of warranty discovered after completion, subject to any limitation of the vendor's liability (see above), a provision is sometimes inserted giving the purchaser the option of either requiring a vendor to pay the purchaser the amount of the diminution in the value of the purchaser's shares, or to pay to the company the loss suffered by it by reason of the breach of warranty. The reason for the alternative is that in certain cases it might be difficult to quantify any diminution in the value of the purchaser's shares, and that in such a case the calculation of loss could give rise to lengthy arguments on valuation and therefore protracted litigation. Where the consideration for the shares is small or nominal, the alternative remedy is essential.

For convenience of discussion of the specific warranties, it may be desirable to classify numerous warranties under one of six major headings (although such classification need not be incorporated into the contract):

1. Constitution and share capital

2. The accounts

3. Assets and liabilities other than land

4. Employees

5. Land and interests in land

6. General

Warranties relating to taxation are dealt with in section C of this chapter. It will be seen that there is a certain overlap between the above classifications. Nevertheless such overlap is customary and it is usual to provide that no warranty shall be limited by reference to any other.

(1) Constitution and share capital

A warranty that all the returns due to be made to the Companies Registry have been, and pending completion, will be made, is inadequate. In the first place most returns are not required to be made for at least 14 days after the event, so that if a special resolution were passed during the week prior to completion to change the company's name, this would not constitute a breach of this warranty. Secondly, many acts of the company require no notification to the Companies Registry, for example the issue of an unsecured debenture giving the debenture holder a right to convert the debenture into shares of the company.

Although it is not strictly speaking a warranty which relates to the company's share capital, it is convenient at this point to include a warranty that the affairs of the company have not been, and pending completion will not be, conducted in a manner unfairly prejudicial to the interests of any member of the company where the purchaser is leaving a minority holding outstanding. Any such conduct would entitle the prejudiced member to apply to the court under section 459 of the 1985 Act and the powers of the court include power (i) to order the purchase of shares of any members of the company by other members or by the company itself and, in the case of a purchase by the company itself, the reduction of the company's capital accordingly; (ii) to regulate the conduct of the company's affairs in the future.

(2) The accounts

Whether the price is negotiated on an asset value basis or a multiple of profits, reference must be made to the most recent available accounts. These should be the most recent audited accounts but it is frequently desirable during the negotiation stage to arrange for the vendors to have more up-to-date accounts prepared and, indeed, they themselves will wish to do so if this will enhance the price. Whichever set of accounts is used as the basis for valuing a company, its contents should be warranted as true and accurate by the vendors and if unaudited accounts are used the same notes should be attached to them regarding, for example, depreciation of fixed assets and provisions for taxation as would be attached to audited accounts so that the notes will be subject to the vendors' warranty. A warranty that the warranted accounts have been prepared on a basis consistent with the audited accounts of previous years is also necessary. Sometimes a vendor will be prepared to give only a limited warranty as to unaudited accounts, i.e. that they are correct to the best of his knowledge, information and belief. A purchaser should insist that a warranty as to audited accounts should be absolute and that any limited warranty as to unaudited accounts is backed by an absolute warranty as to the company's net worth at completion.

(3) Assets and liabilities other than land

The matters to be included will depend substantially upon the nature of the business of the company, and it is likely that the warranties contained in schedule 5, Appendix A will require expansion or modification in any particular case. For example, where a particular piece of machinery and spare parts for it are vital for the company's business special warranties may be required. Paragraphs 26 and 32, schedule 5 Appendix A contain warranties in general terms relating to the company's licences and insurance policies. The purchaser's pre-contract enquiries should reveal details of these and, if so, there is no reason why these details should not be scheduled and specifically warranted by the vendor.

(4) Employees

The position of employees in a take-over situation and the liabilities of the old and new employers are discussed in more detail in chapter 12.

The precedent agreement in Appendix A contains relevant warranties in paragraphs 41 to 48 of schedule 5, but other paragraphs, for example paragraphs 30 and 51 are relevant also. The warranties in effect provide inter alia that pending completion no existing contract of employment will be varied or any new contract entered into without the prior written consent of the purchaser. In the case of a company with a large work force such a provision may be impracticable and in that case the undertaking could be limited either to employees earning over a specified amount and/or employees in key positions and/or by reference to the total wage roll.

Where staff are likely to be sensitive to a take-over the

purchaser may want an early opportunity after exchange of contracts to introduce himself. The contract may for example provide for the purchaser to send all employees a letter in an agreed form immediately after exchange, provided the vendor is satisfied as to the purchaser's ability to complete.

Where any employees or directors of the target are in a pension scheme, specialist pension advice should be obtained both on the adequacy of the scheme's funding and on questions arising from differences between that scheme and any existing scheme of the purchaser.

(5) Land and interests in land

The reader is referred to the general comments under the heading 'Title to the underlying assets' in chapter 6.

The warranties in paragraph 54, schedule 5 in Appendix A are extensive and the vendor should not give them lightly. Indeed no solicitor could advise his client to give such warranties without carrying out a full investigation into the properties and carrying out the usual searches since a charge may have been registered against the property without the vendor's knowledge. Given that a full investigation is necessary, from the vendor's point of view it must be preferable to permit the purchaser to make it at his own expense and for the vendor to give no warranties save (i) as to the correctness of his replies to the purchaser's enquiries relating to the property and (ii) undertakings equivalent to the undertakings required by the Law of Property Act 1925 in the case of a person transferring 'as beneficial owner'. This course need not involve any delay if the purchaser is willing to incur extra expense in making personal local authority searches. It is however difficult where a large number of properties is involved.

(6) General

It is common for the purchaser to insert a widely worded warranty to the effect that the vendor is not aware of any matter or thing which may adversely influence a purchaser of shares in the company. It should be noted that this warranty usually refers to 'a purchaser' and not to 'the Purchaser', i.e. the vendor need not take into account any special requirements or circumstances of his own purchaser as regards this particular warranty.

Nevertheless great care should be taken before a vendor gives such a warranty since it could cover diverse circumstances, for example a major customer about to go out of business. Specific bad debts will be covered by the specific warranty in paragraph 20, schedule 5 Appendix A but the general warranty may be construed as covering loss of profit arising from the customer's collapse. Equally the general warranty may cover a key supplier about to go out of business or even an interruption in important supplies caused by war in an exporting country. Any such warranty should therefore from the vendor's point of view, if he agrees to give it at all, limit his liability to facts of which he has become aware by virtue of his control of the company, not being facts which are public knowledge. Usually, however, a vendor insists that this type of warranty be deleted entirely since it seeks to give a purchaser protection against the ordinary commercial risks of the business.

C. TAXATION

The company whose shares are being acquired may be liable to pay tax beyond that allowed for in the warranted accounts. If the taxation unallowed for is due and payable on completion, the purchaser may rely on the vendor's general warranty on the accounts since taxation is a liability which will have been understated. However, more specific protection is usually obtained either by way of express warranty or by way of indemnity to cover:

1. Liabilities which are unknown or unquantified. These may arise where the returns made to the Revenue have been incorrect; or where any liability of the company is subject to dispute.

2. Deferred and/or contingent liabilities. As regards these, express provision is usually made as follows:

   (i) CGTA 1979, section 115 provides that where a person carrying on a trade or profession applies the consideration received from the sale of qualifying assets used for the trade in the purchase of other qualifying assets to be used for that trade or another trade carried on by the same person, any capital gain made on the sale of the old assets may, at the seller's option, be rolled over by making a corresponding reduction in the acquisition price of the new assets for capital gains tax purposes. For example X Limited buys land which it occupies for the purposes of its trade for £20,000. On moving to larger premises it sells the land for £30,000 and buys a new site for £50,000. If X Limited so elects, instead of paying tax on a gain of £10,000, it may claim to treat the acquisition price of the new site as being reduced to £40,000. Thus if, after X Limited has been sold, the new site is eventually sold for £60,000 the chargeable gain will be £20,000 and not £10,000 as might have been expected from an examination of the company's accounts. Accordingly, it is usual for the vendors to warrant that the company has made no claim under CGTA 1979, section 115. Note should be made that where the replacement asset is a wasting asset, there is a ten-year time limit on the deferment of tax, so that the deferred liability may crystallise before the replacement asset is sold[5].

(ii) A deferred liability may arise under CGTA 1979, section 13 under which a gain made on the disposal of overseas assets will not be chargeable if the person chargeable claims that the conditions specified in the section are satisfied. When the conditions cease to be satisfied (which may be after the purchaser has acquired the company) the gain will be chargeable. The conditions are essentially that the gain could not be transmitted to the UK due to the laws of the territory where the income (sic) arose, or to the executive action of its government or to the impossibility of obtaining foreign currency in that territory. It is usual for the vendor to warrant that no claim has been made under section 13 because, although no tax will be payable until after the company has received the consideration giving rise to the charge, that consideration will have been reflected in the company's accounts at the time the disposal was made and

---

[5] CGTA 1979, s. 117. CGTA 1979, s. 115 is discussed from a vendor's point of view on p. 100.

the price for the shares will therefore have also reflected the gain[6].

(iii) A similar deferred liability as under (i) above can arise under the following provisions:

(a) CGTA 1979, sections 29A and 62 under which market value can be substituted for actual consideration in transactions effected other than by way of arm's length, i.e. where a company has acquired an asset, such as a principal private residence, from its majority shareholder at an over value[7].

(b) CGTA 1979, section 22(2): a loss may be claimed without an actual disposal where the owner of an asset satisfies the Revenue that its value has become negligable. In that event the claimant is treated as having sold, and immediately re-acquired, the asset for a consideration equal to the value specified in the claim. If the asset is subsequently disposed of for a greater consideration a charge to tax will arise. If, however, a claim has been made under this section, it should be reflected in the net asset value of the company shown in its accounts.

(c) There is a similar relief given by CGTA 1979, section 136 in respect of loans to a trader where the lender satisfies the Revenue that the loan is irrecoverable. Where all or part of the loan is subsequently recovered, a charge to capital gains tax will arise, but again the state of the loan should be reflected in the accounts.

(d) The base cost of an asset may be less than its actual cost by virtue of ICTA 1970, section 267 (company re-construction or amalgamation—transfer of assets) or ICTA 1970, section 273 (transfers within a group).

(e) Where a company holds shares in a non-resident company a charge to capital gains tax may arise on

---

[6] ICTA 1970, ss. 418 and 419 contain similar provisions in respect of unremittable overseas income.
[7] CGTA 1979, s. 63(6).

an amount greater than the excess of disposal proceeds over acquisition costs[8].

All the above cases can be covered by a warranty to the effect that the acquisition cost, for capital gains tax purposes, of the company's assets is not less than their value as shown in the warranted accounts. Such a warranty will not and is not intended to cover the inherent capital gains tax liabilities within a company whose assets have appreciated over the years. These liabilities should be reflected in the purchase price.

(iv) It may be appropriate for the vendors to warrant that all expenditure shown in the company's profit and loss accounts is allowable as a deduction in assessing the company's liability to corporation tax. In this connection express warranties are normally taken regarding remuneration paid and benefits provided to or for directors and employees, rent for leased assets and in connection with certain anti-avoidance provisions concerning leased assets[9].

(v) With certain limited exceptions where a company makes a distribution as defined by ICTA 1970, section 233 (and, in the case of close companies, as expanded by sections 284 and 285 of that Act), it becomes liable to pay advance corporation tax. It is usual therefore for the vendors to warrant that no such distribution has been made since 5 April 1965 other than as shown in the warranted accounts. In addition because a bonus issue following a repayment of share capital can give rise to a charge to advance corporation tax[10] a warranty should be taken that there has been since 5 April 1965 no repayment of share capital for the purposes of section 234.

(vi) In relation to the acquisition of a company which is a member of a group, ICTA 1970, section 278 deems the company leaving the group to have sold, and immediately re-acquired, at market value at the time of acquisition all assets acquired within the previous six years

---

[8] ICTA 1970, s. 268A: postponement of charge on transfer of assets to a non-resident company.
[9] ICTA 1970, s. 492.
[10] ICTA 1970, s. 234 and FA 1972, s. 84.

from other members of the group. For this purpose assets exclude trading stock but include assets which have been replaced by other business assets under the roll-over provisions of CGTA 1979, section 115. Since gains on intra-group transfers are rolled over[11], the effect will be to charge to the company leaving the group, and thus indirectly to the purchaser, the whole capital gain arising from the time the asset was acquired by a group member (or from 6 April 1965 if later) to the time when it was acquired by the member leaving the group. It should be noted also that in certain circumstances a company may be charged on capital gains made by another company which is in the same group of companies when the gain accrues[12].

If the company to be acquired has one or more subsidiaries, then any loss on the disposal of a subsidiary may be reduced, if the value of the shares in the subsidiary has been materially reduced by a depreciatory transaction, as defined by ICTA 1970, section 280, effected on or after 6 April, 1965, or if ICTA 1970, section 281 (dividend stripping) applies. A warranty that no such transaction has been effected is usual.

(vii) Where the company to be acquired has tax trading losses, ICTA 1970, section 483 may prevent such losses being carried forward and set against the profits of subsequent accounting periods. A prerequisite of the operation of the section is a change in the ownership of the company. Accordingly, where the target company has tax losses available for carry forward and for which the purchaser is paying, it is usual to ask the vendor of its shares to warrant that no such change has taken place on or after 15 April 1969, before which date any change of ownership for section 483 purposes is irrelevant. When such a change has taken place, the vendor may be asked to warrant that no major change in the nature or conduct of the company's trade has been commenced or completed after 14 April 1969. Because the definition (see below) of 'major change in the nature or conduct

---

[11] ICTA 1970, s. 273.
[12] ICTA 1970, s. 277.

of a trade' is both wide and loose, a vendor needs caution before agreeing such a warranty.

An alternative approach is for the purchaser to agree to pay at a specified rate for tax losses as and when allowed[13], but any purchaser who so agreed shortly before the 1984 Budget, when reductions in corporation tax rates for future years were announced, may well have lost out. An evaluation of that kind of commercial risk is usually best left to the client, giving the professional adviser more time to think about (i) the capital gains tax consequences or deferred consideration; (ii) the time limit, if any, on utilisation of tax losses triggering payments to the vendor; (iii) the consequences of an onward sale of the company by the purchaser prior to expiry of the time limit and (iv) from the vendor's point of view, the security of the purchaser's covenant.

It is convenient at this point to discuss section 483 more generally since the acquisition of a majority holding in the company being acquired will itself constitute a change of ownership for the purposes of that section. Accordingly, if the other conditions of section 483 are satisfied, trading losses (but not capital losses which are outside the scope of the section) incurred prior to the change of ownership may not be available for carry forward. The section states that a loss incurred by a company in an accounting period beginning before the change of ownership will not be carried forward against any income or other profits of an accounting period ending after the change of ownership if:

(a) within any period of three years there is both a change in the ownership of the company and (either earlier or later in that period or at the same time) a major change in the nature or conduct of a trade carried on by the company, or

(b) at any time after the scale of the activities in a trade carried on by a company has become small or negligible, and before any considerable revival of the trade, there is a change in the ownership of the company.

'Major change in the nature or conduct of a trade' includes

---

[13] See Ring and Clark *Tax Warranties and Indemnities* (with precedents).

(a) a major change in the type of property dealt in, or services or facilities provided, in the trade, or (b) a major change in customers, outlets or markets of the trade. Section 483 applies even if the change is the result of a gradual process which began outside the period of three years. It would therefore be appropriate for the vendor to warrant that no such change has taken place during the three years prior to exchange where the company has unrelieved trading losses.

Where, as will usually be the case, the change of ownership occurs in the middle of an accounting period, section 483 is applied as if there were two separate accounting periods, one ending with the change of ownership and the other beginning with it.

Profits or losses of the actual accounting period are usually apportioned to the two deemed periods on a time basis, save that 'if it appears that that method would work unreasonably or unjustly such other method shall be used as appears just and reasonable'[14]. Thus suppose X Limited has an accounting period coinciding with the calendar year and the change of control occurs on 30 June. Up to 30 June, X Limited made losses of £20,000 but from then until the end of the year it made profits of £10,000. The loss for the actual accounting period will be £10,000 of which that part apportioned to the period up to 30 June, namely £5,000, may be unavailable for carry forward. It will be seen that even where section 483 operates part of the loss (75 per cent in the above example) incurred prior to change of ownership is effectively allowed against subsequent profits. The percentage which is effectively relieved in these circumstances depends not only on the relative trading results of the two deemed periods, but their relative length. Suppose in the above example all the figures were the same, but the change of ownership occurred on 30 September. The loss for the actual accounting period will still be £10,000, but that apportioned to the deemed period prior to change of ownership (and therefore potentially unavailable for carry forward) will be £7,500 and that to the subsequent period £2,500.

To take another example, suppose the change as in the first example occurs on 30 June. Again the losses up to this date are £20,000 but under its new management the company earns

---

[14] ICTA 1970, s. 483(2).

second half profits of £20,000, There will be neither profit nor loss for the actual accounting period and therefore no profit or loss to be apportioned to either of the deemed periods. The whole of the loss incurred in the deemed accounting period prior to change of ownership will have been relieved. It will be seen that there are opportunities for judicious timing both in acquiring the company and in making sales and purchases of trading stock subsequently. However, if the change in the nature of the trade takes place shortly after the change in ownership, the Revenue may resist the apportionment of profit of the actual accounting period on a time basis.

Where the purchaser is a company, timing of the acquisition may also need to take into account the group relief provisions contained in ICTA 1970, sections 258 to 264[15] whereby losses of one company within a group may be relieved against the profits of the corresponding accounting period of the other member(s) of the group. As regards date of change of ownership, references to ownership are to be construed as references to beneficial ownership[16]. Beneficial ownership of shares will normally change on exchange of contracts, unless the contract is conditional on a condition precedent in which case it will change when the conditions have been satisfied.

It should be noted that in any event losses incurred in a trade can be carried forward only against profits from the same trade. Even if section 483 is inapplicable because, for example, the change in the nature of a trade takes place outside the three-year period, a loss may be unavailable for carry forward because the company under its new management undertakes a different trade[17].

FA 1972, section 101 contains restrictions on the carry forward of surplus advance corporation tax against mainstream corporation tax liability parallel to those on the carry forward of tax trading losses contained in ICTA 1970, section 483.

The above matters are by no means exhaustive of the warranties which may be required in any particular case and in addition the purchaser will require a tax indemnity in the form set out in the fourth schedule to the Agreement set out in Appendix A. In

---

[15] As amended, particularly by FA 1981, s. 40 and FA 1984, ss. 46 and 47, and by FA 1985, Sch. 9.

[16] ICTA 1970, s. 484(7).

[17] ICTA 1970, s. 177(1).

essence the usual indemnity relates to those events and transactions occurring on or prior to the date of completion of the sale of the shares which could give rise to a tax liability on the company and are not allowed for in the warranted accounts. The liabilities referred to above and covered by specific warranties will not arise solely by reference to events occurring prior to completion and are therefore not covered by the usual form of indemnity. It would serve no useful purpose to list the occasions of charge which an indemnity is designed to cover, first because they are legion, and secondly because they change too frequently for any such list to be instructive. The principal situations other than as above where an undisclosed tax liability may arise are where the company is liable to be assessed as a result of some other person failing to pay tax, i.e. a shareholder on an apportionment of a close company's income to him; or where there has been prior to the acquisition of the company a transfer of capital assets within a group of companies of which the company formed part; or where the company being acquired has participated in some transaction which gives rise to assessment under an anti-avoidance provision, or, under the Ramsay principle, where the substance of a transaction gives rise to a tax liability notwithstanding that its form does not[18]. Accordingly the usual tax indemnity is widely framed and in particular it will be seen that the expression 'taxation' is widely defined in the draft indemnity to cover all existing taxes and some that no longer exist. From the vendor's point of view, however, it is better for the indemnity to relate only to specific statutory provisions which may create or increase tax liabilities, rather than to cover the generality of tax liabilities.

Both parties need to consider the different effects of warranties and indemnities. For example, breach of warranty will require investigation into the loss suffered by the purchaser which may or may not be identical with the additional tax suffered by the target company. Further the purchaser will be under the usual duty to mitigate his loss. Neither of these factors will apply to a straightforward indemnity obligation which is an obligation to pay on the happening of certain events. There is additionally a possible difference in the tax treatment of payments under

---

[18] *W. T. Ramsay Ltd v IRC* [1982] AC 300, [1981] 1 All ER 865; and see *Furniss v Dawson* [1984] AC 474, [1984] 1 All ER 530.

warranty claims, which are treated as adjustments in the price for capital gains tax purposes[19], and payments under an indemnity, which may be made to the target company, in respect of which the capital gains tax consequences are unclear.

3. Liabilities of participators in close companies. An exhaustive definition of the meaning of the terms 'close company' and 'participator' is inappropriate to this book. Suffice it to say that most unquoted companies resident in the UK will be close unless controlled by a non-close company. A participator in a company includes a person having a share or interest in the capital or income of the company. This definition includes, besides shareholders, persons who have unconditionally contracted to purchase shares or who have an option to purchase shares. The enquiring reader is referred to ICTA 1970, Chapter III, Part XI for the relevant definitions.

The principal danger for a purchaser of shares is that under Schedule 16 to FA 1972 there may be apportioned to participators in a close trading company the excess of the company's relevant income for any accounting period over its distributions for that period less the amount which needs to be retained to meet the requirements of the company's business[20]. For accounting periods ending after 26 March 1980 the trading income of a company which is a trading company, or a member of a trading group, will not form part of its relevant income, but investment income can still be apportioned. In the case of a close non-trading company, the whole income may be so apportioned. Income will be apportioned according to the respective interests of the participators in the company, and the consequence will be (inter alia) that the individual to whom income is apportioned will be liable to income tax at higher rates on it as if it were the top slice of his income.

Individuals, who are members of the company at the end of its accounting period, are treated as the participators for the whole accounting period, and could therefore have apportioned

---

[19] CGTA 1979, s. 41.

[20] In determining the requirements of a company's business for shortfall purposes, regard is also to be had to requirements necessary or advisable for the acquisition of a trade or of a controlling interest in a trading company: FA 1978, s. 36 and Sch. 5. The provision applies with respect to accounting periods ending on or after 11 April 1978 irrespective of the date of acquisition.

to them pre-acquisition profits which may have been taken into account in the calculation of the purchase price. Since the requirements of a company's business are taken into account by the Revenue in deciding whether an apportionment is appropriate, a problem can arise for vendors of shares also in that these requirements will in practice be examined in relation to the last accounting period in which the vendors were shareholders after they have sold their shares. If the purchaser is an individual, or itself a close company, it will be unwilling to undertake to avoid an apportionment by the declaration of a sufficiently high dividend. Consideration should be given by the vendor to obtaining formal clearances for all relevant accounting periods under FA 1972, Sch. 16, para. 18, and the purchaser may wish to insist on such clearance being obtained as a condition of the transaction.

As regards capital transfer tax, although a close company's transfer of value may be apportioned among the participants, the apportionment is made according to their respective rights and interests in the company immediately before the transfer. Thus only a transfer of value made between contract and completion of the purchase could adversely affect a purchasing shareholder. This can be covered by a warranty, or will be covered by the usual deed of indemnity provided the deed indemnifies the purchaser in respect of all events occurring up to completion. The company itself may however be liable to pay capital transfer tax in respect of transfers of value made to it, and such liability should be covered by the usual tax indemnity.

5 Stamp Duty

A. CONVEYANCE OR TRANSFER DUTY

Unless a share transfer executed in the United Kingdom is stamped with transfer duty of one per cent on the price paid for the shares (or their market value if higher) the company may not register the transfer so that the transferee will not be entered as a member of the company[1]. Furthermore an unstamped transfer may not be admitted as evidence in any legal proceedings and if a transfer is lodged for stamping after 30 days has elapsed from its execution the Commissioners may impose a penalty over and above the duty originally payable up to the amount of that duty.

FA 1927, section 55 (as amended), provides an important exemption from transfer duty where the consideration for the shares (or for an undertaking or part of an undertaking) to be acquired consists mainly of shares in the acquiring company. The conditions to be satisfied for the exemption to be claimed are:

1. The transaction is in connection with a scheme for the reconstruction of any company or companies or the amalgamation of any companies.

2. A limited company has been registered, or the nominal share capital of a company has been increased, with a view to the

---

[1] *Maynard v Consolidated Kent Collieries Corpn* [1903] 2 KB 121; and CA 1985, s. 183(1).

acquisition of, either the undertaking of, or not less than 90 per cent of the issued share capital of, any particular existing company. The issue of unissued share capital will be treated as an increase of capital for this purpose.

3. The consideration for the acquisition (save such part as consists of the transfer to, or discharge by, the transferee company of liabilities of the existing company) consists as to not less than 90 per cent of shares in the transferee company issued:

   (i) where an undertaking is to be acquired, to the existing company or to holders of its shares, or

   (ii) where shares are to be acquired, to holders of shares in the existing company in exchange for their shares in that company.

4. Both companies are incorporated in Great Britain.

5. A company is not a 'particular existing company' unless:

   (i) the memorandum of association of the transferee company has as one of its objects the acquisition of the undertaking of, or shares in, the existing company or

   (ii) the resolution for the increase of capital of the transferee company shows by its wording that the increase is authorised for the purpose of acquiring the undertaking of, or shares in, the existing company.

6. The transfer of the shares or undertaking is executed within 12 months of the registration of the transferee company or of the date of the increase in the share capital, unless made pursuant to an agreement filed at the Companies Registry within that period.

7. Shares in the transferee company will not be regarded as having been issued unless the persons to whom they are issued are registered in respect of them, i.e. the issue on renounceable letters of allotment will not suffice[2], nor will the issue to nominees of the existing company or of the holders of its shares[3].

8. For there to be a scheme of reconstruction there must be a

---

[2] *Oswald Tillotson Ltd v IRC* [1933] 1 KB 134.
[3] *Brotex Celluloid Fibres Ltd v IRC* [1933] 1 KB 158.

transfer of the undertaking, or part thereof, from an existing company to another company, and the undertaking must continue substantially unaltered. A scheme of amalgamation has been held to exist where the holders of shares in the existing company were obliged to sell one-third of the shares issued to them in the transferee company to a shareholder in the transferee company who at the time of the transaction held that fraction of the transferee company's shares.

9. The exemption will be lost:

   (i) where shares in the transferee company have been issued to the existing company and the existing company ceases (otherwise than in consequence of reconstruction, amalgamation or liquidation) within two years of the registration or the increase in capital of the transferee company to be the beneficial owner of its shares

   (ii) where the exemption has been allowed in connection with the acquisition by the transferee company of shares in another company, the transferee company (otherwise than as above) ceases within two years of its incorporation or increase of its capital to be the beneficial owner of the shares acquired.

10. Where the transferee company already holds more than 10 per cent of the existing company condition 2 above cannot be satisfied[4].

It will be seen that the conditions for claiming exemption are exacting and the Commissioners require a statutory declaration by a solicitor in support of a claim. The requirement that the shares in the transferee company be actually registered in the name of the holders of shares in the existing company, and in the same proportions as they held shares in the existing company, makes FA 1927, section 55 unsuitable where these holders intend immediately after completion to sell their shares. This is likely to arise where a transferee company is listed and desires to issue the vendors with shares as consideration for the purchase, but the vendors require cash. In such a case the purchasers will arrange with the Stock Exchange for the exchange shares to be admitted to listing and will arrange for brokers to place these shares with third parties on behalf of the vendors to raise

---

[4] *Lever Bros Ltd v IRC* [1938] 2 KB 518, [1938] 2 All ER 808.

the requisite amount of cash. This operation is called a 'vendor placing'. Although section 55 can be satisfied on issue of the consideration shares to the vendors, on their subsequent sale by the vendors for cash conveyance on sale duty will be payable on the executed share transfers by the purchasers[5]. In this situation, or wherever purchasers are buying for cash and for some reason the conditions of section 55 cannot be satisfied, it used to be possible to adopt a common avoidance scheme, known as the 'pref-trick', which depended for its success on two principal factors:

(a) the issue of shares on renounceable letters of allotment, since renunciation of such letters did not attract conveyance or transfer duty[6];

(b) the diversion of the main value of the company out of the shares to be transferred by way of dutiable share transfers and into the shares to be issued on renounceable letters of allotment.

The exemption from conveyance on sale duty for renounceable letters of allotment which is provided by FA 1963, section 65(1) has, however, now been restricted by FA 1985, section 81. No exemption will be available where rights to shares (and certain loan stock) in a company are renounced in favour of a person who has control of the company issuing the shares, or who will have control in consequence of the arrangement under which the rights are renounced. A person has control of a company if he, or he with persons connected with him as defined by section 81(6), has power to control that company's affairs by virtue of holding shares in, or possession voting power in relation to, that company or any other body corporate. These provisions apply to renunciations made on or after 1 August 1985 except where the renunciations result from an offer which had become unconditional as to acceptances on or before 27 June 1985.

Earlier renunciations made as part of a tax avoidance scheme, such as the pref-trick, may nevertheless be dutiable since the

---

[5] Exemption from stamp duty may also be obtained where the vendor and purchaser companies are associated within the meaning of FA 1930, s. 42 as amended by FA 1967, s. 27.

[6] FA 1963, s. 65(1).

Revenue regard the decisions in *Ramsay (WT) Ltd v IRC*[7] and *Furniss v Dawson*[8] as likely to apply to stamp duty avoidance schemes, and such schemes will be challenged where the acquiring company had not obtained effective control of more than 50 per cent of the votes in the target company on or before 27 July 1984[9]. The extra-statutory concession announced on that date has now been enacted with certain amendments as FA 1985, section 78. This section applies with retroactive effect to 28 July 1984 where one company issues 'relevant securities' in exchange for shares or convertible loan stock in another company and the first company either has control of the other, or will have control in consequence of the exchange or of a general offer as a result of which the exchange is made. As regards instruments executed after 31 July 1985, section 78 is modified by FA 1985, s. 80. Where section 78 applies instruments transferring the shares in the target company are not chargeable with conveyance on sale duty. Where the issuing company issues or transfers other property as well as relevant securities in exchange for shares in the target, there is provision for partial relief[10]. 'Relevant securities' are registerable shares or other securities 'in relation to which the terms of the general offer or other arrangement providing for the exchange make no provision for partial or total conversion directly or indirectly into money (whether by way of redemption, sale or otherwise) at a time which falls or may fall before the expiry of the period of three years commencing with the day on which the exchange is completed'[11]. If the intruments are executed after 31 July 1985 the terms of a general offer or other arrangement are to be disregarded for this purpose to the extent that they provide for the sale of securities to a person other than the issuing company[12]. This would seem to cover the situation where the agreement provides for the issuer's exchange shares to be listed on the Stock Exchange. Section 78(5) provides that relevant securities shall not be taken to be issued unless registered, in a register kept by or on behalf of the issuing company, either in the name of the persons transferring shares in the

---

[7] [1982] AC 300, [1981] 1 All ER 865, HL.
[8] [1984] AC 474, [1984] 1 All ER 530, HL.
[9] Stamp Duty: Transfer of Shares or a Take over (Inland Revenue Press Release, 27 July 1984).
[10] FA 1985, s. 78(3).
[11] FA 1985, s. 78(4).
[12] FA 1985, s. 80(4).

target by way of exchange, or alternatively (but only in respect of instruments executed after 31 July 1985)[13] in the name of the target company and held on trust for the person so transferring. There is provision for instruments of transfer to be presented for denoting[14]

FA 1985, section 78 therefore provides a simpler route to exemption from stamp duty on a share for share exchange than FA 1927, section 55 particularly because, unlike the latter section, there is no requirement for the issuing company to retain the target company's shares for any particular period, nor for the vendors to retain their shares in the issuing company. FA 1985, section 78 however has no application to the acquisition of an undertaking as opposed to shares and, whereas under that section exemption will be lost to the extent that the consideration is property other than relevant securities, there will be no loss of the exemption under FA 1927, section 55 if up to 10 per cent of the purchase consideration consists of cash.

The Inland Revenue carefully scrutinise claims for relief under FA 1927, section 55 and it should be assumed that it will do so in connection with claims under FA 1985, section 78. In connection with any such claim, therefore:

(i) The Inland Revenue will look closely at all company resolutions to assess their effectiveness[15].

(ii) Any restructuring must be carried out in accordance with the company's memorandum and articles of association and the Companies Acts (including sections 80 and 125 of the Companies Act 1985 so far as relevant), and particular care must be taken to see that a quorum is present at the board and general meetings and that all requisite notices thereof (and consents to short notice if required) have been given.

(iii) A renounceable letter of allotment (if free of duty following enactment of FA 1985, section 81) is free of duty only if the rights thereunder are renounceable not later than six months after the date of its issue[16]. This point is relevant

[13] FA 1985, s. 80(5).
[14] FA 1985, s. 78(10).
[15] For an example of a decision (in another context) as to why a company resolution was ineffective, see *Re Zinotty Properties Ltd* [1984] 3 All ER 754, [1984] 1 WLR 1249.
[16] Stamp Act 1891, Sch. 1.

where the acquiring company issues shares on renounceable letters of allotment. The restriction on the exemption from duty for such letters contained in FA 1985, section 81 and discussed above basically applies where a target company issues them in a takeover situation.

(iv) The acquiring company will have to file a note of any increase of its capital[17] and make a return of allotments[18].

(v) A straightforward share for exchange is unlikely of itself to have adverse tax consequences for the vendors. On the contrary it may result in a deferral of liability to capital gains tax[19]. Where, however, retirement relief would otherwise be available under FA 1985, section 69 on a sale for cash, it will not normally be available on a sale of substituted securities.

B. CAPITAL DUTY

Ad valorem duty of one per cent is chargeable on certain transactions undertaken by a 'capital company' which includes a limited liability company incorporated according to the law of any part of the UK if either (a) the place of effective management of the company is in Great Britain, or (b) its registered office is in Great Britain but its place of effective management is outside the EEC.

The chargeable transactions which are most common in practice are those referred to in FA 1973, Sch. 19, sub-paras (a) to (c) of paragraph 1, namely:

(a) the formation of a capital company;

(b) an increase in the capital of a capital company by the contribution of assets of any kind including the conversion of loan stock into share capital and the issue of shares in satisfaction of a debt owed by the company[20];

---

[17] Companies Act 1985, s. 123.
[18] Companies Act 1985, s. 88.
[19] CGTA 1979, s. 85.
[20] FA 1973, Sch. 19, para. 2(2).

(c) an increase in the assets of the capital company by the contribution of assets of any kind in consideration, not of shares, but of rights of the same kind as those of members of the company such as voting rights, a share in profits or a share in the surplus on liquidation.

Duty is generally chargeable on the actual value of the assets of any kind contributed by members of the company, or the nominal value of the company's shares allotted on the relevant occasion whichever is greater[1]. An issue of bonus shares, unlike an issue of shares for a consideration, is not chargeable to capital duty, however, since although the company's capital will be increased thereby, the issue involves no contribution of assets from outside the company. Furthermore in the case of chargeable transactions falling within sub-paragraphs (a) to (c) of paragraph 1, Schedule 19, where the consideration provided by the capital company for the acquisition of all or any of the assets contributed consists, wholly or partly, of the assumption of liabilities transferred to it or the discharge by the company of any liabilities, the actual value of assets contributed is to be treated as reduced by an amount equal to the liabilities so assumed or discharged.

There is however an important exemption contained in FA 1973, Schedule 19, paragraph 10, which corresponds to, but is not identical with, the exemption from conveyance or transfer duty under FA 1927, section 55 discussed above. For the exemption to apply the following conditions must be satisfied:

(i) a capital company in the process of being formed or already in existence has acquired share capital of another capital company to the extent that, after the transaction, not less than 75 per cent of the other company's issued share capital is beneficially owned by the first company, or has acquired the whole or any part of the undertaking of another capital company;

(ii) the place of effective management or the registered office of the acquired company is in the EEC;

---

[1] It should be noted that where members of a company undertake to pay calls on shares, the liability to pay capital duty arises when the undertaking is given and not when the calls are made or paid: *Cambridge Petroleum Royalties v IRC* [1982] STC 325.

(iii) so much, if any, of the consideration for the acquisition as does not consist of shares in the acquiring company consists wholly of a payment in cash not exceeding 10 per cent of the nominal value of the shares which make up the balance of the consideration. However, no account is to be taken of that part of the consideration as consists of the assumption or discharge by the acquiring company of liabilities of the acquired company.

Unlike the exemption from conveyance or transfer duty under FA 1927, section 55, the exemption from capital duty applies whether or not a scheme of reconstruction or amalgamation is to be effected and therefore it is not necessary for the resolution increasing the capital of the acquiring company to state that the increase is with a view to the acquisition of the shares in, or undertaking of, the acquired company. It will be seen that it is not necessary to acquire 75 per cent of another company's share capital all at once for the exemption to apply. If the first acquisition is of, say, 51 per cent and the second 25 per cent, then an issue of shares to acquire the latter (and issues in respect of subsequent acquisitions) will be exempt from capital duty if the other conditions are satisfied. Any issue of shares in respect of the first acquisition will remain fully chargeable. If, however, the acquisition is in respect of 75 per cent all at once, the whole issue of shares will be exempt. For the exemption to apply, it would seem that by analogy with cases decided in connection with claims for exemption under FA 1927, section 55 there can be an issue of shares in the acquiring company only if the members of the acquired company are registered as holders of the consideration shares.

Care needs to be taken as regards satisfying condition (iii) above wherever any consideration is to be other than of shares in the acquiring company. First any other type of consideration (other than the assumption or discharge of liabilities of the acquired company) must consist of a 'payment in cash'. Thus consideration consisting of loan stock, or the rendering of services, or even a deferred cash consideration, will cause the exemption to be lost. Furthermore the cash payment must not exceed 10 per cent of the nominal value of the shares making up the balance of the consideration. Such nominal value may be substantially less than the actual value of the shares in question with the result that the actual percentage of the consideration which can be paid in cash, without forfeiting the exemption, will be correspondingly lower.

The exemption from capital duty may be lost if within five years of the exempt chargeable transaction the acquiring company ceases to retain at least 75 per cent of the acquired company's share capital.

Although the conditions for exemption in respect of capital duty on the one hand, and conveyance or transfer duty on the other, are not identical, FA 1973, Schedule 19, paragraph 13 provides that if a transfer of assets to a capital company forms part of a chargeable transaction consisting of either the formation or increase in capital of a capital company, and is made in consideration of the issue of shares in the company, no transfer duty shall be chargeable on the transfer except insofar as the consideration is referable to the transfer of (a) stock or securities, or (b) the whole or any part of an undertaking or (c) any estate of interest in land.

6 Investigating Title and Completion

Aside from any express warranties and indemnities given by a vendor, he is often expressed to agree to transfer his shares 'as beneficial owner'. This phrase is a term of art in land transactions, and its use implies certain covenants by the vendor in favour of the purchaser under the Law of Property Act 1925. An agreement for the sale of shares is not usually a conveyance as defined by the Law of Property Act 1925, and it would seem therefore that there will be no covenants automatically implied by virtue of that Act in favour of a purchaser of shares from a vendor expressed to sell 'as beneficial owner'. Nevertheless the phrase 'as beneficial owner' is so well known among lawyers that its use might be regarded by the courts as showing that it was the intention of the parties that the implied covenants should be incorporated insofar as they could be made relevant to a sale of shares. The position however is not clear. Briefly the implied covenants adapted to share sale situations would be approximately:

(a) the vendor is entitled to transfer the shares;

(b) the purchaser's title shall not be called into question by previous owners;

(c) the shares are transferred free from incumbrances;

(d) the vendor will take such steps as may be necessary following completion to perfect the purchaser's title.

Such covenants would all relate to title to shares in the company being sold and not to title of the company to its underlying assets. The covenants are clearly of use to a purchaser and it is advisable to spell them out in the purchase contract rather than hope that they may be implied by use of the phrase 'as beneficial owner'.

The starting point of investigating title to shares is the memorandum and articles of the company in question. In the first place this will show who are the subscribers and how many shares they agreed to subscribe to on incorporation. The 1985 Act, section 22 deems subscribers to be members of the company. Subject to any special or unusual provisions in the memorandum or articles, the subscribers will immediately upon incorporation be the only members of the company and they will at that moment be in sole control of it. It follows, for example, that an appointment of first directors by shareholders other than the subscribers will only be valid if supported by a transfer of the subscribers' shares to the shareholders concerned being a transfer which has been registered before the appointment of the directors.

Secondly, the memorandum and articles will contain any restrictions on the transferability of shares or on the restructuring of share capital and will show what consents, if any, have to be obtained. The articles of many unquoted companies contain some provisions the general effect of which is to forbid the transfer of any share by a member of the company to an outsider if any other member of the company is willing to purchase it at a price calculated by reference to a formula, often a proportion of the company's net tangible asset value. The well-drawn preemption article will contain both a notice procedure, which must be complied with by any intending vendor of shares, and a provision that the restriction will not apply to any transfer to which all the members of the company have consented in writing. A purchaser must satisfy himself that, either the notice procedure has been complied with, or the consents obtained, not only in respect of the proposed transfer to himself but also in respect of transfers to previous owners of the shares in question.

In the case of smaller unquoted companies a purchaser will often find that the formalities have been virtually ignored. Some documents will be incorrect and others missing. It is not of course permissible to backdate or invent documents, but suitable confirmations after the event will at least raise an estoppel and a purchaser will usually be prepared to accept the position if no contrary circumstances are known to exist.

So far as is known, no title indemnity insurance is written to cover a transfer of shares and it would therefore, except in a substantial case, be relatively expensive to have a special insurance contract prepared. Technical defects in title are so frequent in smaller companies that most purchasers are prepared to take a commercial view in the absence of suspicious circumstances. Thus the purchaser need not be concerned if he finds that some years ago all the shareholders of the company simultaneously transferred their respective shares without complying with the pre-emption procedure. The simultaneous transfer to the same person would strongly suggest a mutual consent by all shareholders—if the transfers are each for a different consideration per share, however, further investigation may be necessary.

After reading the company's memorandum and articles the purchaser will know what, if any, special points to look out for when he comes to investigate the company's statutory books. 'Statutory books' is a composite term for the records, other than financial records, which statute and/or a company's articles require it to keep. Specially printed statutory books are cheaply available from all the company registration agents. One type comprises a register of allotments, a register of members, a register of transfers, registers of directors and secretaries, registers of debentures and directors' interests, blank pages to which board minutes can be attached and finally some 20 blank share certificates perforated down one side so that they can be torn out and completed when desired[1].

As he looks through the statutory books, the purchaser should keep in mind that he is concerned with title to the shares he wishes to buy. That is to say, he must investigate the transfer to the vendors of the shares in question and each preceding transfer

---

[1] The reader may practise investigating statutory books by looking at the statutory books of quoted companies. Subject to its power to close the register for 30 days a year every company is obliged to permit anyone to inspect its register of members during normal business hours on payment of 5 pence—or without charge in the case of members of the Company: Companies Act 1985, s. 356. The register of members will usually be kept at the company's registered office—if not the company is obliged to file a notice at the Companies Registry stating where it is kept: s. 353. The statutory books of larger quoted companies are usually immaculate and, therefore, worth studying.

as far back as the original allotment of the shares by the company. If on any such occasion the transfer or allotment required, for example, some resolution of the directors he must satisfy himself that the persons who purported to pass the necessary resolutions were indeed the properly appointed directors of the company at the relevant time. This point needs particular attention when the provisions for rotation of directors, contained in Table A (see below) have not been excluded. Such provisions are quite often found in smaller private companies and are just as often found to have been ignored, so that technically there may have been occasions when the company had insufficient directors for a quorum, or even no directors at all. This type of defect cannot be corrected, but should not be regarded as fatal particularly in the case of a family company where there have been no disputes amongst shareholders and where the vendors are prepared to give a warranty to cover the position[2].

Table A is the specimen form of articles of association for a company limited by shares and is set out in the Schedule to the 1985 Regulations. There is no obligation on any company to adopt all or any part of Table A. In practice however most private companies are likely to adopt the greater part of Table A with modifications to suit their particular circumstances. In practice most target companies investigated for some years to come will be found to have adopted Table A of the 1948 Act, as amended by Companies Act 1980 in the case of companies registered after 21 December 1980.

In addition, the purchaser will need to consider the application of Companies Act 1985, sections 80 and 89 to any allotment of shares which took place after 21 December 1980. Section 80 provides that directors of a company may not allot shares or convertible stock therein unless authorised by the company in general meeting or by the company's articles. Any such authority must state the maximum amount of securities to which it applies and the date of expiry of the authority. The maximum period for an authority is five years, but it may be renewed by the company in general meeting for further periods up to a

---

[2] The provisions for rotation of directors are a nuisance and of little value to the shareholders of most companies, and it is surprising that the 1985 Regulations should have retained them in the new Table A. One advantage of buying a 'ready made' company from company registration agents is that their standard form articles usually exclude these provisions.

maximum of five years and so on ad infinitum. An authority may be revoked or varied by ordinary resolution of the company's members even though it alters the articles. Although it is an offence for a director to permit or authorise a contravention of the provision, the allotment will not thereby be invalidated. Section 80 does not apply to shares taken by subscribers to the company's memorandum or to shares allotted pursuant to an employee's share scheme.

Section (1) provides that a company shall not allot any 'equity securities' unless it first offers to allot the same amongst existing holders of 'relevant shares' pro rata to their existing holdings and on the same or more favourable terms. Offerees must be given at least 21 days' notice before the offer can be withdrawn. 'Relevant shares' are all shares other than those which as respects dividends and capital carry a right to participate only up to a specified amount and shares held under an employees' share scheme. 'Equity security' means a relevant share (or right to subscribe for, or convert securities into, relevant shares) other than a share taken by a subscriber to the memorandum, or a bonus share. A private company may exclude section 89(1) by a provision in its memorandum or articles[3] and that section will not in any event apply to a particular allotment of equity securities which are to be wholly or partly paid up otherwise than in cash[4]. Furthermore, section 89(1) may be made inapplicable, or modified, by the articles or by special resolution so long as the directors have an authority for the purposes of section 80[5].

With the above points in mind, the purchaser should seek at least a title to the shares in question which can be clearly traced by entries in the register of allotments and/or transfers and in the register of members together with either the original registration application forms, where shares have been allotted, or duly stamped share transfer forms, where transfers have occurred. Original documents of this nature should preferably be kept with the statutory books. In addition a purchaser should ensure that share certificates issued to the previous owners of the shares are with the statutory books and endorsed as duly cancelled, or that the company holds a suitable indemnity in the case of a lost certificate.

---

[3] Companies Act 1985, s. 91.
[4] Companies Act 1985, s. 89(4).
[5] Companies Act 1985, s. 95.

The 1985 Act and Table A scheduled to the 1985 Regulations provide assistance in investigating title in the following ways:

(1) The certificate of incorporation is conclusive evidence that all requirements for registration have been complied with and that the company has been duly registered under the Act[6].

(2) The certification by a company of an instrument of transfer constitutes a representation by the company to any person acting on the faith of such certification that there have been produced to the company 'such documents as on the face of them show a prima facie title to the shares ... in the transferor named in the instrument of transfer, but not as a representation that the transferor has any title to the shares ...[7]'. Certain acts may constitute certification by the company[8]. Where, however, a purchaser is effectively buying the company, such certification is of little value.

(3) A certificate under the common seal of the company, or under the special duplicate authorised by Companies Act 1985, section 40, specifying any shares held by a member is prima facie evidence of title of the member to the shares[9]. Note that a duly sealed certificate constitutes only prima facie evidence of a title.

(4) The 1985 Act, section 361 provides that the register of members is prima facie evidence of any matters directed or authorised by the Act to be inserted therein. Such matters include the names and addresses of the members, a statement of the shares held by each of them with their distinguishing numbers and of the amount paid or agreed to be considered as paid on the shares of each member, the dates on which each person (i) was entered in the register as a member, and (ii) ceased to be a member[10].

(5) The 1985 Act, section 382(1) requires the company to keep minutes of meetings of its members and directors, and section 382(2) provides that any such minutes purporting to be

---

[6] Companies Act 1985, s. 13(7).
[7] Companies Act 1985, s. 184(1).
[8] Companies Act 1985, s. 184(3).
[9] Companies Act 1985, s. 186.
[10] Companies Act 1985, s. 352.

signed by the chairman of the meeting, or of the next succeeding meeting, shall be evidence of the proceedings. Where minutes have been made in accordance with this section then, until the contrary is proved, the meeting is deemed to have been duly held and convened, and all proceedings duly had, and all appointments as directors, managers or liquidators to be valid.

(6) The acts of a director are valid notwithstanding any defect that may afterwards be discovered in his appointment or qualification[11]. This does not cover the situation where no appointment at all has been made[12], or where the defect is known at the time of the act in question[13].

(7) Where Regulation 58 of Table A, 1948 Act, or the similar but not identical Regulation 47 of Table A of the 1985 Regulations, applies, an entry in the company's minute book to the effect that the chairman of the meeting of its members has declared a resolution to have been carried, carried unanimously or by a particular majority by a show of hands, is conclusive evidence of that fact.

(8) Regulation 73 of Table A, 1948 Act and Regulation 63 of Table A of the 1985 Regulations, deal with the validity of proxies in the case of the prior termination of the proxy's authority where notice of termination was not received by the company prior to commencement of the meeting.

(9) Where Regulation 106 of Table A 1948 Act, or Regulation 93 of Table A of the 1985 Regulations, applies, a resolution in writing, signed by all directors for the time being entitled to receive notice of a meeting of the directors, is as valid as if it had been passed at a duly convened board meeting. A similar provision concerning written resolutions signed by all of a company's members in relation to general meetings of a company may be incorporated into its articles depending upon the date of the company's registration[14].

---

[11] Companies Act 1985, s. 285.

[12] But see Companies Act 1985, ss. 285 and 292(2).

[13] Compare reg. 105, Part I of Table A of the 1948 Act and the more widely worded reg. 92 of Table A to the 1985 Regulations.

[14] See reg. 5, Part II Table A, 1948 Act; reg. 73A, Table A, 1948 Act; and reg. 53 Table A of the 1984 Regulations.

If the investigation of the statutory books proves satisfactory, the following searches should be made immediately before completion, in addition to any searches which may have been made prior to exchange of contracts:

(a) A search in the Companies Registry against the company being acquired to ensure that no notice of a resolution for winding up has been filed. The 1985 Act, section 576 provides that any transfer of shares (but not of debentures) not being a transfer made to or with the sanction of the liquidator, made after the commencement of a voluntary winding up shall be void. A voluntary winding up is deemed to commence at the time of the passing of the resolution for voluntary winding up[15]. The resolution must be notified by advertisement in the Gazette within 14 days after passing of the resolution[16] and there is no statutory protection for a purchaser if he searches and completes during the intervening period.

There is similar provision in the case of a winding up by the court. Here a transfer of shares after the commencement of a winding up is void unless the court otherwise orders[17].

(b) In the case of the winding up of a company by the court not only are transfers of shares prima facie void but also any disposition of the company's property[18]. Accordingly, before completion a search should be made against any corporate vendor of shares in the company being acquired. Bankruptcy searches against individual vendors should be made in the Land Charges Registry.

There is no requirement for a notice to be filed of an agreement by a company to issue, or of an agreement by its shareholders to secure the issue of, shares at some future date, unless such an agreement is itself contained in a registerable debenture containing conversion rights. Such a possibility must be covered by an appropriate warranty from the vendors. On the other hand a company search will reveal whether the target company has been authorised by special resolution passed within the

---

[15] Companies Act 1985, s. 574.
[16] Companies Act 1985, s. 573.
[17] Companies Act 1985, s. 522.
[18] Companies Act 1985, s. 522.

previous 15 days to enter into a contract to make an off-market purchase, or a contingent purchase, of its own shares[19].

For a list of the items to be physically collected by the purchaser on completion see Clause 5 of the Agreement in Appendix A.

B. TITLE TO THE UNDERLYING ASSETS

(1) Land

Any discussion of the investigation to title of land would be out of place here. Suffice it to say that local authority and Land Charges Registry searches should be made and the vendors should be required to permit to be made Land Registry searches also. These searches however offer formal protection only to purchasers of the land and not to purchasers of shares in the company owning the land. The documents of title should also be examined on completion, but because of the lack of formal Land Registry and Land Charges Registry protection, a purchaser of shares may still in effect acquire land subject to unregistered encumbrances.

Vendors sometimes take the attitude that a purchaser cannot be given the opportunity fully to investigate title as well as warranties as to title. If a purchaser is forced to choose, he will need to consider the following factors among others:

(i) The value of the vendor's covenants.

(ii) The practicability and desirability of a full investigation of title, where numerous titles are involved, e.g. a chain of shops.

(iii) Whether particular premises, or the permitted user thereof, is fundamental to the business of the company, i.e. a company operating a licensed gaming club, or owning land which reflects development value, in which case damages for breach of warranty would be unlikely to be a sufficient remedy.

(iv) The relative value of the land and of the other assets.

In any event a company search should be made immediately

---

[19] Companies Act 1985, ss. 164(2), 165(2) and 380.

prior to completion. This will reveal whether any charges have been registered against the company's assets but is not a total protection since a charge can be registered up to 21 days after its creation and still acquire full protection as against other creditors. Where it is not intended that a charge should be paid off on or before completion, and the charge is not for a fixed amount, a letter from the chargee stating the amount of the indebtedness should be requested.

(2) Other assets

A purchaser should be advised to request his accountants to investigate and report on the company being acquired. Where possible the purchaser should define the areas which he wishes the accountants to investigate. These would usually include the up-to-date position as regards assets and liabilities, including where practicable contingent liabilities, and the current trading position. The investigation will normally have been carried out prior to contract and suitable warranties incorporated in the contract itself, particularly as regards contingent liabilities which by their nature may be incapable of indentification by the purchaser or his advisers.

In appropriate cases it is advisable to have a physical check carried out just prior to completion on stock and fixed plant and machinery. It may be impractical to carry out a check on debtors and work in progress, but a bank certificate as to the amount of cash balances is sometimes requested on completion. Such a certificate could also refer to the amount of any overdraft in appropriate cases, and confirm the level of overdraft facilities which will continue to be available to the company.

A company search for registered charges should be made, and in the case of a floating charge, a certificate both from the company secretary or other officer and the chargee certifying that the charge has not crystallised should be produced on completion.

Amongst a company's assets may be one or more subsidiary companies. In the case of the acquisition of a holding company, subsidiary companies may comprise by far the greater share of the holding company's value. Title to the shares in the subsidiaries should be investigated and the subsidiaries themselves and their assets investigated in the same way as the holding company. The warranties and indemnities given by the vendor in respect of the company being acquired should be extended to its subsidiaries.

C. COMPLETION

Once the investigations are over a purchaser can proceed to complete. The principal matters to be dealt with on completion should be set out in the contract. The Agreement in Appendix A includes a typical clause, but circumstances may dictate variations. Because there may be numerous documents with numerous signatories to be handed over on completion, it is usual for the purchaser's solicitor to prepare a completion agenda. This is submitted to and agreed with the vendor's solicitor prior to completion. The agenda will set out (i) the persons required to attend completion (ii) the documents to be tabled in chronological order (iii) summaries of board and/or company resolutions to be passed. A typical completion agenda is set out in Appendix D together with typical board minutes of the target company and its subsidiaries.

7 The Transfer of a Business

The expression 'business' is used in this book to mean a collection of assets and liabilities making up a commercial enterprise. It is a convenient word, but not a precise one. Does it for example mean just goodwill, or assets and liabilities and, if so, which? The starting point, therefore, in framing any agreement for the sale and purchase of a business is a precise definition of the assets to be transferred.

A. THE ASSETS OF THE BUSINESS

Assuming that a business is being sold as a going concern, and that the intention is to take over all of its assets and liabilities, it will be found that most businesses comprise the following:

1 Premises
2 Plant, Machinery and Vehicles
3 Hire Purchase and leasing agreements
4 Stock
5 Debtors and Creditors
6 Goodwill
7 Benefit of Contracts

The agreement for sale of the business must therefore effectively provide for the vesting of each of these items in the purchaser together with suitable warranties where appropriate[1]. For this

---

[1] A vendor, who is a receiver, will not usually give warranties beyond warranting title to the assets and that he has been properly appointed.

reason it is in the author's view desirable that the first clause of any such agreement should contain a definition of each of the items being sold. Questions regarding employees are discussed in chapter 12.

1. Premises

Matters of title are outside the scope of this book but are nevertheless relevant to the purchase agreement. Where the premises in question are leasehold, their assignment will normally be subject to the landlord's prior written consent. Assuming that either of the current editions of the Law Society's Conditions of Sale or the National Conditions of Sale are, with certain exceptions, incorporated into the agreement (see clause 4.2 of the draft agreement in Appendix E), provision will automatically be made for the agreement to be conditional on such consent being obtained on or before completion, and, if such consent is not so obtained, then the contract may be rescinded and any deposit paid by the purchaser returned.

Several points need to be borne in mind when dealing with the transfer of leaseholds. First, one of conveyancing's rituals is that the licence to assign is prepared by the landlord's solicitors and another regrettably seems to be that they take a long time doing it. The moral is either to obtain licence to assign prior to exchange of contracts, or if for some reason of commercial expediency this is undesirable or impossible, to allow adequate time for the licence to be obtained before the contract can be rescinded. For this reason a fixed completion date may be inappropriate, and it may be better to provide for completion, say, 14 days after the licence has been obtained with an outside date of, say, three months before the contract can be rescinded.

Secondly, assuming that the covenant against assignment is in the usual form, i.e. not to assign the premises without the landlord's consent, such consent cannot be unreasonably withheld because the Landlord and Tenant Act 1927, section 19 so provides. This means, in effect, that unless there is any reason to believe that the assignee will not make a responsible tenant capable of paying rent and performing the tenant's covenants, or that there may be difficulty in enforcing a judgement against the assignee, the landlord is obliged to grant consent on the provisions of satisfactory references from the tenant. Suitable references would be, for example, a bank reference, a landlord's reference and a solicitor's or accountant's reference. There is no reason why all or most of these references should not be obtained in advance of, or immediately after, exchange of contracts, and in the author's view the purchaser should be put under a positive obligation to do so within a stated period of exchange. The difficulty with this from the purchaser's point of view is that he cannot force his bank or anyone else to write a satisfactory reference, or any reference, within a stated time. On the other hand if the purchaser is not under such an obligation, he effectively has an option as to whether to proceed to completion, since if he fails to obtain satisfactory references, he can be reasonably certain that licence to assign will be refused. Possibly a reasonable compromise would be to oblige the purchaser to provide the vendor on exchange with the names of not less than three referees, and then to oblige the vendor to use his best endeavours to obtain the landlord's licence to assign.

Such a provision should be so drafted so as not to prejudice the condition that, if in the event the landlord's licence is refused, either side may rescind. Alternatively, where the purchaser is an unknown company, or one without a record of substantial trading, it may be prudent for the vendor to insist on the contract containing a term that the directors of the purchasing company should unconditionally and irrevocably offer to the landlord jointly and severally to guarantee their company's obligations under the lease. Such provision is essential where the lease in question provides that the landlord may require the guarantees of individual directors of an assignee company as a condition of its granting its licence. A further point in connection with leases, and one which is easily overlooked, is the question of costs. It is common for a contract for the assignment of leasehold premises to provide that the assignee shall pay the tenant's legal costs including the landlord's costs in granting (or withholding) its consent. Many leases of commercial premises provide that the landlord's costs in dealing with any application for a licence under a lease shall be met by the tenant. It is not, however, usual for the purchaser of a business to be made responsible for the vendor's costs and if it is desired that the purchaser should at least bear the costs of the application to the landlord, the agreement should so provide.

Tenants occupying premises for business purposes are entitled to security of tenure provided by the Landlord and Tenant Act 1954, Part II, unless such security has been excluded by agreement and the agreement has been approved by the court. In certain cases where the court is precluded from ordering a new tenancy, the tenant will be entitled to compensation for disturbance. The amount will be six times the rateable value of the holding (rather than the usual three times) if during the 14-year period preceding termination of the tenancy, the premises have been occupied by the occupier for the purposes of a business[2]. Where there has been a change of occupier during that period, the new occupier will be entitled to compensation at six times the rateable value if he succeeded to the business of the predecessor carried on at the premises. It is therefore necessary, inter alia, to assign the goodwill of the business as well as any lease in order to preserve the right to compensation at the higher rate.

Three final points on premises whether freehold or leasehold. First, although it is not proposed to discuss questions of title, nevertheless for most businesses their premises are fundamental to their ability to be sold as a going concern. Consequently, if title cannot be made to the premises, or the landlord's consent to assignment cannot be obtained, the contract should make clear that the purchaser may rescind and recover any deposit, so that there can be no doubt that he may not be obliged to buy the remainder of the assets. The same consideration may be true of other assets where in the particular circumstances of the case monetary compensation will not suffice.

Secondly, it is becoming more usual for the sale contract to contain warranties by the vendor regarding user of the premises and other matters which may make them suitable for use in the business in question. So long as the contract for sale of the business provides that the vendor sells 'as beneficial owner', adequate covenants as to his title to the land are implied into the conveyance by virtue of the Law of Property Act 1925. This cannot apply in a case of the sale of shares since it is not the company's land being transferred but shares in the company itself. In the case of a sale of shares the purchaser's solicitors often incorporate, besides a warranty as to title, warranties as

---

[2] Landlord and Tenant Act 1954 (Appropriate Multiplier) Order 1984, SI 1984/1932.

to user as well (see paragraph 54 (I) of schedule 5 in Appendix A).

Finally, the purchaser should not forget to insure the premises from the moment of exchange of contracts except where the premises are leasehold and the lease obliges the landlord to insure and further provides for abatement of rent in the case of the destruction of, or damage to, the premises. Full abatement of rent will not cover the whole loss where the purchaser is paying a premium for leasehold premises to reflect an actual rent below current market value. In this case, additional cover should be arranged on exchange of contracts. In any event the purchaser should try to have its interest noted on the landlord's policy.

2. Plant, machinery and vehicles

Plant and machinery may be a grand title for a desk, a chair and a typewriter or it may represent substantial investment in industrial plant, office equipment and a fleet of cars. The principles for dealing with their transfer are the same.

First an inventory should be made, and once agreed should be attached to the contract for sale which will then express the sale to be of the equipment specified in the inventory. Since the sale will thus be of specific goods, the risk will, in the absence of agreement to the contrary, or an apparent different intention, pass to the purchaser on exchange of contracts and the purchaser should therefore immediately take out appropriate insurance[3]. This is a question closely connected with the more general question of for whose benefit and at whose risk the business is run pending completion. This is discussed later in this chapter.

A further aspect of this problem as it relates to plant and machinery is its physical condition. A vendor will be well advised to exclude his liability under the Sale of Goods Act 1979 insofar as he may have any and insofar as he may be permitted to do so by virtue of the Unfair Contract Terms Act 1977[4]. Nevertheless a purchaser could reasonably require the vendor to warrant that on completion goods would be in no worse condition than they were at the date of exchange, fair wear and tear excepted.

---

[3] Sale of Goods Act 1979, ss. 18 and 27.
[4] Where the transfer of goods is by way of barter, rather than sale, reference should be made to Supply of Goods and Services Act 1982.

In any event, a purchaser should insure plant and machinery against all normal risks as from exchange of contracts.

The Sale of Goods Act 1979 applies to every contract for sale of goods. Goods are defined as all chattels personal other than things in action and money but exclude things attached to or forming part of the land unless agreed to be severed before the sale or under the contract of sale. It should be noted first that the implied undertaking as to title under section 12 of the 1979 Act can never be excluded[5]. Furthermore the implied undertakings on the vendor's part under sections 13, 14 and 15 of the 1979 Act can only be excluded insofar as the exclusion of liability clause satisfies the requirement of reasonableness of the Unfair Contract Terms Act 1977: section 6(3) Unfair Contract Terms Act 1977. The requirement of reasonableness for the purposes of the 1977 Act is that the term excluding liability 'shall have been a fair and reasonable one to be included having regard to the circumstances which were or ought reasonably to have been known to or in the contemplation of the parties when the contract was made'. Regard is also to be had to the matters specified in Schedule 2 to the 1977 Act. These include the strength of the bargaining positions of the parties.

The 1979 Act, section 15, is concerned with the sale of goods by sample and is unlikely to be relevant in the transfer of a business. Section 13, however, provides that where there is a contract for sale of goods by description, there is an implied condition that the goods should correspond with the description. This will apply to goods listed in an inventory and it is submitted that exclusion of this liability would be unlikely to satisfy the reasonableness test of the 1977 Act. It should be noted that a breach of a condition as opposed to a breach of warranty entitles the buyer to repudiate the contract for sale as an alternative to claiming damages. Whether such a breach would entitle the buyer to repudiate the whole contract or simply that part relating to the goods in question is not clear. One possibility would be to include a clause providing that the breach by the vendor of any condition relating to particular goods shall only entitle the buyer to repudiate the contract insofar as he might otherwise be required to purchase those goods. Thus the buyer will still be obliged to complete the remainder of the contract. Such a

---

[5] Unfair Contract Terms Act 1977, s. 6(1).

provision will itself have to satisfy the test of reasonableness under the 1977 Act[6]. And where the item is fundamental to the business sold it is thought that a purchaser could repudiate the whole contract notwithstanding.

The Sale of Goods Act 1979, section 14(3), implies a condition that the goods shall be reasonably fit for the purpose for which they are required. However, before the buyer can invoke this section he must first show that expressly or by implication he had made known to the seller the particular purpose for which the goods are required unless the buyer did not rely, or it would have been unreasonable for him to rely, on the seller's skill or judgement. This requirement is unlikely to be satisfied in the usual situation of transfer of a business where the buyer has some knowledge—possibly more than the seller—about the goods. Even if the buyer were a novice, the second requirement, namely that the goods are being sold in the course of a business, cannot be satisfied as regards the sale of fixed assets as part of the sale of the business itself.

Section 14(2) implies a condition of merchantable quality where the seller sells goods in the course of a business and again will not therefore apply to a sale of fixed assets where the business itself is being sold.

3. Leasing agreements

Most businesses have certain equipment subject to hire purchase or leasing agreements. Unless the contract otherwise provides, and unless the owner of the goods agrees, the liabilities under such agreement will remain with the vendor who may have no further use for the equipment in question. Assuming therefore that the purchaser wishes to take over the agreement and that the owner of the goods is agreeable to the agreement being assigned, the contract for sale of the business should provide that the vendor has complied with all obligations under the agreement up to completion, and that the purchaser will so comply following completion. Suitable cross indemnities between vendor and purchaser should be incorporated. The purchaser should also require a warranty that the disclosed terms of any such agreement are true and complete. It should

---

[6] S. 13(1)(b).

also be noted that insofar as the hire purchase or leasing agreements, as opposed to the goods themselves, have value, the value is chargeable with conveyance on sale duty if the agreements are assigned[7].

4. Stock

Stock is normally simply described as such and purchased at a valuation made on or shortly before completion. Save for the implied conditions as to title it is unlikely that any of the other conditions implied by the Sale of Goods Act 1979 will apply. Section 13 will only apply if the goods are sold by description. Sections 14(2) and (3) may however apply to stock, even where it is sold with fixed assets of the business, where the stock is sold at its ordinary market value[8]. Frequently, specified professional valuers are agreed between the parties and named in the contract. Whether or not named, valuers need guidance in the contract as to the criterion for valuation, i.e. open market value; cost to the vendor; cost plus or minus a certain percentage depending upon, for example, whether the stock is classed growth claret or daily newspapers.

There are two dangers to a purchaser in agreeing to purchase stock at valuation without qualification. First there is the danger that between contract and completion the stock will be run down and secondly there is the opposite danger, namely that for some reason the vendor will make large purchases of stock just before completion. It may at first sight seem improbable that the vendor would wish to do this, but the situation may be that he is selling one of a number of similar businesses and that he can obtain a substantial discount on the stock purchased for his other businesses by buying in quantity and off-loading surplus stock onto the business being sold. Both dangers may be avoided to some extent by providing elsewhere in the contract that pending completion the vendor will carry on the business in the same way and to the same extent as before, but it would be advisable to reinforce such a provision with specified minimum and maximum amounts of stock.

[7] Stamp Act 1891, s. 59(1) as amended, and see *Drages Ltd v IRC* (1927) 6 ATC 727.

[8] *Buchanan-Jardine v Hamilink* 1983 SLT 149.

5. Debtors and creditors

It often happens that trade debtors and creditors are not taken over by the purchaser. On the contrary, as regards debtors of the business the purchaser usually undertakes to account to the vendor for any sums received, it being left to the vendor to collect in the debts. An assignment of book debts, or an agreement to assign the same, will attract ad valorem conveyance or transfer duty, as will the amount of the vendor's debts which the purchaser undertakes to discharge. No duty will be payable if the agreement provides that the purchaser will discharge the vendor's debts out of the proceeds of book debts collected by the purchaser as agent for the vendor. An obligation on the part of the purchaser to account to the vendor for such sums as may be paid to the purchaser by the vendor's debtors will not attract duty. Where the obligation to account is likely to be onerous, the purchaser may stipulate for a fee based either on the value or the number of the vendor's book debts collected. If, however, an assignment of debts is required, then to make such assignment fully effective as against the debtors, and enforceable by the purchaser in his own name, the purchaser will have to give notice in writing to each of them[9], a possibly time consuming and costly exercise. A schedule of debtors and the amounts owed by each of them would also have to be annexed to the agreement. As regards creditors, the vendor should undertake to indemnify the purchaser in respect of all obligations and liabilities incurred up to completion and this would include trade and other creditors. If the purchaser wishes to ensure that creditors of the business are promptly paid, one solution would be for part of the purchase price to be lodged in the joint account of the vendor's and purchaser's respective solicitors for this purpose. The basis for release of these monies should be set out in the contract. The purchaser will thus know that bills will be met when presented, and the vendor will be assured that his liability to the creditors will be satisfied.

---

[9] Law of Property Act 1925, s. 136. A general assignment of debts by a trader may be void as against his trustee in bankruptcy as regards book debts not paid at the commencement of the bankruptcy, unless the assignment has been registered as if it were a bill of sale given otherwise than by way of security for the payment of a sum of money. This does not apply, inter alia, to an assignment of book debts included in a transfer of a business made bona fide and for value. See Bankruptcy Act 1914, s. 43.

The purchaser will not however be concerned with any unsecured overdraft or other loan facility given to the vendor, and if any assets of the business are charged, the purchaser will require all charges to be removed on or before completion. Usually any such charge will be over land and the usual conveyancing searches will be made prior to completion to ensure that the vendor's title is free from encumbrances. Where the vendor is a company a company search should be made to see whether any charges are registered, although such a search confers no automatic protection.

6. Goodwill

Goodwill has been defined as 'the probability that the old customers will resort to the old place'[10].

Not every business has goodwill; indeed some proprietors are at pains to point out that the business is 'under new management'. Many agreements disposing of a business make no express provision for the disposal of goodwill, the purchaser preferring to rely on non-competition covenants by the vendor. This still leaves the goodwill theoretically assignable to a third party, and the better method is to take an assignment of goodwill, together with, if necessary, a covenant by the vendor not to compete with the business being sold. Such a covenant must not represent an unreasonable restraint of trade, but the courts lean in favour of the covenantee in deciding this issue where he is the purchaser of a business (per contra where he is an employer and the covenantor is an employee). Nevertheless the covenants should contain some sensible limitations in three respects (i) geographical area (ii) time and (iii) type of business.

The first two will vary with the type of business being sold and it is suggested that the scope of the covenant should be no wider than to protect the business from wholesale desertion by its customers to the vendor. A fair limitation should be expressed to be in accordance with the actual type of business being sold and not what the purchaser hopes it may develop into.

The vendor should be asked also to give a separate, but related, covenant not to solicit any employees of the business

---

[10] Per Lord Eldon in *Cruttwell v Lye* (1810) 1 Rose 123.

being taken over, nor any person who is at the date of sale a customer, or has been within a stated period prior to that date a customer, of the business. If there is any doubt about the enforceability of a non-competition clause, it should nevertheless be possible to enforce independently a non-solicitation clause provided that it is drafted so as to be severable from the former.

A further separate covenant should be required by the purchaser forbidding the vendor from using the name of the business or any similar name and from holding himself out as being, or as having been, connected with the business. With effect from 26 February 1982, a person or persons with a place of business and carrying on business in Great Britain commits an offence if he, they or it so carries on business other than under a name which (i) is not his, their or its own name and (ii) which would be likely to give the impression that the business is connected with H.M. Government or with any local authority, or includes any word or expression for the time being specified in regulations made under the Business Names Act[11]. No offence is committed by a person to whom the business has been transferred on or after 26 February 1982, and who carries on the business under the name which was its lawful business name immediately before that transfer for up to 12 months beginning with the date of the transfer[12].

In addition the vendor may be required to covenant that pending completion he will not do anything to diminish or prejudice the goodwill of the business. Such a covenant is related to the covenant referred to above in connection with stock-in-trade, namely that pending completion the vendor will carry on the business in the same way and to the same extent as before. This assumes that there will in fact be a material period of time between exchange of contracts and completion, as there usually will be where premises and or licences are to be transferred.

Finally the vendor should be required to yield up all records of the business including lists of customers and all copies of the same.

---

[11] Business Names Act 1985, s. 2(4).
[12] Business Names Act 1985, s. 2(2).

7. Benefit of contracts

Where certain contracts are fundamental to the business being acquired, for example, agency or licensing agreements, provision should be made for these to be either novated or assigned to the purchaser with the agreement of the third party and for completion to be conditional on such novation or assignment. The contract will provide that, pending completion, the vendor will not vary or release its rights without the purchaser's prior consent. Service agreements are discussed separately in chapter 12. Assignments, other than assignments of foreign rights executed and retained abroad, will be subject to stamp duty (see below) so it is preferable from this point of view for the sale agreement to provide for cancellation of the original agreement and for its novation with the purchaser. Care needs to be taken however that such cancellation does not itself give rise to liabilities or, if it does, that these liabilities are waived. Furthermore if a purchaser enters into a new agreement on precisely the same terms as those in the old, he will in all likelihood acquire some precompletion liabilities. The safe course, therefore, is for the purchaser to see if the third party will enter into an entirely new agreement rather than simply to agree to treat the former agreement as subsisting between them.

B. APPORTIONMENT OF THE PURCHASE PRICE

It has already been seen that a business is a collection of assets and where the parties have agreed a global figure for the whole concern (usually plus stock-in-trade at valuation) it is usual to apportion the price between the constituent assets. An apportionment will have tax consequences for both vendor and purchaser because of the differing tax treatment of the assets being transferred, as the following examples show:

(1) Plant and machinery used as fixed assets will qualify for a writing down allowance of 25 per cent of their cost[13] in the

---

[13] With respect to capital expenditure incurred on plant and machinery after 31 March 1985 and before 1 April 1986, a purchaser may claim a first year allowance of 50 per cent of the cost. Subsequent writing down allowances will

accounting year in which the cost is incurred and further allowances each year thereafter of 25 per cent of the reducing balance. Such allowances can be set against the purchaser's taxable profits from the business in the relevant year. On the other hand, if the amount received for plant and machinery by the vendor exceeds its written down value, the excess will be subject to a balancing charge thus increasing the vendor's liability to income tax or corporation tax.

(2) A vendor who has reached the age of 60 and who can therefore take advantage of the retirement relief provisions contained in FA 1985, section 69, may be particularly concerned to load the price onto assets the gains of which will be subject to capital gains tax but not to balancing charges. The purchaser on the other hand will wish to keep as low as possible the acquisition cost of assets subject to capital gains tax and conversely pay more for trading stock.

(3) Any transfer of premises or assignment of goodwill will attract stamp duty up to 1 per cent payable by the purchaser, whereas no duty is payable on a transfer of moveable plant and machinery capable of transfer by delivery.

(4) Any profit received on the disposal of trading stock will be taxable in the vendor's hands as income. If, however, the purchaser's acquisition cost of trading stock is low, his eventual taxable profit will be that much higher. The anti-avoidance provisions contained in ICTA 1970, sections 485 and 486 (transactions between associated persons) should be noted.

(5) In the case of a company which is close, capital gains are left out of account in arriving at its distributable income for shortfall purposes[14]. This may be significant where such a company has substantial non-trading income.

---

be claimable against the remaining 50 per cent at the rate of 25 per cent per year on the reducing balance, i.e. 12.5 per cent of the original cost in the first year following that in which the expenditure was incurred, 9.375 per cent in the second year and so on.

[14] FA 1972, Sch. 16, para. 10(2).

For these reasons and others, the question of the apportionment of the purchase price, which probably neither the vendor nor purchaser thought of at the commencement of negotiations, often assumes importance at a later stage. Where some of the assets qualify for capital allowances, CAA 1968, sections 77 and 81 require a just apportionment of the total sale proceeds.

The author would not wish to give the impression that in agreeing an apportionment between themselves, the vendor and purchaser can take figures out of the air to suit their respective tax positions, or that the Inland Revenue would accept such figures. On the contrary the apportionment should correspond with reality. Nevertheless, there is always room for an honestly held difference of opinion on values. If an apportionment cannot be agreed, each side will negotiate for itself with the Revenue which is in any event entitled to question even an apportionment agreed between the parties.

C. VALUE ADDED TAX

Value Added Tax Act 1983, section 33 provides that where the business carried on by a taxable person is transferred to another person as a going concern, then

(a) For the purpose of determining whether the transferee is liable to be registered for VAT, he is to be treated as having carried on the business before as well as after the transfer, and supplies by the transferor are treated accordingly; and

(b) Any records relating to the business which under Schedule 7 of the Act are required to be preserved for any period after the transfer, are to be preserved by the transferee, unless the Commissioner for Customs and Excise at the request of the transferor otherwise directs. The current requirement is for records of all transactions occurring on or after 1 August 1982 to be kept for six years.

The purchaser should therefore obtain on completion all VAT records of the business for a period of six years prior to completion[15].

As regards whether VAT is chargeable on assets sold on the

---

[15] See also the VAT (General) Regulations 1985, SI 1985/886, para. 4.

transfer of the business, the position is now set out in the VAT (Special Provisions) Order 1981, SI 1981/1741.

Under that Order the following supply will be neither a supply of goods, nor of services, and therefore not subject to VAT, namely the supply by a person of assets of his business where:

(a) the business or part thereof is transferred as a going concern, and

(b) the assets are to be used by the transferee in carrying on the same kind of business as that carried on by the transferor, and

(c) the transferee is, or immediately becomes as a result of the transfer, a taxable person, and

(d) where part only of the business is transferred, that part is capable of separate operation.

A mere transfer of assets without transfer of goodwill will generally not constitute transfer of a business as a going concern. For such a transfer to occur there must be continuity of both suppliers and customers as well as a continuity of trading in the same line of goods[16]. The fact that the purchaser's post-completion actions may be relevant to deciding whether a supply at the time of completion is chargeable to VAT creates a difficulty, but it is possible to apply for written clearance from Customs and Excise. Where it is clear that the VAT (Special Provisions) Order 1981 does not apply, VAT should be charged on the price of all assets including goodwill, but interests in land are exempt. Where the Order is likely to apply, a provision in the sale agreement on the lines of Clause 13 of the precedent in Appendix E should be included, and action taken accordingly on or before completion.

D. STAMP DUTIES

Any instrument by which any property, or any interest in property is transferred to or vested in a purchaser, or a nominee for a purchaser, is subject to duty on the amount of the consideration. In the case of a deed of transfer incorporating a certificate

---

[16] *Caunt v Customs & Excise Comrs* (1984) unreported.

for value there is a nil rate of duty where the consideration does not exceed £30,000. (Transfers of shares do not however enjoy this exemption.) Where the consideration exceeds £30,000, the deed is stampable on the whole amount thereof at the rate of 1 per cent.

Thus, on the sale of a business any instrument vesting an interest in land in the purchaser will be taxable if the consideration exceeds £30,000. Furthermore any deed assigning goodwill will be similarly taxable and in deciding whether such deeds are liable to be stamped at nil rate the consideration for the land and goodwill must be aggregated. An agreement for sale of goodwill is chargeable (unless the business is carried on entirely outside the UK) and so is an agreement for the sale of the tenant's fixtures[17] and an agreement to sell debts. As regards goodwill it should be noted that the giving of a covenant by a vendor not to operate a business in a specified area has been held to be dutiable because it was equivalent to an agreement for the sale of goodwill[18]. In addition, with certain exceptions, the Stamp Act 1891, section 59 charges with ad valorem duty, as if it were an actual conveyance on sale, an agreement for sale of:

(i) any equitable interest in property and

(ii) any estate or interest in any property other than:

(a) land

(b) non-UK property

(c) goods, wares or merchandise

(d) shares

(e) ships.

Among the assets chargeable are cash on deposit (which should therefore be transferred to current account before the date of the agreement), books debts, trade marks and similar industrial property. The contract for sale is therefore itself dutiable except insofar as it deals with property in one of the exempted categories. In practice, however, purchasers do not

---

[17] *Lee v Gaskell* (1876) 1 QBD 700.

[18] *Eastern National Omnibus Co Ltd v IRC* [1939] 1 KB 161, [1938] 3 All ER 526.

stamp the agreement unless it is required to be enforced in the courts.

There is however no double duty where, for example, an agreement for the sale of goodwill is followed by its assignment to the purchaser. This is because the Stamp Act 1891, section 59(5) provides that the agreement need not be stamped under that section if a conveyance or transfer in conformity with the agreement is presented for stamping within six months of execution of the agreement, and either the agreement bears a fixed duty of 50p or it would not be chargeable apart from section 59. In such a case duty is paid on the conveyance or transfer.

No duty is chargeable on stock-in-trade provided that it is transferred by physical delivery and not by an instrument of transfer.

It will be appreciated that where the agreement involves the sale of a number of assets (as it usually will in the case of the sale of the business) an apportionment must be made between dutiable and non-dutiable assets. The apportionment must be made bona fide and may have other tax consequences (see above under the heading 'Apportionment of the purchase price'). The apportionment should be made on Form 22 which is supplied by the Stamp Office of the Inland Revenue. Where the purchase price in respect of the dutiable assets does not exceed £30,000, an appropriate certificate of value should be included in both the agreement and in any subsequent conveyance. Where, for example, the dutiable assets consist of freehold land valued at £22,000, and goodwill valued at £7,000, both documents should contain a certificate of value that the consideration does not exceed £30,000.

An exemption from conveyance on sale duty may be available where the consideration for the business being acquired consists of an allotment of shares in the acquiring company. An explanation of this exemption is contained in chapter 5: Stamp Duty. It should be noted that the company making the allotment must within one month thereafter file with the Registrar of Companies the duly stamped written contract. Where the contract is not in writing, there must be delivered the prescribed particulars of the contract stamped with the same duty as would have been chargeable on the contract had it been reduced to writing[19].

---

[19] Companies Act 1985, s. 88.

Finally, the Stamp Act 1891, section 59(6) provides that any ad valorem duty paid under the section shall be returned if the contract is subsequently rescinded or annulled or for any other reason is not substantially performed.

8 Tax Payable by Vendors

A. CAPITAL TRANSFER TAX

Normally where a transaction is at arm's length and not intended to confer any gratuitous benefit on any person no charge
to capital transfer tax will arise[1]. In the case, however, of the
sale of unquoted shares or debentures, the above does not apply
unless it is shown that the sale was at a price freely negotiated
at the time of the sale or at a price such as might be expected to
have been freely negotiated at the time of the sale. Since a
transferee, as well as the transferor, may be liable for the tax[2] it
is in both parties' interests that any negotiations as to price be
documented[3].

B. CAPITAL GAINS AND CORPORATION TAX ON CAPITAL GAINS

Assuming that the vendor is not a dealer in the assets being
sold, then, subject to ICTA 1970, sections 460 and 488, any gain
made on the sale (whether the sale be of shares or of assets other
than trading stock) will be chargeable in the hands of an individual to capital gains tax, and in the hands of a body corporate
to corporation tax—but in the latter case only on a fraction of
the gain so that the effective rate is reduced to the maximum

---

[1] Capital Transfer Tax Act 1984, s. 10(1).
[2] Capital Transfer Tax Act 1984, s. 199.
[3] But note Capital Transfer Tax Act 1984, ss. 199(3) and 200(2) as regards a
purchaser's liability for capital transfer tax.

rate payable by individuals, presently 30 per cent. In either case capital losses made in the same or previous periods of assessment may be set off against the gain insofar as they are unrelieved. Gains or losses made before 6 April 1965 (when capital gains tax was introduced) are not taxable or allowable. In the case of shares in unquoted companies or assets of a business acquired before that date[4], the amount of gain or loss will be apportioned on a time basis over the whole period of ownership and only the gain or loss made since 6 April 1965 will be taxable or allowable unless the taxpayer elects under CGTA 1979, Schedule 5, paragraph 12 for the shares to be valued as at 6 April 1965. The position of non-resident vendors is discussed in chapter 11.

Where part of the gain on a sale of shares in a close company is attributable to a profit on assets transferred to the company by any of the persons having control, or by a connected person, prior to disposal of the shares, the period over which the gain (but not any loss) is to be treated as growing at a uniform rate may, depending upon the identity of the vendor of the shares, begin with the time when the assets were transferred to the company: CGTA 1979, Schedule 5, paragraph 16. The result is that part of a gain on a sale of shares acquired prior to 6 April 1965 may be wholly chargeable if it is attributable to a profit on assets transferred to the company after 5 April 1965.

Three important reliefs are available to vendors who are individuals:

(1) CGTA 1979, section 5 (as amended by FA 1982, section 80(2)) exempts the first £5,900 of an individual's taxable amount in the year of assessment 1985/86[5]. This amount will be increased annually by reference to the Retail Price Index[6].

An individual's taxable amount for a year of assessment is defined as the gains for which he is chargeable for that year less any capital losses of that or previous years available for set-off or carry forward. There is provision so that any available losses are not wasted in reducing an individual's taxable amount below the exempt amount[7].

---

[4] See also CGTA 1979, Sch. 5, para. 9 (land having development value).
[5] Capital Gains Tax (Annual Exempt Amount) Order 1985, SI 1985/428.
[6] CGTA 1979, s. 5(1B).
[7] CGTA 1979, s. 5(4).

(2) An individual who has attained the age of 60 (or who has retired on ill-health grounds below the age of 60) and who disposes of the whole or part of a business, or of one or more assets which, at the time at which a business ceased to be carried on, were in use for the purposes of that business, or of shares or securities in a company, may claim relief under FA 1985, section 69 if the relevant conditions have been fulfilled throughout a period of at least one year ending with the disposal[8].

The relevant conditions are, in the case of a sale of a business, that the business in question is owned either by the individual, or by a trading company which is the individual's family company, or a member of a trading group of which the holding company is the individual's family company, and the individual is a full-time working director of that company, or if that company is a member of a group or commercial association of companies, of one or more companies which are members of the group or association. In the case of a sale of shares, the relevant conditions are that the company is the individual's family company and is either a trading company, or the holding company of a trading group, and the individual is a full time working director of the company, or of any member of the group. Relief is preserved where the business owned by the company at the date of disposal was not owned by it throughout the one year qualifying period but was owned by the individual making the disposal.

A 'family company' in relation to an individual means one in which the voting rights are held either (i) as to at least 25 per cent by the individual, or (ii) as to more than 50 per cent by the individual or a member of his family and as to at least 5 per cent by the individual himself.

The period during which the relevant conditions are fulfilled is called the qualifying period, and the maximum relief is £100,000 where the qualifying period is ten years or more. If it is less than ten years, the maximum relief is a percentage of £100,000 equal to the percentage which the qualifying period (subject to a one year minimum) bears to ten years. Thus, if the qualifying period is six years, three months, the maximum relief will be £62,500. Where the qualifying period is less than ten

---

[8] In the case of the disposal of shares in a company which has ceased to be a trading company before the disposal, then subject to certain other conditions, the one year qualifying period ends on the date of cesser: FA 1985, s. 69(6).

years, but during that period the individual making the disposal was concerned in carrying on another business, then, subject to certain conditions, the period of carrying on the other business may be aggregated with the period relevant to the business being disposed of in order to recalculate the qualifying period. Any time between the end of the first period and beginning of the second is ignored for the purposes of the recalculation, but if the lapse between the two exceeds two years the earlier period cannot be aggregated at all.

FA 1985, Schedule 20, paragraph 16 contains further provision for lengthening the qualifying period where (i) the assets in question were acquired in whole or in part by an individual from his spouse; (ii) the acquisition was under the spouse's will or intestacy or by lifetime gift and the spouse and individual were living together at the date of death or of the gift, as the case may be; (iii) the individual acquired the whole of the spouse's interest in the assets; and (iv) within two years after the disposal by the individual, he elects that paragraph 16 should apply. The qualifying period will then be extended by applying the conditions which have to be satisfied for relief (i.e. full-time working directorship etc.) to the individual or his spouse, instead of just to the individual making the disposal. However, where the individual's acquisition from his spouse was by lifetime gift, the maximum relief is limited to the lower of (i) the amount by which £100,000 exceeds the relief given to the spouse up to and including the gift, and (ii) the amount which would have been available for relief if the gift had not occurred, and the individual's disposal had been made by the spouse, and anything done by the individual relating to the business after the gift had been made had been done by the spouse.

It should be noted that relief will be given only on gains accruing on the disposal of chargeable business assets or, in the case of a disposal of shares, so much of the value of the shares as reflects the value of chargeable business assets of the company. Chargeable business assets are those assets used for the purposes of the trade in question and include goodwill but exclude assets held as investments. Since assets held as investments are excluded, shares in trading subsidiaries as such will not qualify as chargeable business assets[9]. However assets used in a trade

---

[9] FA 1985, Sch. 20, para. 12(2).

by a member of a trading group of which the holding company is the individual's family company will qualify.

As under the retirement relief provisions formerly contained in CGTA 1979, section 124, the individual's retirement is not a condition of the relief. He need only attain the age of 60. Where however relief is claimed by an individual retiring below that age on ill-health grounds, he must satisfy the Inland Revenue that he has ceased to engage in the business and, by reason of ill health, is incapable of engaging in similar work, and is likely to remain permanently so incapable.

Where an individual is entitled to retirement relief on the sale of an interest in a partnership or shares in a family company, he can also claim relief on gains from associated disposals, i.e. of assets owned by him personally which have been used for the purposes of the business of the partnership or company. It is a condition for such relief that the individual should withdraw from the business[10].

(3) FA 1980, section 37 provides that, subject to the provisions of the section, where an individual who has subscribed for shares in a qualifying trading company incurs an allowable loss (for capital gains purposes) on their disposal, he may claim income tax relief on the amount of the loss, but he will thereby forfeit the amount claimed as a deduction for capital gains tax purposes. Relief is given against earned income before other income. Reference should be made to the legislation for the full definition of 'qualifying trading company', but it may be noted that there are excluded from the definition, among others, quoted companies and other companies whose trade consists wholly or mainly of dealing in shares, securities, land, trades or commodity futures. The relief is extended to disposals by investment companies on or after 1 April 1981 by FA 1981, section 36.

The relief under FA 1980, section 37 is distinct from that provided by FA 1983, section 26 ('the Business Expansion Scheme') whereby, subject to fulfilment of certain strict conditions, an individual may claim income tax relief on the amount subscribed for shares in a qualifying company in respect of the year of assessment in which the shares are issued. Disposal of

---

[10] FA 1985, s. 70.

the shares in certain circumstances can lead to the relief being withdrawn. A full discussion of the complex provisions of the Business Expansion Scheme is outside the scope of this book. Adequate summaries of the provisions can usually be found in the prospectuses published by the promoters of B.E.S. share issues. In some cases such summaries (together with the printer's name and address) comprise the more reliable parts of their contents.

Two further reliefs in connection with capital gains tax are available both to individuals and others. The first, commonly known as roll-over relief, does not relieve tax, but only defers its payment by providing in essence that, if the consideration received on the disposal of assets used in a trade is applied in the acquisition of other assets to be used in the same or another trade, the disposal proceeds are deemed to produce neither a gain nor loss and the acquisition costs of the new assets are treated as reduced by the amount of the gain which would have been chargeable on disposal of the old assets[11]. There are restrictions on the relief where only part of the consideration is applied in acquiring new business assets or where the assets sold were not used wholly for business purposes. In addition both the old and new assets must be within certain classes, although it is not necessary that assets in one class be replaced by other assets in the same class. The classes are (a) any building or land occupied and used for the trade; (b) fixed plant and machinery; (c) ships aircraft and hovercraft; (d) goodwill. A further condition is that the acquisition of the new assets must take place, or an unconditional contract for the acquisition entered into, within the period beginning one year before and ending three years after the disposal of the old assets. The relief also applies to a case where an individual disposes of an asset used in a trade by that individual's family company[12] and the new asset is acquired after 11 April 1978[13]. By extra-statutory concession expenditure incurred on improving an existing asset, or on acquiring a further interest in an existing asset will, subject to

---

[11] CGTA 1979, s. 115.
[12] Within the meaning of Sch. 20, para. 1(2) of FA 1985.
[13] CGTA 1979, s. 120.

certain conditions being satisfied, be treated as expenditure on a new asset[14].

The second relief is known as the indexation allowance and applies on the disposal by a company on or after 1 April 1985, or by anyone else on or after 6 April 1985, of an asset of any kind. However, where loan stock or similar security is disposed of before 28 February 1986 no indexation allowance is given for an increase in the Retail Price Index in the first year of ownership, nor can the indexation allowance create an allowable loss[15]. The allowance operates by index-linking by reference to the Retail Prices Index for March 1982 or the month in which the relevant expenditure was incurred, whichever is the later, all expenditure relevant in computing the gain other than disposal costs. There is provision for index-linking to be in an upwards only direction[16]. Contrary to the rules applicable to disposals before 1 April (companies) or 6 April (others) 1985, the indexation allowance may create or increase an allowable loss. Further, where shares were acquired after 5 April 1965 and before 1 April 1982 a claim may be made for the indexation allowance to be calculated by reference to their market value on 31 March 1982.

Exchange of shares

CGTA 1979, section 85 provides that, if certain conditions are satisfied, where a company issues shares or debentures to a person in exchange for shares in or debentures of another company it shall not be treated as involving the disposal of the original shares or the acquisition of the new shares, but the new shares shall be treated as having been acquired at the same time and for the same consideration as the original shares. Thus no taxable gain or allowable loss will arise on the occasion of the exchange of shares, nor on any subsequent exchanges so long as the conditions are satisfied.

The conditions are:

(1) the company issuing the shares or debentures holds, or in

---

[14] The text of the relevant concessions (which have not yet been assigned a number by the Revenue) are set out as concessions X6 and X7 in Inland Revenue Practices and Concessions, Dearden Farrow.

[15] FA 1985, s. 68(2)(b).

[16] FA 1982, s. 87(3).

consequence of the exchange will hold, more than one quarter of the ordinary share capital of the other company; or where the first-mentioned company issues the shares or debentures in exchange for shares as a result of a general offer made to members of the other company, the offer being made in the first instance on condition that the first mentioned company will control the other.

(2) the exchange must be affected for bona fide commercial reasons and must not form part of a scheme which has the avoidance of capital gains tax or corporation tax as its main purpose or one of its main purposes. This condition has no application to a person holding not more than 5 per cent of, or of any class of, shares or debentures in the company being acquired[17]. There is a clearance procedure provided by CGTA 1979, section 88 and either the acquiring company or the company being acquired may apply to the Board of Inland Revenue thereunder. The Board must clear or refuse the proposed transaction within 30 days of receipt of the application, or within 30 days of receipt of any further particulars which the Board may require in consequence of the application (see also chapter 3, section B above)[18].

ICTA 1970, section 461, paragraph E applies where two companies under the control of five or fewer persons and unquoted are involved in a transaction in securities and the person in question (the vendor of shares) receives consideration in the form of shares or securities which represents the value of assets of such a company and does not pay tax on it as income. A share exchange is within this provision and clearance under ICTA 1970, section 464[19] should be sought at the same time as that under CGTA 1979, section 88. In the case of a reverse takeover (where the vendors will have control of the purchaser company) clearance is unlikely to be given where the consideration includes loan stock, debentures or redeemable shares.

---

[17] CGTA 1979, s. 87(2).
[18] Application for clearance should be made to Technical Division (Capital Gains), Room 28 New Wing, Somerset House, London WC2R 1LB.
[19] See above, pp. 27-9.

Consideration due after time of disposal

CGTA 1979, section 40(1) provides that if the consideration, or part of it, taken into account in computing capital gains, is payable by intalments over a period of at least 18 months beginning not earlier than when the disposal was made, the capital gains tax may be paid by intalments over a period of up to eight years, if the person making the disposal satisfies the Revenue that he would otherwise suffer undue hardship. In considering whether undue hardship may arise, the Revenue will 'look primarily to the question whether the vendor ... could reasonably be expected to pay the tax on the full amount immediately, in the light of the resources made available by the particular transaction involved'[20]. No discount for postponement of the right to receive any part of the consideration is allowed, nor, in the first instance, for the risk of any part of the consideration being irrecoverable or for the right to receive it being contingent although there is provision for subsequent adjustment[1].

Where the amount of the consideration, or part of it, cannot be determined at the time of the disposal (because for example the price is to be determined by reference to future profits), the gain will be computed by reference to the fixed sum immediately payable, if any, plus the value at the date of disposal of the shares of the contingent right to receive the deferred consideration. It has been held that such a right is an asset, and that the payment of the deferred consideration is a capital sum derived from that asset and so chargeable to capital gains tax[2]. Any contingent liability of the vendor in respect of a warranty or representation made on a sale of shares is, however, granted no allowance in computing capital gains in the first instance. There is provision for subsequent adjustment if the contingent liability becomes enforceable: CGTA 1979, section 41.

Transfer of a business to a company

Where an individual transfers to a company a business as a going concern, together with all the assets of the business (other than cash), in exchange wholly or partly for shares the

[20] Official Report, Standing Committee E, 27 June 1972, col. 1544.
[1] CGTA 1979, s. 40(2).
[2] *Marren* (Inspector of Taxes) *v Ingles* [1980] 3 All ER 95, [1980] STC 500.

chargeable gains of the transferor on the disposal are calculated. The gain is apportioned between the value of the exchange shares and the value of other consideration received. The part of the gain apportioned to the shares is not charged to tax but is deducted from the acquisition cost of the shares so that payment of tax on that part is deferred until the shares are disposed of. The part of the gain attributable to the remaining consideration is assessed normally save that the assumption of liabilities by the transferee company is not treated as part of the remaining consideration for this purpose[3]. Since all the assets of the business, other than cash, must be transferred for the deferral to operate, there may be adverse stamp duty consequences, where the assets include book debts (see chapter 7).

Where the whole or part of a UK resident company's business is transferred to another such company in a scheme of reconstruction or amalgamation and the transferor company receives no consideration (other than the assumption of liabilities of the business by the transferee company), the transferee company is treated as having acquired the assets at their cost to the transferor. Effectively, therefore, the gain or loss is deferred until a disposal by the transferee company. Clearance under ICTA 1970, section 267 (3A) should normally be obtained.

C. INCOME TAX AND CORPORATION TAX ON INCOME PROFITS

The most likely applications of ICTA 1970, sections 460 and 488 are discussed in chapter 3, section B. Both sections contain clearance procedures whereunder the Board of Inland Revenue must within 30 days of being supplied with the requisite particulars declare whether it is satisfied that the section in quesion is not applicable[4].

The transfer of a business results in the transferor being treated as discontinuing the trade. Where the transferor is an individual or partnership, consideration needs to be given to the discontinuance provisions contained in ICTA 1970, section 118. The Revenue can elect to substitute the actual profits of the two fiscal years prior to the cessation for the profits of those years as assessed on the normal basis. The normal basis is to assess as

---

[3] CGTA 1979, s. 123, and I.R. Statement of Practice 4/1971.
[4] ICTA 1970, ss. 464 and 488(11).

the profit for a year of assessment the profits of the accounting period ending in the previous year of assessment. A Revenue election will have adverse tax consequences for the vendor where the profits of the business have been rising in the years prior to the transfer. Where a change in the partners carrying on a business would result in a deemed cesser of that business, the business will be treated as continuing if all the partners, new and old or their personal representatives, so elect within two years of the change[5]. If an election could have been made, but is not, the new partnership will be assessed to tax in accordance with ICTA, section 116 if the change of partners took place before 20 March 1985 and in accordance with that section as amended by FA 1985, section 47 if the change occurred after 19 March 1985.

On cesser of a business, trading stock must be brought into account in the calculation of the final accounting period profit or loss. If the stock is transferred for valuable consideration to a person who carries on, or intends to carry on, a trade in the UK and the cost of the stock will be a deductible expense for tax purposes in the purchaser's hands, the value of the consideration for the stock will be the amount brought into the vendor's final accounts. In any other case the stock will be valued at its market value[6]. Where the agreement for sale of a business declares the effective transfer date to be some prior date and the purchaser undertakes to indemnify the vendor in respect of liabilities of the business from that date, the liabilities of the vendor for basic rate income tax on the sale of stock to the purchaser as at the actual transfer date will be a liability covered by the purchaser's indemnity[7]. Any indemnity given by the purchaser should be limited to exclude such tax.

Normally, trading losses can be carried forward only against profits of the same trade. Thus on the sale of a business, since the trade is deemed to cease, losses unrelieved under the carry across or terminal loss provisions or under FA 1978, section 30 (loss relief for individuals in early years of trade) cannot be carried forward. There are however two exceptions:

---

[5] ICTA 1970, s. 154(2).
[6] ICTA 1970, s. 137(1).
[7] Re Hollebone's Agreement [1959] 2 All ER 152.

(a) ICTA 1970, section 172 provides that where a business carried on by an individual, (or individuals in partnership) has been transferred to a company in consideration solely or mainly of shares in the company, then unrelieved losses of the business can be set off against income derived by the individual from the company during any year of assessment throughout which (i) he is the beneficial owner of the shares and (ii) the company carries on the business. The income may be from dividends or remuneration or any other type of income derived from company profits.

(b) ICTA 1970, section 252 provides that where one company ceases to carry on a trade and another company begins to carry it on, unrelieved trading losses and capital allowances on the predecessor's written down values[8] may be taken over by the successor company and deducted from taxable profits of the same trade if

(i) on, or at any time within two years after the event, not less than a three-quarters' interest in the trade belongs beneficially[9] to the same persons as it did at some time within the year preceding the transfer

(ii) during the period referred to in (i) above when the three-quarters' interest is maintained, the trade is carried on by a company assessable to UK tax.

It is not possible for the successor company to obtain relief under this section and for the predecessor company to obtain terminal loss relief under ICTA 1970, section 178.

Two points should be noted where the company being sold is a member of a group of companies. First, group relief is not available in the accounting period when arrangements are in existence for the surrendering company to leave the group[10]. 'Arrangements' means arrangements of any kind whether in writing or not[11]. Therefore, negotiations for the sale of a group company with losses available for surrender should not begin

---

[8] I.e. the actual proceeds passing between the companies in respect of relevant capital equipment is ignored.

[9] ICTA 1970, s. 253(3)(a).

[10] FA 1973, s. 29, but see Extra Statutory Concession C12 in connection with 'first refusal agreements' between members of a consortium.

[11] FA 1973, s. 32(6), and see *Pilkington Bros Ltd v IRC* [1982] 1 All ER 715, [1982] 1 WLR 136.

until after the end of its accounting period when the surrender takes place.

Secondly, a company to which advance corporation tax has been surrendered must remain a 51 per cent subsidiary throughout the accounting period when the dividend giving rise to the payment of advance corporation tax was paid, and no arrangements (see above) must be in existence whereby another person could obtain control of the subsidiary but not of the parent[12]. Otherwise the subsidiary will not be treated as such for the purposes of the surrender to it of the benefit of advance corporation tax.

D. DEVELOPMENT LAND TAX

Development land tax is abolished in respect of disposals occurring, and projects of material development commencing, after 18 March 1985.

An outline of the tax consequences arising from the apportionment of the purchase price between various assets on the sale of a business will be found in chapter 7.

---

[12] FA 1972, s. 92(9).

9 The Position of Minority Shareholders

For the purposes of this section a minority shareholder is any holder of shares in a private company whose holding is not on its own sufficient to prevent another or others controlling the composition of the board of directors and the management of the company's business. A minority shareholder may hold the majority of the company's issued shares but, if these shares have no voting or restricted voting rights he will fall within the above definition. In the absence of special rights or disadvantages attaching to any particular class of shares control of the composition of the board may be exercised by the holder(s) of a simple majority of issued shares. Thus any holder of shares with less than such a majority will be a minority shareholder. Further any holder of shares of 25 per cent or less of the issued shares will be unable to prevent other members of the company from passing those resolutions, called special resolutions, which are required by the 1985 Act to be passed before certain fundamental changes can be made to a company's constitution—for example, change of name, alteration of objects, alteration of articles, reduction of share capital and voluntary winding-up.

In the absence of an agreement between the majority and minority shareholders for the protection of the latter, the minority shareholder will only have limited protection. The forms of protection can be summarised as follows:

(1) The doctrine of fraud on the minority. The general principle

that the majority governs a company is known as the Rule
in *Foss v Harbottle* (1843) 2 Hare 461. The object of the Rule
has been expressed in another case by the learned Judge as
follows:

'In my opinion if the thing complained of is a thing which in
substance the majority of the company are entitled to do, or
if something has been done irregularly which the majority of
the company are entitled to do regularly, or if something has
been done illegally which the majority of the company are
entitled to do legally, there can be no use in having litigation
about it the ultimate end of which is only that a meeting has
to be called, and then ultimately the majority gets its wishes[1].

Thus since a breach of a director's fiduciary duty to a company is capable of ratification by the company it cannot be
subject to a minority shareholder's action[2]. An action based on
a fraud on the minority constitutes an exception to the general
rule, but a number of tests must be passed before a minority
shareholder can successfully invoke this protection which is
therefore of limited use. First, the effect of the action complained
of must be to discriminate between the majority shareholders
and the minority shareholders as shareholders so as to give the
former an advantage of which the latter are deprived. Secondly,
the act complained of must be dishonest or improper, or, if
merely negligent, must confer some advantage on the wrong-
doer, e.g. by the sale of corporate assets to a director at an
undervalue[3]. A minority shareholder will not succeed in a claim
based on bad management by the directors in the absence of

---

[1] Mellish LJ in *Macdougall v Gardiner* (1875) 1 Ch D 13 at 25.

[2] *Bentley-Stevens v Jones* [1974] 2 All ER 653, [1974] 1 WLR 638. And a director
who is removed from the board by his co-directors in an alleged breach of
their fiduciary duty to exercise a power under the company's articles cannot
maintain an action in his own name to restore himself to office. The remedy
would be a derivative action on behalf of the company to right a wrong done
to it: *Samuel Tak Lee v Chou Wen Hsien et al.* (PC).

[3] *Daniels v Daniels* [1978] Ch 406, [1978] 2 All ER 89. But no impropriety was
alleged in *Clemens v Clemens Bros Ltd* [1976] 2 All ER 268, where it was held
that a majority shareholder's right to vote as she pleased was subject to
equitable considerations which may make it unjust to exercise it in a particular
way, and in certain circumstances the court will interfere with the majority
voting in a way which it may reasonably believe to be in the best interests of
the company: *Estmanco (Kilner House) Ltd v Greater London Council* [1982]
1 All ER 437, [1982] 1 WLR 2.

manifest bad faith[4] unless the directors themselves benefit from their own negligence[5]. Thirdly, a minority shareholder's representative action (the usual method of proceeding) must show that because the wrong-doers are in control of the company, the plaintiff cannot sue in the name of the company[6]. (There are disadvantages for a minority shareholder suing in the name of a company which are not within the scope of this book to discuss.) Finally, the court will consider the conduct of a plaintiff in a minority shareholder's action; a particular plaintiff may not be a proper person because his conduct is tainted in some way which under the rules of equity may bar relief[7].

(2) Provisions of the 1985 Act permitting applications to the court to cancel company resolutions:

(a) Section 5. The holders of not less than 15 per cent in aggregate in nominal value of the company's issued share capital, or any class thereof, may apply to the court for an alteration to the company's memorandum to be cancelled. Such application must be made within 21 days after the date of the resolution for the alteration of the memorandum.

(b) Section 54. The holders of not less than 5 per cent in aggregate in nominal value of the company's issued share capital or any class thereof, or not less than 50 of the company's members, may apply to the court for cancellation of a special resolution by a public company to be re-registered as a private company.

(c) Section 127. Where the share capital of the company is divided into different classes of shares and the rights attached to any class are varied pursuant to provisions for variation contained in the memorandum or articles, the holders of not less than 15 per cent in aggregate of the issued shares of that class may apply to the court to have the variation cancelled within 21 days of the resolution for variation being passed. The court may disallow the variation if it is satisfied, having

---

[4] *Pavlides v Jensen* [1956] Ch 565, [1956] 2 All ER 518.
[5] *Daniels v Daniels* [1978] Ch 406, [1978] 2 All ER 89.
[6] The question whether a company is under the control of those practising an alleged fraud on it should be determined before a representative action is heard: *Prudential Assurance Co Ltd v Newman Industries Ltd (No 2)* [1982] Ch 204, [1982] 1 All ER 354.
[7] *Nurcombe v Nurcombe* [1985] 1 All ER 65, [1985] 1 WLR 370, CA.

regard to all the circumstances of the case, that the variation would unfairly prejudice the shareholders of the class represented by the applicant. It should be noted that it is not sufficient for the applicant to be prejudiced—the applicant must show that his class of shareholders as a whole will be prejudiced. Where rights attached to a class of shares are varied under the Companies Act 1985, section 125(2) (which applies where the rights are attached otherwise than by the memorandum and the articles contain no provision for variation), section 127 applies to such variation also[8].

(d) Section 157(2) contains provision for the holders of not less than 10 per cent in aggregate in nominal value of a company's issued share capital, or any class thereof, to apply to the court for cancellation of a special resolution passed pursuant to section 155 of the 1985 Act approving the giving of financial assistance by the company in connection with the acquisition of its shares. Section 155 applies only to private companies.

(e) Section 176 provides that where a private company passes a special resolution approving for the purposes of Chapter VII of the 1985 Act any payment out of capital for the redemption or purchase of any of its shares, any member of the company other than one who consented to or voted in favour of the resolution, and any creditor of the company, may within five weeks of the date on which the resolution was passed apply to the court for cancellation of the resolution. The court's powers include power to adjourn the proceedings in order that an arrangement may be made to the court's satisfaction for the purchase of the interests of dissentient members[9]. (The purchase by a private company of its own shares is further discussed on pp. 117–118.)

(3) Other provisions of the 1985 Act relating to the management of a company's affairs:

(a) Section 16. Unless the member otherwise agrees in writing at any time, no alteration in the memorandum or articles of association made after he became a member shall bind him

---

[8] Companies Act 1985, s. 127(1)(b).
[9] Companies Act 1985, s. 177(1).

insofar as the alteration requires him to take or subscribe for more shares than the number held by him at the date on which the alteration is made, or in any way increases his liability as at that date to contribute to the share capital of, or otherwise pay money to, the company.

(b) Section 89(1) provides that a company shall not allot any 'equity securities' unless it first offers to allot the same amongst existing holders of 'relevant shares' pro rata to their existing holdings and on the same or more favourable terms. Offerees must be given at least 21 days before the offer can be withdrawn[10]. 'Relevant shares' are all shares other than those which as respects dividends and capital carry a right to participate only up to a specified amount in a distribution and shares held under an employee's share scheme[11]. 'Equity security' means a relevant share (or right to subscribe for, or convert securities into, relevant shares) other than a share taken by a subscriber to the memorandum, or a bonus share[12]. A private company may exclude section 89(1) by a provision in its memorandum or articles[13] and that section will not in any event apply to any particular allotment of equity securities which are to be wholly or partly paid up otherwise than in cash[14]. Furthermore, section 89(1) may be made inapplicable or modified by the articles, or by special resolution, so long as the directors are generally authorised for the purposes of section 80 (authority of company required for allotment of certain securities by directors).

(c) Section 359. If the name of any person is, without sufficient cause, entered in or omitted from the register of members, or there is default or unnecessary delay in entering on the register the fact of any person having ceased to be a member, the person aggrieved, or any member, or the company, may apply to the court for rectification of the register. In an appropriate case, this will be an essential preliminary step in seeking the court's assistance pursuant to those provisions of the 1985 Act available only to members of the company.

---

[10] Companies Act 1985, s. 90(6).
[11] Companies Act 1985, s. 94(5).
[12] Companies Act 1985, s. 94(2).
[13] Companies Act 1985, s. 91.
[14] Companies Act 1985, s. 89(4).

(d) Section 368. On the requisition by the holders of not less than 10 per cent of the company's paid up voting capital, the directors of the company must convene an extraordinary general meeting of the company's members. This provision may be appropriate for quoted companies with a widely disbursed share ownership, but is of little use to the minority shareholders of a private company. This applies similarly to the court's power under section 371 to order a general meeting of the company to be called, and to section 378 which requires a company to circulate members' resolutions to members of the company if a certain minimum number of members, or of members with a certain minimum fraction of voting rights, so requests. The right of a minority to demand a poll at general meetings of the company cannot be excluded by anything in the company's articles: section 373. The minority must be of the size specified by that section.

(e) Section 431. On the application of not less than 200 members or of members holding not less than 10 per cent of the issued shares, the Department of Trade may appoint one or more Inspectors to investigate a company's affairs. The Department may require the applicants to give security for the costs of the investigation up to £5,000, but this does not apply to a Department investigation under section 442 as to the true beneficial ownership of the company's share capital. The Department may in addition on its own initiative institute enquiries into a company's affairs under section 432(2) of the 1985 Act. The Department's discretion under section 432(2) arises if it appears to it that there are circumstances suggesting, inter alia, that the company's affairs are being or have been conducted in a manner unfairly prejudicial to some part of its members, or that any actual or proposed act or omission of the company is or would be so prejudicial, or that persons concerned with its formation or management have been guilty of fraud, misfeasance or other misconduct towards the company or its members. The Department of Trade, however, is sparing of its use of its powers under these provisions.

(f) Section 459(1) provides that 'a member of a company may apply to the court by petition for an order ... on the ground that the company's affairs are being or have been conducted in a manner which is unfairly prejudicial to the interests of some part of the members (including at least himself) or that any actual or proposed act or omission of the company (including an act or omission on its behalf) is or would be so prejudicial'.

It may be noted that:

(i) The expression 'member' is extended to include a person who is not a member but to whom shares in the company have been transferred or transmitted by operation of law: section 459(2).

(ii) The conduct of the company's affairs need only be 'unfairly prejudicial' rather than 'oppressive' which was the test under section 210 of the 1948 Act.

(iii) Although a shareholder must show that he is aggrieved in his capacity as a shareholder, it is not necessary to show that any other shareholder is unfairly prejudiced.

(iv) A single unfairly prejudicial act or omission of the company may be the subject of an application under section 459.

(v) The specific remedies available to the court under section 461(2) are clearly expressed to be without prejudice to the generality of section 461(1) which permits the court to make such order as it thinks fit for giving relief in respect of the matters complained of. The specific remedies include power to authorise civil proceedings to be brought in the name and on behalf of the company by such person and on such terms as the court may direct and power to order the purchase of the shares of any members of the company by other members of the company or by the company[15]. In decisions under section 210 of the 1948 Act, which was the law applicable prior to 22 December 1980, it had been held that a complaint by a shareholder/director that he had been excluded from board meetings would not be within the ambit of the section because the conduct complained of

---

[15] When the court orders that a petitioner's shares be bought at their fair value, generally the fair value will be determined on a pro rata basis rather than a discounted basis: *Re Bird Precision Bellows Ltd* [1984] Ch 419, [1984] 3 All ER 444.

must relate to the petitioner qua shareholder and not in some other capacity[16]; and that disapproval of management policy was an insufficient ground to invoke the section[17]. It is thought that similar decisions would be made in respect of petitions presented under section 461 of the 1985 Act[18].

Where it is commercially possible minority shareholders should seek to negotiate an agreement detailing a number of obligations on the part of the majority shareholder and restrictions on his conduct. The following are examples, by no means exhaustive, of situations in which an agreement should be negotiated on behalf of the minority.

(1) A Limited incorporates a subsidiary, B Limited, to carry out a new manufacturing process using the expertise of Messrs. X and Y whom A Limited has poached from a rival company. The Board of B Limited consists of three nominees of A Limited and X and Y each of whom, besides being given a three year service agreement, are permitted to subscribe to 10 per cent of B Limited's share capital at par, the remainder being held by A Limited. At the end of three years, the Board of B Limited decides not to renew X and Y's service agreements since the manufacturing process has been established and only administrative and financial management is required. A Limited votes to remove X and Y from the Board of B Limited and offers to purchase their shares at a value which X and Y consider derisory, but which A Limited maintains is a proper value having regard to the fact that the holdings are minority holdings and that there is no market for them.

(2) A and B are designers and incorporate a company AB Limited through which to conduct their business. They come up with an idea capable of substantial commercial exploitation but lack the necessary funds. They are unable to borrow from a bank. They approach an established company X Limited, which undertakes to make a medium-term loan to B Limited in return for inter alia 51 per cent of that company's equity. The product is successful, but management fees charged by X Limited starve AB Limited of funds and the product cannot be fully exploited and the development of new products is severely limited.

---

[16] *Re Bellador Silk Ltd* [1965] 1 All ER 667.
[17] *Re Five Minute Car Wash Service Ltd* [1966] 1 All ER 242, [1966] 1 WLR 745.
[18] See for example *Re a Company* [1983] Ch 178, [1983] 2 All ER 36.

(3) D Limited incorporates a subsidiary in which it subscribes to 75 per cent of the shares, and Mr S is the managing director (the other two directors being D Limited nominees) and holder of the other 25 per cent of the company's capital. In the first years of operation the subsidiary makes a loss which would be available for set off against its subsequent profits. However the board of the subsidiary votes to surrender the losses to D Limited in return for inadequate consideration.

Possibly in these examples the minority could successfully petition the court under section 459 of the 1985 Act, and such a petition may be tactically effective. Nevertheless contractual rights in a minority shareholder's agreement may be easier to enforce than rights under section 459.

The precedent contained in Appendix F is designed to give the minority some protection in these and other situations, and in addition it contains a put option for the minority so that if its shares acquire value, such value can be realised. If any such option is included, it is in the author's view preferable as far as possible to include a valuation formula. This can be based on a multiple of profits in which case there must be defined:

(1) What is meant by profits.

(2) The multiple itself.

(3) The accounting period(s) the profits of which are relevant.

(4) How losses are to be treated, i.e. whether they are to be treated as nil profits or carried forward and deducted from subsequent periods.

Alternatively the valuation can be related to asset values in which case it must be decided whether to include goodwill; how assets are to be depreciated; how the value of the shares in question are to be related to the value of the underlying assets.

Certain other provisions of the precedent call for special comment. Clause 1(2) requires the majority to keep the minority informed should the latter not exercise its option to appoint nominees to the board. If the conduct of the company through the majority of the board is improper vis-à-vis outsiders, the minority may well wish to resign from the board. The clause is therefore designed to overcome the difficulty of obtaining information experienced by shareholders who are not directors, but of course it cannot be effective against a majority determined to keep their unofficial discussions secret.

Clauses 1(2)(s) and 1(5) of the precedent deal with the tax position of minority shareholders and this is discussed in section B of this chapter.

Another possible area of negotiation has arisen since 15 June 1982 when section 162 of the 1985 Act (formerly section 46 of the Companies Act 1981) became operative. Section 162 permits a company to buy its own shares subject to the conditions of that and other sections being satisfied. The company must be authorised to purchase its own shares by its articles although the terms and manner of such purchase need not be specified. The same problem of valuation arises as on an option agreement between shareholders. Provision in the articles for the company to buy its shares 'at a fair price to be determined by the auditors', merely defers consideration of the problem.

A private company is in a privileged position when it comes to purchasing its own shares. Such a company is not restricted to financing the purchase only from its distributable profits, or the proceeds of a fresh issue of shares made for the purpose, but may, if authorised by its articles and insofar as distributable profits are unavailable, use its capital. There are, however, a number of safeguards for shareholders and creditors[19] which make the exercise complicated, and certain time limits must be adhered to. These include the requirement for the directors to make a statutory declaration of solvency in accordance with section 173 of the 1985 Act, and the right of any creditor to object to the court. Since these are matters which cannot be controlled by the company, an undertaking by the company to buy out a minority shareholder is less than cast-iron. Indeed, the 1985 Act provides that a company is not liable in damages for failing to buy back its shares, nor can specific performance be ordered if the distributable profits of the company are insufficient[20]. Although the failure to purchase may be enforced in a winding up, the shareholder's right to be bought out will be subject to the prior claims of creditors, and the value of the shares themselves may be less on a break-up basis than on a going concern basis. Even where the company complies with its

---

[19] Companies Act 1985, ss. 171–177.
[20] Companies Act 1985, s. 178.

obligation to buy back without there being a winding up, the vendor, (and the directors) may be required to contribute to any deficiency in the company's assets in the event of a winding up within one year of the company using capital to buy back its own shares.

A further disincentive, if one were needed, to making use of the buy back provisions lies in the tax treatment of the transaction. Unless the transaction falls within one of two cases the payment by the company to the shareholders will be treated as a distribution, so that the company will be charged to advance corporation tax, and the shareholder to income tax under Schedule F. The relevant provisions are contained in FA 1982, section 53, and a clearance procedure is available. The first case is where substantially the whole price is applied by the recipient in discharging a capital transfer tax liability, and that liability could not without undue hardship have been discharged except by selling shares back to the company or another similar company[1]. Where, however, capital transfer tax is payable in instalments over eight years, it may be difficult to satisfy the undue hardship condition.

The second case is where the main purpose of the company's purchase is to benefit its trade, and reference should be made to the Inland Revenue Statement of Practice SP2/82 for the Revenue's view of the type of transaction likely to qualify. A purchase will nevertheless not qualify unless the vendor/shareholder satisfies certain conditions including one that he must have owned the shares throughout the previous five years[2].

Finally, where an individual purposes to subscribe to shares in a company whose shares are not quoted on the Unlisted Securities Market nor listed on the Stock Exchange and the shares are to be issued before 6 April 1987, consideration should be given to the provisions of the Business Expansion Scheme[3] to see if income tax relief can be claimed on the amount of the subscription monies.

---

[1] FA 1982, s. 53(2).

[2] The problems arising under FA 1982, s. 53 and its relationship to ICTA, s. 460 are discussed in an Institute of Taxation Technical Paper 'The Business Start-Up Scheme and the purchase by a Company of its own shares', Taxation Practitioner (1983), vol. 8, pp. 26–28.

[3] FA 1983, s. 26 and Sch. 5.

B. TAX PROTECTION FOR MINORITY SHAREHOLDERS [4]

A shareholder owning or proposing to acquire a minority of a private company's issued share capital may obtain, by agreement with the majority shareholder, certain additional protection and rights specifically designed to ensure that there is no discrimination between the majority and minority shareholders in the tax treatment of the company.

(1) Surrender of Advance Corporation Tax ('ACT')

FA 1972, section 92 as amended permits a company which has in any accounting period paid ACT in respect of a dividend, the ACT not having been repaid, to surrender all or part of the ACT to any 51 per cent subsidiary company. The subsidiary can then set off against its own corporation tax liability the ACT surrendered to it. Although a minority shareholder in a holding company would receive an indirect benefit from an advantage accruing to a subsidiary, it may be that the majority shareholder in the holding company also holds shares directly in the subsidiary. Unless, therefore, the holding company is fully compensated for the surrender, the majority shareholder would thereby receive a share of the benefit accruing to the subsidiary disproportionate to his share in the holding company. This would not be the case were the holding company to carry back or forward surplus ACT to reduce its own corporation tax liability under FA 1972, section 85 as amended by FA 1984, sections 52 and 53 in relation to accounting periods ending after 31 March 1984.

(2) Group relief for trading losses and other amounts

Under the provisions concerned with surrender of ACT, a holding company may surrender to a subsidiary, but not vice versa, and the subsidiary need only be a 51 per cent subsidiary; moreover, one subsidiary cannot surrender surplus ACT to another. This position should be contrasted with that appertaining to group relief for losses. Leaving aside the special provisions dealing with consortia, ICTA 1970, section 258 basically provides that a company and its 75 per cent subsidiaries form a group

---

[4] This section is based on an article by the author published in the British Tax Review [1973] BTR 69.

for group relief purposes. Furthermore, the group relief provisions enable a 75 per cent subsidiary to surrender losses to a holding company or vice versa, and also to surrender losses to another 75 per cent subsidiary of its own holding company. Losses surrendered have value to the surrendering company because, for example, they could (were it not for the surrender) be carried forward to reduce the surrendering company's own future taxable profits.

Thus, a 75 per cent majority shareholder which is itself a company, may procure the surrender to itself, or to another of its 75 per cent subsidiaries, of all or part of the trading losses or other items eligible for surrender of the company in which the minority shareholder has an interest. To the extent that the subsidiary is not fully compensated for such surrender, the minority shareholder will be disadvantaged. Alternatively, the majority shareholder of a parent company may have a direct interest in a 75 per cent subsidiary of that parent and may therefore, in the same way as with the surrender of ACT, receive a disproportionate benefit from a surrender of losses by that parent company to its subsidiary.

(3) Capital gains tax—transfer within a group

For capital gains tax purposes, the general position under ICTA 1970, section 273 is that where a member of a group of companies disposes of an asset to another member of the group, both members are to be treated as if the asset were acquired for such consideration as would secure neither a gain nor a loss on the disposal. The liability to tax arises on a disposition outside the group. For these purposes a group is basically defined as a company and its 75 per cent subsidiaries and the 75 per cent subsidiaries of those subsidiaries ad infinitum.

The statutory provisions relating to inter-group transfers of capital assets enable a corporate 75 per cent majority shareholder in effect to inflict on the minority shareholder a part of the tax liability on its own capital gains. For example, the majority shareholder X Limited may wish to sell a capital asset at a gain for £A, its current market value, to Z who is a person outside the group. A direct transfer by X Limited to Z would result in a tax liability to X Limited in respect of the capital gain. X Limited therefore procures Y Limited, its 75 per cent subsidiary to buy the asset from it for £A and immediately to resell it at the same price to Z. Y Limited will then be treated and taxed as if it had made the gain which in fact accrued to X Limited to the detriment of the minority shareholder in Y Limited.

The above matters are not exhaustive of the tax considerations which a draftsman acting for a minority shareholder may have to bear in mind, because particular circumstances may demand protection of a particular type. These circumstances may relate to the characteristics (from a tax point of view) of the minority shareholder. For example, the draftsman may wish to provide for a dividend policy of one sort or another (particularly where the company concerned is close) depending on the taxable status of the minority shareholder; or he may wish to exempt from any pre-emption provisions relating to the shares in question a transfer by the minority shareholder to members of his family or to trustees of a family settlement.

The particular characteristics of the majority shareholder should be considered also. For example, consideration will have to be given to the tax consequences (as well as the commercial consequences) of sales at an undervalue and of purchases at an overvalue by the company to and from the majority shareholder if the majority shareholder is not resident in the United Kingdom, or is so resident but not trading in the class of assets bought or sold. Such sales and purchases can result in the company's receipts and expenses being respectively increased and reduced in computing its liability to corporation tax[5].

---

[5] ICTA 1970, s. 485.

10 Sales and Purchases by Quoted Companies and Public Limited Companies

Although it is Stock Exchange take-overs which make the headlines the majority of company acquisitions are in respect of unquoted companies.

Where the company being acquired is quoted on the Stock Exchange reference should be made to the Stock Exchange and to the City Code on Takeovers and Mergers[1]. More common is the situation where the vendor or purchaser is a quoted company but the target company is unquoted. In such a case where the quotation is on the Official List reference should be made to the chapter on Acquisitions and Realisations contained in the Stock Exchange's *Admission of Securities to Listing* (known as 'the Yellow Book'), copies of which can be obtained from Quotations Department, PO Box No. 119, The Stock Exchange, Throgmorton Street Entrance, London EC2P 2BT. The Quotations Department issues a separate booklet in respect of companies quoted on the Unlisted Securities Market. The Yellow Book now includes the statutory requirements imposed by the Stock Exchange (Listing) Regulations 1984 on companies quoted on the Official List, and on applicants for such status, the Council of the Stock Exchange having been appointed as the competent authority for the purposes of those regulations.

---

[1] The Code applies also to unlisted public companies and certain classes of private company. Copies can be obtained from the Panel on Take-overs and Mergers, PO Box No. 226, The Stock Exchange Building, London EC2P 2JX.

In the Yellow Book relevant transactions are divided into five categories summarised as follows:

1. Class 1 transactions: These are transactions where the relative figures amount to 15 per cent or more in respect of (a) the value of the assets acquired or disposed of compared with the assets of the acquiring or disposing company, or (b) net pre-tax profits (excluding extraordinary items) attributable to the assets acquired or disposed of compared with those of the acquiring or disposing company, or (c) the aggregate value of the consideration given or received compared with the assets of the acquiring or disposing company, or (d) equity capital issues as consideration by the acquiring company compared with the equity capital previously in issue.

Once terms have been agreed between the parties, if the transaction falls within Class 1 certain specified particulars must be given to the Quotations Department of the Stock Exchange and an announcement given to the Company Announcements Office for the release to the market and which, if desired, may be released simultaneously to the press. In addition a circular must be sent to the shareholders containing prescribed particulars. In certain limited circumstances, described in the Yellow Book, the Committee on Quotations may relax these requirements, but where any comparison on the basis of the tests set out above shows a figure of 25 per cent or more, the transaction, whether an acquisition or realisation, should be made conditional on approval by shareholders in general meeting[2]. In the case of an acquisition by a listed company, there is an additional test for the purpose of ascertaining whether the 25 per cent figure has been reached, namely by comparing on the one hand the market value of the equity capital and all other listed securities of the acquiring company (or nominal value of such of its securities as are unlisted) aggregated with the values of its fixed liabilities, minority interests, deferred taxation and excess of current liabilities over current assets with, on the other hand, the aggregate of similar values of the company or business being acquired, save that the value of the consideration payable will be taken instead of the equity capital at market value. The aggregation is made on the basis that 100 per cent

---

[2] Yellow Book, section 6, ch.1, para. 3.4.

of the equity capital is to be acquired, whether or not such is the case.

2. Class 2 transactions: These are transactions where the relevant figures are more than 5 per cent and less than 15 per cent. The requirement is for an announcement to be given to the Companies Announcements Office (which may be released simultaneously to the press) containing prescribed information.

3. Class 3 transactions: Broadly speaking to come within this category the relevant figures must be less than 5 per cent. No announcement will be required unless the consideration for the acquisition is being satisfied wholly or partly in securities for which a listing is being sought.

   In deciding whether a circular should be sent to shareholders, the Stock Exchange may aggregate acquisitions or realisations that have taken place since either the publication of the last accounts, or the issue of the last circular, whichever is the later.

   In any of the above situations it is for the advisers to the quoted company to ensure that the Stock Exchange requirements are complied with, but the solicitor for the other party should reserve the right for his clients to approve the contents of any announcement or circular prior to publication.

   It should be noted that transactions of a revenue nature including transactions by investment dealing companies in the ordinary course of their business are expressly excluded from the requirements mentioned above.

4. Class 4 transactions: A transaction within this class involving an acquisition or disposal will overlap with a transaction within another class, and is basically one between a quoted company on the one hand and any of its directors or substantial shareholders, past or present, on the other. A transaction is a Class 4 transaction if it falls within any of the following classes:
   (a) An acquisition or disposal of assets by the company or any one of its subsidiaries from or to a director[3] or substantial shareholder or an associate thereof;

---

[3] A management buy-out from a listed company will usually be a Class 4 transaction.

(b) A transaction under which the company or any one of its subsidiaries is to take an interest in a company, any part of the equity share capital of which has recently been, or is to be, acquired, whether by subscription or otherwise, by a director or an associate thereof;

(c) A transaction a principal purpose or effect of which is the granting of credit (including the lending of money) by the company or any one of its subsidiaries to a director or substantial shareholder or an associate thereof, excluding a granting of credit upon normal commercial terms in the ordinary and usual course of business;

(d) The company or any one of its subsidiaries making a takeover offer any acceptance of which, to its knowledge after making all reasonable enquiries, could result in a significant acquisition from a director or substantial shareholder or associate thereof;

(e) The company or any one of its subsidiaries accepting a take-over offer which to its knowledge, after making all reasonable enquiries, would thereby result in a significant disposal to a director or substantial shareholder or associate thereof.

The following definitions are relevant:

The word 'director' means and includes any person who is, or was within the preceding 12 months, a director of the company (or of any of its subsidiaries or its holding company or of a fellow subsidiary of its holding company) and includes a 'shadow director' as defined by Companies Act 1985, section 741(2).

The words 'substantial shareholder' mean and include any person who is, or was within the preceding 12 months, a holder of 10 per cent or more of the nominal value of any class of capital of the company (or any other company which is its subsidiary or holding company or a subsidiary of its holding company) having rights to vote in all circumstances at general meetings of the relevant company.

The word 'associate' means and includes (i) in relation to a director or substantial shareholder being an individual, his or her spouse and any child under the age of 18 years ('family interests') and the trustees (as such) of any trust of which the individual or any of his or her family interests is a beneficiary or discretionary object and any company in which the individual and/or his or her family interests taken together are directly or indirectly interested so as to exercise, or control the exercise of, 30 per cent or more of the voting power at general meetings of the company, or to control the composition of a majority of the board of directors of the company; and (ii) in relation to a substantial shareholder, being a company, any other company which is its subsidiary or holding company or a fellow subsidiary of any such holding company or, save in relation to a take-over offer, one of the equity capital of which it and/or such other companies taken together are directly or indirectly interested as aforesaid.

If a transaction is within Class 4, the Quotations Department of the Stock Exchange must be consulted prior to any contract being entered into or take-over offer made, or the discretion to accept a take-over offer being exercised, and, where it is proposed to enter into a contract the Quotations Department must be supplied with a copy of the draft. The Stock Exchange will normally require shareholders to be circularised and that the transaction be subject to the approval of the shareholders in general meeting. Further it may require that the director, substantial shareholder or associate concerned shall abstain from voting at the general meeting and that a statement to that effect be included in the circular to shareholders. Where, however, the Class 4 transaction is one within (d) above, it is possible for the requisite consent of shareholders to be sought after the offer has been made, provided that the offer is expressed as being conditional on such consent being obtained and the applicable rules of the City Code on Take-overs and Mergers so permit.

It follows that any transaction falling within Class 4 will in the agreement for sale normally be made conditional upon shareholders' consents being obtained. The solicitor acting for the director, substantial shareholder or associate will therefore be concerned:

(i) to review the right to approve the contents of any circular to shareholders (although the circular must contain certain information to satisfy Stock Exchange requirements);

(ii) to oblige the company to act expeditiously in seeking the consent of its shareholders, i.e. to convene an extraordinary general meeting by a stated future date.

(iii) where possible to obtain undertakings from those directors permitted to vote to cast their votes in favour of the transaction. Directors must act in the best interest of their company but directors who negotiate a deal and who recommend it to shareholders by way of circular cannot reasonably refuse to endorse it by their own votes.

The right to approve press announcements and shareholders' circulars is usually readily conceded but equally usually made subject to the proviso that such approval shall not be unreasonably withheld. Some care should be exercised in accepting such a proviso since, unlike in cases, for example, of landlord's consent to assign a lease, the criteria for deciding what is, or is not, reasonable in this context are not clear. The practical answer may be to agree drafts of any announcement and circular before exchange of contracts and for the agreement to provide that no announcement or circular other than in the terms agreed shall be issued.

5. Very substantial acquisitions or reverse take-overs: The Committee on Quotations require these to be subject to the approval of shareholders in general meeting. Listing for the acquiring company's securities will usually be suspended until such approval has been obtained, and will then be cancelled prior to publication of listing particulars (as to which see section 3 of the Yellow Book). A transaction will be within this class where the relative figures as referred to in the description above of Class 1 transactions would be 100 per cent or more, or which would result in a change of control through the introduction of a majority holder or group of holders, and in either case the company or companies to be acquired are not listed.

Where certain conditions are satisfied the company will not be treated as a new applicant for listing, and listing will normally be restored before shareholders' approval has been obtained but after publication of full information. The conditions are (a) the company (or business) to be acquired is of a similar size to that of the acquiring company; (b) the two companies are in a similar line of business; (c) the enlarged group is suitable for listing (as to which see section 1 of the Yellow Book); and (d) there will be no material change of boardroom or voting control, or in the management.

Whichever class a transaction is within, if the purchase consideration is to be satisfied by the issue of shares in a quoted company, the sale contract should provide for the purchaser to procure such shares to be admitted to listing by the Stock Exchange. Listing particulars will be required if there are to be issued shares which would increase the shares of a class already listed by 10 per cent or more, or debt securities of any amount, and such particulars may not be published until they have been approved by the Stock Exchange.

USM Companies

In the case of a company quoted on the Unlisted Securities Market, it is required to notify the Quotations Department of the Stock Exchange of particulars of acquisitions or realisations of assets immediately after the relevant event, wherever any of the following tests amounts to 5 per cent or more, viz (i) the value of assets acquired or disposed of, compared with the assets of the acquiring or disposing company; (ii) net pre-tax profits attributable to the assets acquired or disposed of, compared with the profits of the acquiring or disposing company; (iii) the aggregate value of the consideration given or received, compared with the assets of the acquiring or disposing company; (iv) equity capital issued by the company as consideration for the acquisition, compared with equity capital already in issue.

If one of the above tests amounts to 25 per cent or more, in addition to notification to the Quotations Department, the company must circularise its shareholders in accordance with the requirements of section D of the booklet 'The Stock Exchange Unlisted Securities Market'. Where the relative tests amount to 100 per cent or more, or where a change of control may result, the Department must be consulted in advance.

Transactions which involve, or involve an associate of, a director, substantial shareholder, or past substantial shareholder of the company (or any other company being its subsidiary, holding company or a subsidiary of its holding company) must be first approved by the company in general meeting and be the subject of an explanatory circular. The Quotations Department requires to be consulted as soon as possible on any proposal to enter into such a transaction, and prior to any contract being entered into.

B. PUBLIC LIMITED COMPANIES

Any Stock Exchange requirements are additional to the obligations imposed by the purchasing company's articles and to statutory requirements, for example section 80 of the 1985 Act (authority of company required for certain allotments of shares) and section 320 thereof (substantial property transactions involving directors etc.). Those sections are discussed elsewhere in this book. Other sections of the 1985 Act, although only catching public companies, will concern vendors to a public company, whether or not its shares are quoted on the Stock Exchange.

These are:

(1) Section 101. Although it would be unusual for vendors to accept other than fully-paid shares in the purchasing company, this section prohibits a public company from allotting any share except as paid up at least as to one-quarter of its nominal value and the whole of any premium on it. The broad prohibition on any company, public or private, issuing shares at a discount remains[4].

(2) Section 102(1) prohibits a public company from allotting shares as fully or partly paid up (as to their nominal value or any premium payable on them) otherwise than in cash, if the consideration for the allotment is, or includes an undertaking which is to be, or may be, performed more than five years after the allotment date. Where there is a contravention of section 102(1), the allottee and every subsequent holder (other than a holder for value and without notice, or a successor in title to such a holder)[5] will be liable to pay to the company the aggregate of the nominal value of the shares and of any premium, or so much of the amount treated as paid up thereon by virtue of the undertaking.

The section therefore prohibits the acquisition by a public company of shares in consideration, inter alia, of a covenant by

---

[4] Companies Act 1985, s. 100.
[5] Companies Act 1985, s. 112(5).

the vendors not to compete with the business of the target company for a period exceeding five years.

Section 102(5) provides that where the consideration is or includes an undertaking to be performed within five years, but the undertaking is not performed within 'the period allowed by the contract for the allotment of the shares', similar sanctions apply as apply to a contravention of section 102(1). Section 102(5) presupposes there having been an allotment of shares, so that undertakings by a vendor to be performed prior to completion will in practice not be caught. However, all positive undertakings to be performed by the vendor or anyone else on or after completion will be caught if given in consideration of the allotment and not performed in accordance with the contract. The purchasing company will thus have a statutory remedy (subject to the provisions for relief under section 113) as well as its contractual remedies. Where no proportion of the amount paid up on the consideration shares is treated (presumably by the contract for allotment) as paid up by the undertaking, it would seem that section 102(5) cannot bite. Nevertheless, solicitors will need to be extra cautious about giving undertakings on completion in these circumstances.

(3) Where an expert's report on valuation is required under section 103, the report must state the extent to which the nominal value of the shares and any premium are to be treated as paid up by (i) cash, (ii) non-cash consideration[6]. Section 103 will not, however, apply to a share for share exchange so long as it is open to all the holders of shares, or of shares of a particular class, in the target company to take part[7], nor will it apply to a proposed merger of one company with another, being a proposal by one to acquire all the assets and liabilities of the other in exchange for shares or other securities of the one to shareholders of the other, with or without any cash payment[8]. A proposal to acquire assets, but not liabilities, or some only of the assets and/or liabilities, will not be exempt from section 103 which prohibits a public company from allotting shares, otherwise than for cash, unless:

---

[6] Companies Act 1985, s. 108(4)(d).
[7] Companies Act 1985, ss. 103(6) and 112(1).
[8] Companies Act 1985, s. 104.

(a) the consideration has been valued in accordance with the provisions of the section

(b) a report of the valuation has been made to the company within six months preceding the allotment, and

(c) a copy of the report has been sent to the proposed allottee.

Where there is a contravention of the section, the allottee and every subsequent holder (other than a holder for value without notice, or a successor in title to such a holder) will be jointly and severally liable to pay the issuing company a sum up to the nominal value of shares and any premium thereon or such proportion as is treated as paid up by the non-cash consideration[9], subject to the relief provisions of section 113.

(4) There are special provisions applicable to the acquisition by a public company of non-cash assets, whether for shares or otherwise, from subscribers to its memorandum within two years of the company being issued with a certificate entitling it to do business under section 117 of the 1985 Act[10]. In the case of a company (other than an old public company as defined by the 1980 Act) registering or re-registering as public, the two-year period commences from the date of registration or re-registration.

---

[9] Companies Act 1985, s. 103(4).
[10] Companies Act 1985, s. 103(5).

11 Non-Residents

A. TAXATION

The term 'non-resident' means different things in different contexts. For taxation purposes it means not resident in the United Kingdom of Great Britain and Northern Ireland.

In the absence of statutory definition, the question whether an individual is resident is a question of fact[1] and there is abundant case law to which reference may be made. A useful starting point on taxation questions is the Inland Revenue pamphlet 'Residents and Non-Residents—Liability to Tax in the United Kingdom' (IR20 1983).

The Inland Revenue practice may be summarised as follows:

(1) Where a place of abode is maintained in the UK available for the individual's use, the individual will be treated as resident for any year of assessment in which he sets foot in the UK, and ordinarily resident if he is resident for three years or his visits become habitual and substantial.

(2) Where no such place of abode is maintained an individual will be treated as resident for any year of assessment in which his visits to the UK total six months or more, or if his visits are habitual and substantial. Visits to this country are regarded as becoming habitual after four successive years. An average visit of three months per year is regarded as substantial.

---

[1] *IRC v Lysaght* [1928] AC 234.

(3) The question of residence is determined without regard to the maintenance of a place of abode if the individual works full time outside the UK. In such a case, so long as his absence includes a complete tax year, he will be treated as neither resident nor ordinarily resident unless his visits to the UK amount to six months or more in any tax year, or average three months or more per tax year.

(4) In the case of individuals going abroad the practice is as above save that if the period abroad does not include at least one complete tax year, the individual will be regarded as resident and ordinarily resident throughout[2]. In connection with the years of commencement or cessation of residence of an individual, liability to tax will usually be computed by reference to the individual's period of residence during the fiscal year in question, and not on the basis that he is resident for the whole year[3]. For capital gains tax purposes a disposal by a person who is treated as UK resident for any year of assessment will not be chargeable if made before his arrival in the UK or after his departure if he would then be treated as neither resident nor ordinarily resident[4].

(5) For some purposes the Taxes Acts distinguish between persons who are 'resident' and 'ordinarily resident', and the Revenue practice is to treat as resident and ordinarily resident any person whose visits to the UK are habitual and substantial even if no place of abode is maintained.

(6) The residence of a partnership or a company will be determined according to the place where its control and management are actually situated as opposed to where its articles may provide for it to be situated[5]. In the case of a company, the place of incorporation is not conclusive[6]. As a rule of thumb, the place of a company's central management and control will be the place where its board of directors meets,

---

[2] See also ICTA 1970, s. 49 which was held not to apply on the facts to the pop-star Dave Clark: *Reed v Clark*, op. cit. For individuals coming to the UK, see also Statement of Practice SP3/81.

[3] Extra Statutory Concession A11.

[4] Extra Statutory Concession D2.

[5] *Unit Construction Co Ltd v Bullock* [1960] AC 351, [1959] 3 All ER 831, and see I.R. Statement of Practice SP6/83.

[6] *Egyptian Delta Land and Investment Co Ltd v Todd* [1929] AC1.

so that where for example one or more parties to a purchase transaction wishes to maintain non-resident status, simultaneous completions may need to be arranged in different countries if board resolutions are to be passed on completion. It is therefore possible for a company incorporated in England or Scotland, to be resident abroad, and for a company incorporated abroad to be resident in the UK[7].

(7) In relation to settled property and capital gains tax (but not capital transfer tax) trustees are treated as resident and ordinarily resident in the UK unless the general administration of the trust is ordinarily carried on outside the UK and the trustees, or a majority of them, are not resident or not ordinarily resident there. Professional trustees, however, will be treated as non-resident if the whole settled property consists of or derives from property provided by a person who at the date of the settlement was not domiciled, resident or ordinarily resident in the UK. In such a case, if the trustees or a majority of them are treated as not resident, the general administration of the trust will be treated as ordinarily carried on outside the UK with the result that any non-professional co-trustee will in relation to the settled property also be treated as non-resident[8].

When a vendor of shares is neither resident nor ordinarily resident in the UK, no capital gains tax will normally be chargeable on disposal of the shares[9]. Where disposal takes place pursuant to a contract, the disposal is effected when the contract is made and not on completion unless the contract is conditional in which case the disposal is effected when the condition is satisfied[10]. A person who is neither resident nor ordinarily resident in the UK, but who is carrying on a trade through a branch or agency, will however be chargeable on gains arising from the disposal of assets situated in the UK and used for the purposes of the trade, or of the branch or agency, and of other assets acquired for use by or for the purposes of the branch or

---

[7] In connection with determining whether a company is a 'controlled foreign company' for the purposes of FA 1984, s. 82, residence is determined in accordance with s. 84 of that Act.

[8] CGTA 1979, s. 52(1).

[9] But see ESC D2 referred to at p. 133 above.

[10] CGTA 1979, s. 27.

agency[11]. Although shares are assets, they are unlikely to be of the type described in CGTA 1979, section 12 which for practical purposes therefore can be taken to refer to those assets realised on the sale of an undertaking.

ICTA 1970, section 246(2)(b) contains a corresponding provision for capital gains arising to non-resident companies[12]. To prevent UK companies ceasing to be resident in the UK anti-avoidance provisions are contained in ICTA 1970, section 482. Breach of the section is a criminal offence punishable by fine or imprisonment or both. Not only will the UK resident company be guilty of an offence but also 'any person who does or is party to the doing of any act which to his knowledge amounts to or results in or forms part of a series of acts which together amount to or result in or will amount to or result in an unlawful act'.

The following acts are unlawful without Treasury consent:

(1) A UK resident company ceasing to be so resident. For the purposes of section 482[13] a company is deemed to be resident in the place where the central management and control of its trade or business is exercised. Where, however, it has been established for tax purposes as between the Crown and the company that the company is UK resident for any period of assessment, it will be taken to be so resident for that period and at all times thereafter. It will be seen that care is required where the purchasers propose to appoint to the board of the company being acquired a majority of non-resident directors. Any alteration of the company's articles providing for board meetings to take place outside the UK will be unlawful if acted upon.

(2) The trade or business or any part of a trade or business of a UK resident company being transferred from the company to a non-resident[14]. However, a mere transfer of assets not resulting in a substantial change in the character or extent of the trade or business of the transferring company is

---

[11] CGTA 1979, s. 12.
[12] Gains accruing to a non-resident company which would be close were it resident can be apportioned to UK resident participators: CGTA 1979, s. 15 and to non-resident trustees owning shares in the company where the gain accrues to it after 9 March 1981; FA 1981, s. 85.
[13] ICTA 1970, s. 482(1)(a).
[14] ICTA 1970, s. 482(1)(b).

excepted[15]. The profits of a UK business transferred abroad would continue to be subject to UK tax if carried on through a branch or agency in the UK but a foreign business so transferred would, but for section 482, escape.

(3) Certain acts done by a non-resident company controlled by a resident company are deemed to be unlawful acts by the resident company, but these are outside the scope of this book[16].

The Treasury has given general consents to transactions falling within certain classes of which those relevant to this book can be summarised:

1. Transactions where the UK resident company has been formed after 1 August 1951 for the purpose of carrying on a new business and where more than 50 per cent of the company's issued shares of all classes at the time of the transaction in question are beneficially owned by persons not ordinarily resident in the UK, and were so owned when issued.

2. Transactions consisting of the outright sale of a business or part thereof to a non-resident where (a) the sale is for full consideration paid in cash (b) the price does not exceed £50,000 (c) the buyer is not a company controlled by persons ordinarily resident in the UK (d) the buyer and seller are not associated (e) the sale is not associated with any other transaction whereby the business may revert to the seller or any person having an interest in the business of the seller.

When the transaction does not fall within a category for which general consent has been given, application should be made to the Secretary, H.M. Treasury (AP), Parliament Street, London, SW1P 3AG, although in practice the application will be considered by the Board of Inland Revenue[17].

---

[15] ICTA 1970, s. 482(9).
[16] See ICTA 1970, s. 482(1)(c) and (d).
[17] Details of the method and contents of an application are contained in Simon's Taxes, D4.118.

B. EXCHANGE CONTROL

Since 24 October 1979 there has been no requirement to obtain
exchange control consent for transactions between residents and
non-residents. The Exchange Control Act 1947 is nevertheless
still on the statute book and all or any of the requirements for
consent thereunder can be re-imposed at short notice by H.M.
Treasury.

12 Employees and Directors

Whenever the company or business to be acquired has employees, a number of considerations arise. Can the purchaser be certain of retaining the services of key employees? What are the liabilities of the vendor and the purchaser to employees generally as a result of the transfer of the company or the business, in particular in relation to planned redundancies? It is proposed to consider first contracts of employment generally, albeit in a necessarily abbreviated way, and then to deal with some special situations.

A. THE EFFECT OF MERGERS AND SALES OF UNDERTAKINGS ON
   EMPLOYMENT CONTRACTS

It has been seen that the sale and purchase of a commercial enterprise may be effected, broadly speaking, in one of two ways. First, the shares in the company undertaking the enterprise may be sold. Secondly the individual, partnership or company running the business may sell the undertaking itself. In the first case, the sale of shares does not affect the employee's contract of employment. He continues to be employed by the same company, notwithstanding that the character and aims of the new controlling shareholders may be radically different to those of the old. In the absence of other factors no question of redundancy or dismissal arises on a sale of shares and the mutual obligations of the company and employee continue. As has been pointed out, this is not a complete protection for the employee who may find as a result of the merger that his promotion prospects or long-term job security are adversely affected, or that non-contractual fringe benefits are withdrawn or reduced[1].

The acquisition of shares in an employing company will not therefore of itself involve either the company or the purchaser in meeting redundancy or dismissal claims, except in the unusual case of a service contract providing that the employee may treat a takeover as a termination giving rights to compensation[2]. A purchaser will nevertheless be concerned to have full details of the company's workforce, their terms of employment including details of any pension schemes, and non-contractual items, i.e. staff discounts, customary bonuses, promotion arrangements. Details of any trade union recognition agreement will also be required. These details can be incorporated into the purchase contract by the vendor warranting a schedule of employees with their names, dates of birth, dates of commencement of continuous service (both relevant for redundancy payments and dismissal compensation calculations), job titles, duties, remuneration, proposed increments and review dates, frequency of payment and place of work (where the company has more than one). The vendor should also be asked to provide a copy of all standard terms of employment and to state to which employees such terms apply and whether written particulars have been delivered in accordance with the EPCA 1978. In the case of employees with individual service contracts, copies of these may be annexed to the contract. These details will enable the purchaser to assess

(i) his potential liabilities as regards redundancy claims

(ii) the period of notice to which each employee is entitled

(iii) an important element in his cash flow including PAYE.

---

[1] Paul Davies *The Regulations of Take-overs and Mergers.*

[2] Note the duty of employer to consult with recognised trade unions in respect of redundancy proposals: Employment Protection Act 1975, s. 99, and where either the transferor or transferee envisages 'taking measures' in relation to employees: 1981 Regulations, reg. 10(5). Whether or not measures are proposed to be taken, there is a duty to inform trade union representatives before a transfer takes place of the matters referred to in the 1981 Regulations, reg. 10(2). The duties under reg. 10 need not be fully performed if there are special circumstances rendering it not reasonably practicable to perform a duty: reg. 10(7).

Where the business itself is sold, and in the event that the Transfer of Undertakings (Protection of Employment) Regulations 1981 do not apply, it is clearly established that, because of the personal nature of the contract of employment, an employee cannot be obliged to work for the new owner of a business without the employee's consent[3]. It should be noted that the employee's consent is required for the transfer of his employment but not for the transfer of the remainder of the undertaking. Secondly, the sale of the undertaking does not necessarily result in the employee's dismissal since it may be that the vendor intends to, and does, retain the services of certain employees. Where, however, the contract for sale provides for the undertaking to be sold as a going concern and for the vendor to cease its business on completion, the sale itself will operate as a termination of the contract of employment[4]. Again, where the sale is of assets without which the employee cannot continue to work in the job for which he was employed, the employee may in limited circumstances treat the sale as a wrongful repudiation of his contract of employment[5].

Where, on transfer of a business, an employee accepts employment with the transferee and is subsequently made redundant, the continuity of employment in relation to statutory redundancy pay entitlement will not be broken even if the employee could have claimed a redundancy payment from the original employer.

The above applies where the 1981 Regulations do not, that is to say, for example, where the undertaking transferred is not in the nature of a commercial venture[6]. The position is radically different where the 1981 regulations do apply.

The common law position as it applied to the transfer of undertakings has been fundamentally altered by the Transfer of Undertakings (Protection of Employment) Regulations 1981, all the provisions of which came into force by 1 May 1981. In the following discussion, the expressions 'vendor' and 'purchaser'

---

[3] *Nokes v Doncaster Amalgamated Collieries Ltd* [1940] AC 1014, [1940] 3 All ER 549.

[4] *Re Foster Clark Ltd's Indenture Trusts, Loveland v Horscroft* [1966] 1 All ER 43, [1966] 1 WLR 125.

[5] *Collier v Sunday Referee Publishing Co Ltd* [1940] 2 KB 647, [1940] 4 All ER 234.

[6] 1981 Regulations, para. 2(1).

are used where the 1981 Regulations refer to 'transferor' and 'transferee' respectively.

Excepting 'hive-downs' by receivers and liquidators which are the subject of special rules in regulation 4, the 1981 Regulations apply to any 'relevant transfer' which expression includes any transfer by sale from one person to another of an undertaking, or part of an undertaking, situated within the UK immediately before the transfer. 'Undertaking' includes any trade or business but excludes any undertaking which is not in the nature of a commercial venture, and references to the transfer of part of an undertaking are references to a transfer of a part which is being transferred as a business. The 1981 Regulations do not therefore seem to apply to a mere transfer of tangible assets[7], and it has been held that, for there to be a transfer within the meaning of the 1981 Regulations, there must be a transfer of goodwill[8]. It has been argued that undertakings within the public and charitable sectors are outside the scope of the Regulations by reason of the exclusion of undertakings not in the nature of a commercial venture. The words 'in the nature of' may be significant. The inference may be made that, to be within the 1981 Regulations, an undertaking need not in fact be a venture carried on for commercial profit so long as it is in the nature of a commercial venture, so that, for example, a shop selling second-hand goods on behalf of a charity may be an undertaking within the Regulations.

The key provisions for the purpose of this discussion are paragraphs (1), (2) and (3) of regulation 5, which read as follows:

'5. (1) A relevant transfer shall not operate so as to terminate the contract of employment of any person employed by the transferor in the undertaking or part transferred but any such contract which would otherwise have been terminated by the transfer shall have effect after the transfer as if originally made between the person so employed and the transferee.

---

[7] There is a similar distinction between a transfer of assets on the one hand and of a business as a going concern on the other for the purposes of EPCA 1978, Sch. 13 (formerly contained in Contracts of Employment Act 1972) in respect of which it has been held that there is no transfer of an undertaking where transferred assets are used by the transferee for different purposes than previously: *Woodhouse v Peter Brotherhood Ltd* [1972] 2 QB 520, [1972] 3 All ER 91.

[8] *Robert Seligman Corpn v Baker* [1983] ICR 770 EAT.

(2) Without prejudice to paragraph (1) above, on the completion of a relevant transfer:

(a) all the transferor's rights, powers, duties and liabilities under or in connection with any such contract shall be transferred by virtue of this Regulation to the transferee; and

(b) anything done before the transfer is completed by or in relation to the transferor in respect of that contract or a person employed in that undertaking or part shall be deemed to have been done by or in relation to the transferee.

(3) Any reference in paragraph (1) or (2) above to a person employed in an undertaking or part of one transferred by a relevant transfer is a reference to a person so employed immediately before the transfer, including, where the transfer is affected by a series of two or more transactions, a person so employed immediately before any of those transactions.'

Regulation 5(1) does not transfer to the purchaser all contracts of employment between the vendor and its employees. Only those contracts which satisfy three conditions will be transferred. These conditions are, first that the contract is of a person employed in the undertaking or the part transferred, and secondly that the contract 'would otherwise have been terminated by the transfer'[9]. The second condition is probably intended to mean that the contract of any employee whom the vendor ceases to employ on the transfer taking place will be transferred. This interpretation is wider than justified by a narrow interpretation of the phrase which would cover only those employees constructively dismissed by the occurrence of the transfer per se. For example, a cleaner may be employed to clean one of two adjacent factories owned by the same employer. The sale of one of the factories, whether or not as a going concern, is unlikely per se to terminate the cleaner's employment although he may be redundant so far as the vendor is concerned who therefore ceases to employ him. At the other end of the employment scale, a

---

[9] The meaning of these words is discussed in the article referred to in footnote 14 below.

director of a vendor company may be an employee for the purposes of the 1981 Regulations[10]. He may be employed in the management of other undertakings of the vendor besides the one being transferred. Regulation 5(1) will not transfer his service contract to the purchaser. The third condition is that the employee should be one employed 'immediately before the transfer'[11].

Given the difficulty of interpreting the Regulations and the fact that every transfer will be governed by its own circumstances, vendor and purchaser should schedule to their agreement all persons employed in the undertaking, distinguishing between those whose services the vendor will retain and those whom it will cease to employ. As between vendor and purchaser the agreement will thus specify those contracts of employment which will be transferred to the purchaser by virtue of regulation 5(1). Where such a contract is transferred, the purchaser of the undertaking is deemed to have contracted with the relevant employee on the same terms and conditions (save as to pension rights as to which see below) as applied between the employee and the vendor. The effect of regulation 5(2) is that there is also transferred to the purchaser the accrued seniority of employees for the purposes of their individual statutory employment rights (i.e. minimum notice, redundancy entitlement) and the vendor's liabilities in tort (as well as in contract) to his employees. The wording appears wide enough to transfer to the purchaser accrued holiday liabilities and liabilities in respect of the vendor's having given notice to, or affected a wrongful or unfair dismissal of, an employee still in employment at the date of transfer, subject to regulation 8 (described below). When the transfer results in redundancies, regulation 5(2) will operate to make the purchaser liable for the redundancy payments[12]. Criminal liabilities are, however, expressly excluded from the transfer[13] and there is some doubt whether statutory rights and liabilities, such as under the health and safety at work legislation, are transferred. It has been held that an employer's 'duties and liabilities

---

[10] 1981 Regulations, reg. 2(1).
[11] 1981 Regulations, reg. 5(3).
[12] *Premier Motors (Medway) Ltd v Total Oil Great Britain Ltd* [1984] 1 WLR 377, [1984] ICR 58 EAT.
[13] 1981 Regulations, reg. 5(4).

under or in connection with' a contract of employment do not include the duty under Employment Protection Act 1975, section 9 to consult trade union representatives on proposed redundancies since the duty did not arise in connection with any contract with an individual employee[14]. If statutory duties are expressly incorporated into an employment contract, or implied by the circumstances, they will be duties 'under' the contract. If an employer's duty to maintain personal injury liability insurance were a duty in connection with a contract of employment[15], would the vendor's rights under a liability insurance policy be transferred under regulation 5(2) as rights 'in connection with' an employment contract? The point could be important where, say, an employee contracts some disease whilst in the vendor's employ and as a result of its negligence but the disease does not show itself until after the business has been sold. A purchaser will need to check that its own liability insurance covers such pre-transfer liabilities. Presumably, an employer's duty to pay statutory sick pay would be regarded as transferable under regulation 5(2) because the duty can only be quantified by reference to individual contracts of employment.

A further difficulty which arises in the interpretation of regulation 5 is in deciding when the transfer occurs, in particular whether it occurs on exchange of contracts or on completion. Some commentators consider that the transfer takes place on exchange of contracts, with the result that where a vendor makes or purports[16] to make an employee redundant after exchange of contracts, the purchaser, and not the vendor, would be entitled to the redundancy rebate. This interpretation is, however, inconvenient since a vendor' other than a receiver, will be reluctant to declare redundancies prior to exchange. It would seem to mean, for example, that between exchange and completion the purchaser will be responsible for the salaries and the control of relevant employees. Besides the practical problems this may have, what would the position be were completion never to take

---

[14] *Angus Jowett & Co Ltd v National Union of Tailors and Garment Workers* [1985] ICR 646, [1985] IRLR 326. See the discussion of this and other cases by John McMather in *The Law Society's Gazette* (24 October 1985).
[15] See Employers Liability (Compulsory Insurance) Act 1969.
[16] If an employment contract is transferred on exchange of contracts, the vendor will be unable to dismiss the individuals concerned who will have become the purchaser's employees.

place? Could such a non-event be deemed itself to be a relevant transfer so that employees would once again be employed by the vendor, or would the purchaser be stuck with the employees and the vendor with the assets? A sub-sale would further complicate the picture.

The 1981 Regulations contain support for the alternative view that the transfer takes place on completion. In particular regulation 3(4) declares that a transfer may be effected by a series of two or more transactions between the same parties. The regulation further provides that in determining whether such a series constitutes a single transfer, 'regard shall be had to the extent to which the undertaking was controlled by the transferor and transferee respectively before the last transaction, to the lapse of the time between each of the transactions, to the intention of the parties and to all the other circumstances'. If contract and completion are regarded as two transactions in a series, and if in fact control of the business passes only on completion, as will usually be the case, the more practical result of transfer on completion will be achieved. To put the matter beyond doubt, however, the parties could declare their intention in the agreement, as they are in effect invited to do by regulation 3(4).

If, as is argued here, transfer of employment contracts would usually take place on completion, the employees covered by regulation 5 are those employed by the vendor immediately before completion. In addition, however, those so employed immediately before exchange of contracts, but who for some reason leave their employment before completion, are also within regulation 5. This is because regulation 5(3) provides that where the transfer is effected by a series of two or more transactions (i.e. contract and completion) a reference in regulation 5(1) and (2) to a person employed in an undertaking transferred by a relevant transfer includes reference to a person so employed immediately before any of those transactions[17]. If the view that the transfer is effected on exchange of contracts were correct, it would have the odd result that a person whose employment contract with a vendor commences between contract and completion would be outside the scope of regulation 5. Nevertheless, until the question of the effective date of transfer is settled by

---

[17] 1981 Regulations, reg. 5(3).

the courts[18], it will be safer for a purchaser to proceed on the assumption that he may take over service contract obligations as from exchange, so that the agreement for sale of the business should provide that, pending completion, as between vendor and purchaser, the vendor will make all payments due to employees. There can, however, be no question of service contract obligations being transferred on exchange of a contract subject to a condition precedent until the condition has been satisfied, so that such a provision is unnecessary if the condition can be satisfied only on completion.

The expression 'immediately before the transfer' has been the subject of judicial decision. Where an employee was dismissed on a Friday and the business sold on the following Monday, it was held that the interval of time between dismissal and transfer was minimal so that the employee was employed in the undertaking transferred immediately before the transfer for the purposes of the 1981 Regulations[19]. It followed therefore in that case that the purchaser took over any financial liabilities arising from the dismissal.

Regulation 5(5) preserves any right of an employee 'arising apart from these Regulations to terminate his contract of employment without notice if a substantial change is made in his working conditions to his detriment; but no such right shall arise by reason only that (under regulation 5(1)) the identity of his employer changes unless the employee shows that, in all the circumstances, the change is a significant change and is to his detriment'. It is thought that if the employee can show that he will have, say, materially reduced promotion prospects under the new employer, he can treat this as constructive dismissal.

In respect of most pension rights the terms of employment are not carried across to the new employment. Regulation 7 provides that regulation 5 shall not apply to so much of an employment contract as relates to an occupational pension scheme within the meaning of the Social Security Pension Act 1975. If

---

[18] It has, however, been decided that where a proposing purchaser takes over management of a business during negotiations for its sale, but prior to conclusion of any contract, no transfer of employment takes place: *SI (Systems and Instrumentation) Ltd v Grist* [1983] ICR 788, [1983] IRLR 391.

[19] *Apex Leisure Hire Ltd v Barratt* [1984] ICR 452, [1984] IRLR 224 (EAT) in which incidentally both parties assumed that the transfer of employment occurred on completion, not on exchange of contracts.

the transfer results in some material prejudice to the employee's pension rights, including prospective rights, he can treat the transfer as a constructive dismissal if such prejudice involves a breach of the employment contract by the employer. Where an employer undertakes in a contract of employment to pay contributions to a pension scheme in accordance with the scheme rules, and terminates its contributions in accordance with those rules, it is thought that there will be no breach of the contract of employment. Where, as in such a case, the constructive dismissal arises from the fact of the transfer itself, the ordinary law relating to dismissal will apply, and not that qualified by regulation 8 which applies to dismissal before or after a relevant transfer. Furthermore, since regulation 5 is made inapplicable in these circumstances, the liability in respect of the employee's lost pension rights will remain with the vendor. Where any employees of the business being required are in a pension scheme, actuarial advice should be obtained by both vendor and purchaser.

So far the discussion has been concerned with the circumstances in which rights and liabilities under contracts of employment may be automatically transferred to a purchaser on acquisition of a business, and it should be noted that regulation 6 contains provisions for the transfer of collective agreements (insofar as such agreements may be enforceable at all). In addition, however, the 1981 Regulations significantly modifies the rights of an employee who is dismissed because of a relevant transfer.

Regulation 8(1) makes the dismissal of any employee of the vendor or purchaser (including employees who are not transferred) before or after a relevant transfer automatically unfair if the transfer of the undertaking, or a reason connected with it, is the reason or principal reason for the dismissal. Regulation 8(2) however provides that regulation 8(1) shall not apply to any dismissal where 'an economic technical or organisational reason entailing changes in the workforce of either the transferor or the transferee before or after a relevant transfer is the reason or principal reason for dismissing an employee'. The effect is that a dismissal for such a reason before or after a relevant transfer will be fair so long as the employee dismissed has not been unfairly selected and the proper procedures for dismissal have been followed, and so long as the courts do not require the condition of regulation 8(2) to be satisfied by an objective, as opposed to subjective, test[20]. However, the expression 'changes in the workforce' in regulation 8(2) means a change in the personnel employed, not merely a change in its conditions of service, so that where after a transfer had taken place an employee had his payment terms altered by the new employer, this was held to be a constructive dismissal which was automatically unfair under regulation 8(1)[1].

The following comments may be made in connection with the preparation of assets sale agreements:

(1) Where a vendor or purchaser wishes to make redundant part of the workforce of the business being transferred, so long as proper notice of termination of employment is given (i.e. the greater of what is required by statute or contract), and the proper procedures followed, including not making any unfair selection for redundancy, the liability to the affected employees will be for a redundancy payment, because it is difficult to envisage circumstances where redundancies arising from the transfer will not be for an 'economic, technical or organisational reason entailing changes in the workforce[2].' Where the redundancy is affected after the transfer of employment (see above) the purchaser will be liable for the redundancy payment and will be able to claim a redundancy rebate in respect of any payment which the redundant employee has receipted on Form RP3 issued by the Department of Employment. On the other hand, the amount of the redundancy payment will be calculated by reference to the employee's accrued seniority with the vendor as well as the purchaser. Whether the payment is to be borne by the vendor or purchaser by, say, some adjustment in the price of the business will be a matter of negotiation. It is however important that the vendor should be obliged to warrant the

---

[20] See, for example, *Hollister v National Farmers' Union* [1979] ICR 542, [1979] IRLR 238, (CA) and *Anderson v Dalkeith Engineering Ltd* [1985] ICR 66, [1984] IRLR 429, (EAT).

[1] *Delabole Slate Ltd v Berriman* [1985] IRLR 305, CA.

[2] But see *Canning v Niaz and McLoughlin* [1983] IRLR 431 where it was held by EAT in Scotland that, applying the words of reg. 8(2)(b), a successful defence by an employer under reg. 8(2) would disentitle the employee from claiming a redundancy payment. The decision has been widely criticised and not followed by the EAT in England or Scotland, i.e. *Gorictree Ltd v Jenkinson* [1985] ICR 51, [1984] IRLR 391.

accuracy of the information on which the redundancy calculation is based.

(2) The liability of the purchaser for redundancy payments described at (1) above will not be automatically extinguished by the vendor affecting the redundancies prior to the transfer for employment, unless redundancy payments are actually made by the vendor and receipted on Form RP3 by the employees. The purchaser will therefore require such receipts to be produced on completion.

(3) The liability of the vendor or purchaser as described at (1) above applies where the dismissals take place before or after the transfer. Where they take place simultaneously with the transfer, regulation 8 will, arguably, be inapplicable; the employees affected may claim to have been constructively dismissed; and the dismissals will be prima facie unfair dismissals. This is subject to regulation 5(5) which provides in effect that a change in employer by virtue of the 1981 Regulations will not by itself be capable of constituting a constructive dismissal.

The most probable cause of a constructive dismissal is likely to be where as a result of a transfer, an employee's terms of employment are worsened such that the purchaser repudiates what will have become his contractual obligations to the employee on the transfer taking place. A purchaser will therefore be on safer ground in making an employee redundant than in reducing his salary or perks even by a small amount. When a relevant transfer operates as a constructive dismissal, regulation 5(1) places the liability for such dismissal on the purchaser, save as mentioned in the next paragraph.

(4) Insofar as the worsening of terms of employment involves some prejudice to actual or prospective pension rights, the liability to the employee will be that of the vendor. If possible, the vendor will therefore wish the purchaser to undertake to procure all employees to be offered immediate membership of the purchaser's scheme on the basis that:

(i) their existing rights will be fully transferable to the new scheme and

(ii) the terms of the new scheme are at least as good as those of the old.

(5) Save in respect of pension rights, the 1981 Regulations will fix the purchaser with the liability for actions and omissions of the vendor relating to the employment contracts of employees of the undertaking, or part thereof, transferred. Such acts may include (wrongful) notice of dismissal. In any event, the purchaser will take over the liability for salary accrued but not yet paid and accrued holiday entitlement among other things. It is essential therefore that the vendor be required to give full information of the terms on which relevant employees are employed including perks, that the information be warranted as true and complete and that the vendor warrants that he will perform and observe all the terms of employment contracts up to completion.

(6) An undertaking by the purchaser to the vendor is advisable to cover the possibility of a claim by employees in respect of their preserved rights under regulation 5(5). The undertaking would be to make no substantial change in the employees' working conditions to their detriment. The second limb of regulation 5(5) preserves an employee's right to treat a change in his employer as a constructive dismissal if the change is significant and to his detriment, and a vendor should require an indemnity in respect of employees' claims. In addition, since the 1981 Regulations do not expressly extinguish the rights of an employee against the vendor (e.g. for accrued pay up to the time of transfer), an appropriate indemnity should be taken from the purchaser to the extent that the parties contemplate the purchaser taking over accrued liabilities.

(7) Where no redundancies are contemplated, the purchaser need not offer new employment contracts to persons employed in the business being transferred, because their existing contracts will continue with the purchaser being substituted for the vendor as employer on the transfer taking place.

(8) Regulation 12 provides that any agreement, whether in a contract of employment or not, to contract out of regulations 5 and 8, among others, shall be void.

The 1981 Regulations contain provisions where the employees of either the vendor or purchaser are represented by a recognised trade union. Regulation 10(2) requires the employer of any affected employees to inform representatives of the union concerned of the matters set out in the regulation including the measures which the employer envisages he will take in relation to affected employees in connection with the transfer. The information must be given 'long enough before a relevant transfer to enable consultations with the union to take place', and an 'affected employee' means, in relation to a relevant transfer, any employee of the vendor or purchaser, whether or not employed in the undertaking to be transferred, who may be affected by the transfer or by measures taken in connection with it. An affected employee could presumably include members of the purchaser's head office staff whose workload may be increased by the acquisition of the new business.

Regulation 10(5) imposes a duty to consult with trade union representatives. The duty is additional to the duty to inform under regulation 10(2) and arises where either the vendor or purchaser envisages taking measures in relation to any affected employees.

The duties to inform and consult are qualified in regulation 10(7) if in any case there are special circumstances which render it not reasonably practicable for an employer to perform them.

Finally a relevant transfer will effect the automatic transfer of rights and obligations under a collective agreement[3]. However, Trade Union and Labour Relations Act 1974, s. 18 creates a statutory presumption that collective agreements are not intended to be legally enforceable, so that their automatic transfer will be significant only where they are expressed to be legally enforceable, or where the operation of a collective agreement has created implied terms in individual employment contracts. In this last case, however, such implied terms will be transferred by virtue of regulation 5, the collective agreement simply being evidence of those terms.

B. KEY EMPLOYEES

Key employees may be either those whose services the vendor wishes to retain, or those whose services the purchaser wishes to

---

[3] 1981 Regulations, reg. 6.

acquire, and in either case their loss or non-acquisition would be so critical to one or other of the parties that special provision is required in the contract.

Where a vendor wishes to retain an employee's services, such retention will involve the termination of the employee's service contract with the target company and a new service contract being concluded between the vendor and employee. Where a vendor is selling assets, but not an undertaking to which the 1981 Regulations apply, the employee's service contract will continue. In these cases the contract between vendor and purchaser may provide that the purchaser will not offer to employ or engage the relevant employee for a specified period.

Where the 1981 Regulations, regulation 5 has effect, the contract between vendor and purchaser will need to provide for dismissal of the employee by the purchaser on completion and his re-employment by the vendor immediately thereafter on the former terms of employment or better. The purchaser will have acquired obligations to the employee under the 1981 Regulations and will therefore require an indemnity. The employee's consent will also be required, and it would therefore seem better in the case of a key employee where a sale of the undertaking is contemplated to persuade him prior to exchange of contracts to enter into a new service contract with, say, an associate of the vendor which will lend his services to the vendor.

A purchaser of shares is unlikely to agree to a vendor's request that the contract be made conditional on a particular employee's engagement by the vendor, since the business being retained by the vendor is not relevant to the subject matter of the sale. When, however, the key employee's services are to be acquired or retained by the purchaser it is usual for the contract to be conditional on the employee entering a new service contract (possibly on different terms) with the company being acquired or, in the case of acquisition of an undertaking, with the new employers, on completion.

Since a conditional contract will normally be rendered void by non-fulfilment of the conditions, it is important that any condition inserted for the purchaser's protection be expressly capable of waiver at the purchaser's option. In the case of the key employee's death between contract and completion the purchaser may nevertheless wish to complete in the certain knowledge that the employee's services will be unavailable to the competition. Where the employee's life is insured, the vendor should be asked to undertake to maintain the policy in force pending completion. If the employee is insured by the company being acquired the policy proceeds will accrue to the company but not necessarily to the purchaser if, for example, the vendor's only warranty is that the company's net assets will not be less than a stated figure and the company distributes the policy proceeds before completion. If the sale is of an undertaking, the purchaser may wish the contract to provide that he can elect either to rescind, or to complete with the purchase price being reduced by an amount equal to the sum insured.

C. COMPENSATION FOR LOSS OF OFFICE

Except where an employee's conduct justifies summary dismissal, or where the circumstances specified in his service contract entitling an employer to terminate it early have happened (e.g. absence from work for a specific period) an employee will be entitled to claim compensation for wrongful dismissal if his contract of employment is ended without adequate notice or, in the case of a fixed term contract, before expiry of the fixed term.

The starting point in calculating the amount of compensation is to apply the measure of damages applicable to breach of contract, namely the damages resulting naturally from the breach and also reasonably foreseeable by the parties. The usual principles of mitigation of damages apply. Subject to this, in practice the measure of damages may be calculated by assessing the annual value of the employee's remuneration package and for this purpose there will be taken into account both salary and fringe benefits, for example, a pension scheme, a company car available for private use, membership of private medical schemes etc. The annual value is then multiplied by the fraction of a year or years representing the notice period or unexpired part of the fixed term. Where no notice period is stipulated in the contract, the period will be the greater of the notice period required under the EPCA 1978 or whatever is a reasonable period of notice. The latter is a matter for negotiation but the principal factor is the employee's seniority. From the gross figure a deduction should be made to allow for any failure of the employee to mitigate his loss, i.e. to seek alternative employment. The deduction will be greater in the case of a younger employee, but will also depend on the job market for employees in similar, but not necessarily identical, employment. A further deduction may be made equivalent to the value of the accelerated payment (often a single figure percentage) and another deduction equal to unemployment benefit entitlement.

Although all or part of a compensation payment may be tax free in the employee's hands (see below)[4] damages awarded by the courts will take into account both the tax which would have been paid on the tax-free element had it been received as salary[5], and, it seems, the employee's tax liability on the net sum so calculated which must then be grossed up to determine the sum of damages actually payable[6]. If, for example, the Gourley principle were to reduce damages of £100,000 to £60,000, and if the tax payable on compensation of £60,000 were £7,500, then following the decision in *Shore v Downs Surgical plc* the sum of damages actually to be awarded would be £67,500. In assessing the likely tax liability, the employee's personal circumstances will be taken into account.

Compensation in excess of £25,000 will be taxable and, if paid prior to termination of the employment, the excess will be subject to deduction of tax at source under the PAYE regulations. The excess over £25,000 will be taxed as follows: tax will be charged on the first £25,000 of the excess of one-half the amount which would have been charged had that excess been the employee's income for the relevant fiscal year; the next £25,000 of the excess will attract three-quarters of the tax otherwise so chargeable; so much of any compensation payment as exceeds £75,000 will be fully chargeable as income of the relevant year. Compensation for which provision is made in the service agreement is in principle taxable in full, but in practice the Revenue will in genuine redundancy cases tax only the excess over £25,000 as above[7].

Where the termination of the employment is by reason of redundancy, the employee, if he has been continuously employed for over two years after the age of 18, may be entitled to a redundancy payment in addition to compensation for loss of

---

[4] ICTA 1970, s. 188(3) as amended by FA 1981, s. 31(1).
[5] *British Transport Commission v Gourley* [1956] AC 185, [1955] 3 All ER 796.
[6] *Shove v Downs Surgical plc* [1984] 1 All ER 7, [1984] ICR 532.
[7] I.R. Statement of Practice SP1/81.

office[8]. The amount of the payment is a multiple calculated by reference to the employee's age, the number of years' continuous employment and the gross weekly wage. The maximum weekly wage to be taken into account is £152[9]. In addition the employee may be entitled to benefit from redundancy arrangements agreed between employer and employee beyond the statutory requirement. For each year of employment between 18 and 21, the multiple is one-half of the gross weekly wage; from age 22 to 40 inclusive the multiple is one, and from age 41 to 64 it is one and one-half[10]. Termination, and even non-renewal of a fixed term service contract, may give rise to a claim for unfair dismissal under the provisions of Part V of the same Act, but except where an employee may have been unfairly selected for redundancy[11], redundancy and unfair dismissal are mutually exclusive. It is not proposed to consider the latter, save to mention that, with certain exceptions, an agreement by an employee not to bring proceedings before an industrial tribunal, even if made in consideration of a compensation payment, will be void[12]. An industrial tribunal is likely to take into account any compensation payment received by the employee in assessing the amount of its award. An employee, or ex-employee, will only be precluded from making an application to an industrial tribunal if he has first signed ACAS Form COT3 before a conciliation officer of ACAS. When termination of employment is contemplated, therefore, the employer should make an early approach to ACAS. In some cases proposed redundancies must be notified in advance to trade unions and the Department of Employment.

Payments in respect of compensation for loss of office are not usually deductible in computing the payer's profits for tax purposes when they are negotiated as part of the terms of a takeover, since they will not have been made wholly and exclusively for the purposes of the trade[13]. Where an agreement for the sale of shares obliges the parties to procure the target company to

---

[8] Employment Protection (Consolidation) Act 1978, Part VI.
[9] Where the contract of employment terminates after 1 April 1985 or would have so terminated had the employer given the minimum period of notice required under Employment Protection (Consolidation) Act 1978, s. 49(1): Employment Protection (Variation of Limits) Order 1984, SI 1984 2019.
[10] EPCA 1978, Sch. 4.
[11] *McGrath v Rank Leisure Ltd* (1983) *Times*, 25 February.
[12] EPCA 1978, s. 140.
[13] *Overy v Ashford, Dunn & Co Ltd* (1933) 17 TC 497.

pay compensation to shareholder directors for loss of office, such compensation will not be deductible[14] and may be financial assistance within the meaning of Companies Act 1985 section 152.

Similarly compensation payments made in connection with the discontinuance of the taxpayer's trade will not be deductible[15].

On the other hand where the compensation payment is arrived at independently of the bargain for sale of shares and is made solely in the interest of the trade, it will be deductible. It will be easier to show this where the employees in question have long-term service contracts which cannot in any event be prematurely terminated by the employer without compensation becoming payable. However, redundancy payments made in accordance with EPCA 1978, and additional payments of up to three times the amount of such redundancy payments, will be deductible even if in connection with the discontinuance of the trade. Any redundancy rebate will be taxed as a receipt of the trade[16].

By Companies Act 1985, section 719 the powers of a company are deemed to include a power to make provision for employees and former employees of the company or any of its subsidiaries in connection with the cessation or transfer of the whole or part of the undertaking of that company or its subsidiaries. The power may be exercised notwithstanding that its exercise is not in the best interests of the company—this reverses the decision in *Parke v Daily News Ltd*[17] in which shareholders restrained a company from making such provision. The power may, however, only be exercised after compliance with any relevant requirement of the company's memorandum and articles and only if sanctioned by (a) a resolution of the directors if so authorised by the memorandum or articles, or (b) a resolution of the members, requiring more than a simple majority if so required by the memorandum or articles, or (c) in any other case by an ordinary resolution of the members. On a winding up a liquidator may make any payment which the company has, before the commencement of winding-up, decided to make under section 719[18].

---

[14] *James Snook & Co Ltd v Blasdale* (1952) 33 TC 244.
[15] *Godden v A Wilson's Stores (Holdings) Ltd* (1962) 40 TC 161.
[16] ICTA 1970, s. 412(2); FA 1980, s. 41.
[17] [1962] Ch 927, [1962] 2 All ER 929.
[18] Companies Act 1985, s. 659.

The powers may not be exercised by a liquidator so as to prejudice creditors, since payment may be made only out of the assets available to members of the company on a winding up.

D. DIRECTORS

Although the 1985 Act, section 303 provides that a company may remove a director by ordinary resolution notwithstanding anything in its articles or in any agreement between it and him, subsection (5) preserves the director's right to compensation for loss of office. The above principles as regards calculation of compensation, including calculation of the redundancy payment, apply to directors as they do to employees, but note should be made of the 1985 Act, section 319. This section provides that a term in a director's service contract whereby his employment is to continue, or may be continued, otherwise than at the instance of the company, for a period exceeding five years will be void to the extent that it contravenes the section unless it has been first approved by the company in general meeting. Where the director concerned is also a director of a holding company, the term must in addition be approved by the members of the holding company in general meeting, but where the director is a director only of a wholly owned subsidiary, the section does not apply. A company resolution approving such a term may not be passed unless a written memorandum setting out the proposed agreement incorporating the term is available for inspection by shareholders both at the meeting and at the company's registered office for at least the previous fifteen days[19]. A short notice procedure for convening the necessary shareholder's meeting is therefore inappropriate[20].

Where a term is so avoided, the agreement will be deemed to contain a term entitling the company to terminate the agreement at any time by the giving of reasonable notice[1]. The director will, however, remain bound for the full term of the agreement. In addition, where a subsequent service agreement is concluded more than six months before the expiration of an existing service

---

[19] Companies Act 1985, s. 319(5).
[20] The contrary has, however, been argued—see Law Society Gazette, vol 80, p. 3085—but an affected director will wish to see all formalities observed.
[1] Companies Act 1985, s. 319(6).

agreement which cannot be terminated by the company by notice, or can be so terminated only in specified circumstances, the unexpired period of the original agreement will be added to the term of the subsequent agreement in calculating whether the five year period is exceeded by the latter[2]. It should be borne in mind that the expression 'director' includes any person occupying the position of director by whatever name called[3], and for the purposes of section 319, a person in accordance with whose directions or instructions the directors of a company are accustomed to act, unless by reason only that they do so on advice given by him in a professional capacity[4]. Where there is no employment, whether under a contract of service or contract for services[5], the section does not apply.

The 1985 Act, section 312 makes it unlawful for a company to make any payment of compensation for loss of office to any director without particulars of the payment being disclosed to, and approved by, members of the company. Where such a payment is made in connection with the transfer of the whole or any part of the company's property or undertaking, without approval by the members of the company, the director is deemed to hold the amount received by him in trust for the company[6].

Section 314 imposes a duty on any director to whom a compensation payment is to be made in connection with certain transfers of any shares in a company, including one resulting from an offer made to the general body of shareholders, or an offer by another company with a view to the first company becoming its subsidiary, or an offer by an individual for one-third or more of the company's voting shares. The director's duty is to take all reasonable steps to secure that particulars of the proposed payment are sent with any notice of the offer for their shares given to any shareholders, and, if he fails in this duty, he is liable to a fine. In addition the payment received by the director will be held in trust for any persons who have sold their shares as a result of the offer unless the payment has been approved by the members of the company, or holders of the

---

[2] Companies Act 1985, s. 319(2).
[3] Companies Act 1985, s. 741(1).
[4] Companies Act 1985, ss. 319(7) and 741(2).
[5] Companies Act 1985, s. 319(7)(a).
[6] Companies Act 1985, s. 313.

relevant class of shares, at a meeting summoned for that purpose[7].

The above provisions do not apply to a bona fide payment by way of damages for breach of contract or by way of pension in respect of past services[8]. With that exception certain other disguised payments of compensation for loss of office are also subject to these provisions[9]. In addition, there should be considered the general fiduciary duty of directors.

---

[7] Companies Act 1985, s. 315.
[8] Companies Act 1985, s. 316(3).
[9] Companies Act 1985, s. 316.

Agreement for Sale of Shares*

THIS AGREEMENT is made the ... day of .... 1986 BETWEEN the persons whose names and addresses are set out in column 1 of Schedule 1 ('the Vendors') of the one part and Armada Hotels Limited whose registered office is at .... ('the Purchaser') of the other part.

WHEREAS:

(1) Transglobal Adventures Limited ('the Company') was incorporated on the First day of September 1984 under the Companies Acts 1948 to 1983[1] with registered number ...... and at the date hereof has an authorised share capital of 5,000 divided into

---

* Warning: all precedents can be dangerous. Do not swallow whole without modification to suit the particular circumstances. Do not take at all except under strict legal supervision. Keep firmly closed and out of reach of impulsive clients and thoughtless advisers. This and the following precedents have not been drafted from the point of view of either a purchaser or a vendor. Nor can they fairly be said to be neutral since some clauses would in many cases be unacceptable to some vendors and others unacceptable to purchasers. The purpose of the precedents is firstly to illustrate common forms of agreement and secondly to draw attention to some of the matters usually found in agreements of the type illustrated. None of the characters in these precedents is intended to resemble any existing company or individual.

[1] Since it is likely to be some years before companies incorporated under Companies Act 1985 become the subject of purchase agreements, the precedent adopts a pre-1985 incorporation date. Since the 'agreement' is concluded in 1986, references in the precedent are nevertheless to the 1985 Act ('the Companies Act') the definition of which is extended by Clause 1(d) to include the earlier legislation.

five thousand ordinary shares of £1 which said shares are issued as fully paid or credited as fully paid and are beneficially owned by the Vendors in the numbers shown against their respective names in column 2 of Schedule 1 and which said shares are hereinafter called 'the Sale Shares'.

(2) The Company is the beneficial owner of the whole issued share capital of the companies listed in Schedule 2 ('the Subsidiaries') the authorised capital and issued capital and registered shareholders of which are shown against the respective names of the Subsidiaries in columns 2 3 and 4 respectively of Schedule 2 and the Company is neither the registered nor beneficial owner of any other shares or securities whatsoever.

(3) The only directors and the secretary of the Company and of the Subsidiaries are the persons whose names and addresses appear in Schedule 3.

(4) The Company is a private company.

(5) Each of the Vendors has agreed to sell and the Purchaser has agreed to purchase all the Sale Shares upon the terms and subject to the conditions hereinafter contained.

NOW IT IS HEREBY AGREED as follows:

1. IN this Agreement and in Schedule 5:

(a) 'the Act' means the Income and Corporation Taxes Act 1970 and 'FA' is an abbreviation of 'Finance Act'

(b) 'the Companies Act' means the Companies Act 1985

(c) save as herein otherwise expressly provided expressions defined in the Act or in the Companies Act have the meanings therein given to them.

(d) reference to any statute or statutory provisions are to such statutes or provisions as from time to time re-enacted or (with effect from a date on or before the date hereof) amended and reference to any statute or statutory provision which has replaced another statute or statutes or a corresponding provision of another statute or statutory provision is to be read as or as including reference to that other statute statutes or statutory provision.

(e) references to the masculine include the feminine

(f) 'tax' includes income tax corporation tax advance corporation tax capital gains tax development land tax development gains tax national insurance and earnings related contributions estate duty capital transfer tax stamp duty and value added tax and all costs charges interest penalties surcharges and expenses relating to any disallowance of relief or claim for taxation[2].

(g) 'the Price' means the sum of £100,000 and 'the Deposit' means the sum of £10,000 referred to in Clause 5(3) hereof

(h) 'the Completion Date' means .... 19... and 'completion' means completion of the sale and purchase of the Sale Shares

(i) 'the Disclosure Letter' means the letter dated .... from the Vendors to the Purchaser (a copy of which signed by the parties and marked 'A' is annexed hereto)

(j) 'the Guarantee' means the guarantee dated .... and given by the Vendors to .... Bank plc of ....

(k) 'the Balance Sheets Date' means .... 19 ... and 'the Balance Sheets' mean the respective audited Balance Sheets of the Company and of the Subsidiaries and their respective audited profit and loss accounts for the [year] ended on the Balance Sheets Date together with the consolidated balance sheet and profit and loss account for the said period[3] (a copy of which signed by the Vendors and marked 'B' is annexed hereto).

(l) 'the Completion Accounts'[4] mean the balance sheets and profit and loss accounts of the Company and each of the

---

[2] This definition does not include overseas taxation and will therefore require expansion in appropriate cases.

[3] I.e. the most recent audited accounts.

[4] The precedent assumes that the price has been negotiated by reference to the Completion Accounts which are unaudited but more up-to-date than the most recent audited accounts. See note 6 on p. 183 below.

Subsidiaries for the period of .... months ended on .... 19 ... ('the Completion Accounts Date') (a copy of which signed by the parties and marked 'C' is annexed hereto).

2. SUBJECT to the terms of this Agreement the Vendors simultaneously shall sell[5] and the Purchaser (if the Vendors simultaneously shall sell) shall purchase the respective holdings of the Vendors of the Sale Shares as specified in Schedule 1 free from all liens charges or incumbrances and with all rights which are now or which at any time prior to completion hereunder may become attached thereto.

3. THE Purchase price for each of the Sale Shares shall be £20.00p and the total purchase price for the Sale Shares is the Price.

4. PENDING completion the Purchaser its accountants and agents shall be allowed reasonable access to all of the financial and customer records of the Company and the Subsidiaries (but any access to or investigation of such records shall not affect the warranties representations and indemities hereby given or agreed to be given on the part of the Vendors)[6].

5. SUBJECT to the provisions of this Agreement the purchase of the Sale Shares shall be completed at the offices of the Vendors' solicitors at .... on the Completion Date when and where:

(1) The Vendors will deliver to the Purchaser:

(a) duly executed transfers of the Sale Shares in favour of the Purchaser or its nominees together with the relative share certificates

---

[5] A director of a company must give it written notice of any agreement to sell any shares or debentures in the company by himself, his spouse or minor children: Companies Act 1985, ss. 324(2)(b) and 328. It seems that a further notice is required on completion: s. 324(2)(a).
[6] The bracketed words may be disputed by the vendor, and quaere whether the discovery of some adverse matter after contract could affect warranties given on contract.

(b) such other documents[7] as may be required to vest in the Purchaser the entire beneficial ownership of the Sale Shares and to enable the Purchaser to procure them to be registered in the name of the Purchaser or its nominees on completion (including without prejudice to the generality of the foregoing all such consents as are referred to in Article ... of the Company's Articles of Association), provided that the Vendors shall not be required to stamp the transfers of the Sale Shares

(c) letters of resignation under seal from each of the directors and the secretary of the Company and the Subsidiaries incorporating in each case an acknowledgment that he has no claim whatsoever against the relevant company together with ACAS Form COT3 signed by each of the said directors and secretary acknowledging that he has no claim to redundancy payment or in respect of unfair dismissal.

(d) letters of resignation from the auditors of the Company and of the subsidiaries in accordance with Companies Act 1985, section 390 incorporating an acknowledgment in each case that they have no claim against the relevant company.

(e) a duly executed Deed of Indemnity in the form of the draft set out in Schedule 4.

(f) duly executed transfers in favour of the Purchaser or its nominees of such of the shares of the Subsidiaries as shall not be registered in the name of the Company on the Completion Date.

(2) The Vendors will deliver to the Purchaser as agent for the Company and the Subsidiaries all papers documents records and

---

[7] I.e. consents in connection with any pre-emption rights conferred on the shareholders. A term incorporated in the agreement whereby the vendors waive their own pre-emption rights is insufficient in a case where not all shares are being acquired simultaneously. Where such consents are required, they will form part of the purchaser's title to the shares, so that to incorporate consents (as opposed to an undertaking to give or procure consents) into the body of the purchase agreement will mean disclosing that document to a subsequent purchaser.

accounts belonging to or in the possession or under the control of the Company or any of the Subsidiaries including:

(a) the statutory and minute books of the Company and the Subsidiaries duly made up-to-date and the common seals and certificates of incorporation thereof together with up-to-date prints of the memoranda and articles of association and the share certificate books together with all unissued or cancelled share certificates of the Company and the whole issued share capital of the Subsidiaries

(b) all books of account or reference as to customers and other records and all insurance policies in any way relating to or concerning the respective businesses of the Company and each of the Subsidiaries

(c) all deeds and documents of title to all assets and properties of the Company and the Subsidiaries

(d) the bank cheque books and paying-in books of the Company and the Subsidiaries

(e) all employment and PAYE records and service agreements or hire purchase leasing or other agreements of any kind entered into by the Company or by any of the Subsidiaries

(f) certificates from all of the bankers mortgagees or other lenders (other than ordinary trade creditors) as to the state of all accounts maintained by the Company or any of the Subsidiaries as at the Completion Date

(3) The Vendors shall deposit the sum of £10,000 with the Purchaser's solicitors on the terms of Clause 6(10) hereof

(4) The Vendors shall procure the boards of directors of the Company and of the Subsidiaries each to hold a meeting at which there shall be transacted such business and only such business as the Purchaser may require[8] including the appointment of such directors as the Purchaser may nominate and the registration (subject to due stamping) of the Sale Shares in the

---

[8] Most vendors will correctly seek to limit the business of completion board minutes to specific matters.

name of the Purchaser or its nominees and the alteration of all authorities in respect of the bank accounts of the Company and the Subsidiaries

(5) Subject to the above the Purchaser will:

(a) deliver to the Vendors a duly executed counterpart of the Deed of Indemnity referred to in Clause 5(1)(e) hereof and

(b) pay the Price to the Vendors' said solicitors (whose receipt shall be a good and sufficient discharge to the Purchaser) and

(c) procure the release of the Vendors from the Guarantee or if it shall after using its best endeavours be unable so to do the Purchaser shall keep the Vendors and each of them indemnified against all claims liabilities and costs arising thereunder and

(d) procure the repayment by the Company or one of the Subsidiaries as the case may require to the Vendors of the amounts owing to the Vendors and disclosed as such in the Disclosure Letter.

6. (1) SUBJECT to the matters specified in the Disclosure Letter (which matters the Vendors hereby warrant to be true) the Vendors hereby warrant and represent to the Purchaser in the terms set out in Schedule 5 (and so that none of the paragraphs of Schedule 5 shall be limited or restricted by reference to or inference from the terms of any other of these paragraphs) as terms and conditions of this Agreement (and notwithstanding any information the Purchaser may have received or been given or have had as actual implied or constructive notice prior to the signing hereof other than that contained in the Disclosure Letter) and that insofar as any of the said terms and conditions relate in whole or in part to present or past matters of fact they shall be deemed to constitute representations upon the faith of which the Purchaser has entered into this agreement

(2) The Vendors hereby warrant to the Purchaser that the warranties and representations set out in Schedule 5 will be true

as if given immediately prior to completion with reference to the facts then existing as well as at the date hereof[9].

(3) If there shall be any breach of any of the said warranties or representations the Purchaser shall (without prejudice to any right to rescind this agreement) be entitled to compensation in respect of any loss resulting from such breach. If at any time after the date of actual completion it shall be found that any matter the subject of a warranty hereinafter set out was not at that date as warranted and that the Vendors are in breach of warranty in respect thereof and the effect of such breach is that either:

(i) the value of an asset of the Company or of any of the Subsidiaries is less than its value would have been had there been no such breach of warranty or

(ii) the Company or any of the Subsidiaries has incurred or incurs any liability or contingent liability which would not have been incurred had there been no such breach of warranty

then the Vendors will make good to the Company or to the relevant Subsidiary the amount of the diminution in the value of the asset(s) or the loss occasioned by such liability by payment in cash to the Company or to the relevant Subsidiary or (if the Purchaser shall so elect) pay to the Purchaser an amount equal to the diminution thereby caused in the value of the Sale Shares Provided always that these provisions shall be without prejudice to any other remedy which the Purchaser may have by reason of a breach of any such warranty or representation

(4) Each of the Vendors will forthwith disclose in writing to the Purchaser any matter relating specifically to the Company or to any of the Subsidiaries which becomes known to him between the date hereof and completion which is inconsistent with any of the said warranties or representations and which is material to be known by a purchaser for value of the Sale Shares

(5) Without prejudice to any other right or remedy of the Purchaser in respect of any breach or non-fulfilment of any of

---

[9] Where the period between contract and completion is significant, the vendor should pause before agreeing this sub-clause in relation to certain warranties, i.e. in particular those contained in paragraphs (13), (20), (24), (30) and (90).

the said warranties and representations whensoever occurring any breach or non-fulfilment thereof before completion or the happening or discovery before completion of any event or circumstance which would render untrue or misleading any of the said warranties or representations shall entitle the Purchaser to rescind this agreement without liability of any kind[10].

(6) In any claim for breach of any of the said warranties or representations the Vendors shall be entitled to reduce the amount of any such claim by the amount by which at the date of such claim:

(a) any current assets included in the Completion Accounts have prior to completion or within [[11]] thereafter been realised in excess of the amount attributed thereto and/or

(b) any liability disclosed in the Completion Accounts has prior to completion or within [   ] thereafter been discharged or satisfied below the amount attributed thereto and/or

(c) any contingency provided against in the Completion Accounts has prior to completion or within [   ] thereafter been ascertained and proved to be over provided for in the accounts

(7) In relation to the warranties and representations contained in this agreement:

(a) the liability of each of the Vendors shall not in any event exceed the amount of the consideration received by him hereunder less any amounts already paid by him in respect of any other claim thereunder[12].

(b) the Purchaser shall reimburse to the Vendors an amount equal to any sum paid by the Vendors under any of the

---

[10] This is a harsh clause unless applicable only to substantial breaches.

[11] It seems appropriate that the periods in this and the following two paragraphs of Clause 6(6) should end on the date specified in Clause 6(8) for notification of claims.

[12] Clause 6(7)(a) should be read in conjunction with Clause 9(b). If two 50/50 shareholders sell a company for a total consideration of £100,000, the liability of each of them cannot exceed £50,000. Up to this figure they will each be jointly and severally liable.

said warranties or representations which is subsequently recovered by or paid to the Purchaser or the Company or any of the Subsidiaries from or by any third party less the Purchaser's or the Company's or the Subsidiary's reasonable costs and disbursements

(c) any amount paid by the Vendors or any of them in respect of any breach of any of the said warranties or representations shall be treated as a reduction in the price[13].

(d) if any person shall have both such debts as are referred to in paragraph (20) of Schedule 5 hereof ('warranted debts') and other debts to the Company or to any Subsidiary any payment made to the Company or to any Subsidiary by such person and not appropriated by him shall be treated as being applied in discharge of warranted debts in priority to other such debts.

(8) Any claim by the Purchaser arising out of breach of any of the said warranties and representations reasonable particulars of which shall not have been notified in writing to the Vendors' solicitors on or before [14] and in respect of which proceedings shall not have been issued and served within one year after such notification shall be deemed to have been waived and any claim or claims which do not in aggregate amount to or exceed £   shall be waived.

(9) In the event of any claim to tax arising against the Company or any of the Subsidiaries the Purchaser shall make no claim in respect thereof under the said warranties and representations unless it shall have first procured the Company or the Subsidiary in question with due expedition to notify the Vendors in writing of such claim and to permit the Vendors at their cost (but with due expedition and indemnifying the Company the Subsidiaries and the Purchaser against tax in question) to resist such claim in the name of the Company or Subsidiary and to have the conduct of any appeal and any incidental negotiation and the Vendors so resisting such claim and conducting any

---

[13] I.e. for capital gains tax purposes; and see CGTA 1979, s. 41.
[14] See discussion on pp. 23-4.

appeal neither the Company or the Subsidiary in question shall do anything which shall or may admit or resist any such claim[15].

(10) (a) Subject to the following provisions of this sub-clause the Purchaser may apply all or part of the Deposit in recouping any amount properly due to it under or by reason of any breach of any of the said warranties or representations or any other obligation of the Vendors herein contravened or in paying to the Company or the Subsidiaries any amount properly due to it under the terms of the Deed of Indemnity and any amount so applied shall pro tanto satisfy the liability concerned.

(b) The Purchaser shall procure its solicitors to deposit the Deposit with a clearing bank selected by it and any interest earned thereon shall accrue to and form part of the Deposit

(c) If the Purchaser shall not have notified the Vendors in writing of any claims hereunder or under the Deed of Indemnity within [......] after completion[16] the Deposit and accrued interest shall be paid to the Vendors' said solicitors whose receipt shall be a good discharge to the Purchaser. If the Purchaser shall have so notified the Vendors of any claim then upon final determination of the total amount (if any) falling to be applied by the Purchaser hereunder (which the Purchaser shall use reasonable endeavours to calculate as soon as possible) any balance of the deposit shall be released to the Vendors' said solicitors provided that no amount shall be released before the expiry of the period of [   ] after completion.

7. (1) THE sale and purchase agreed herein is conditional upon

---

[15] In agreeing a clause of this type the purchaser accepts a risk that a claim for tax against the target will lead to inclusion of an additional liability or contingent liability in a post-completion balance sheet without right of recourse against the vendor until the claim has been determined.

[16] Logically the period should coincide with the limitation period in Clause 6(8), but few vendors are likely to agree to a deposit being held for any extended period applicable to tax warranties.

and subject to the undermentioned conditions being satisfied on or before the Completion Date

(a) the Vendors deducing and exhibiting to the solicitors for the Purchaser to their reasonable satisfaction a good and marketable title of the Company or of one of the Subsidiaries free from any incumbrances to each of the properties described in Schedule 10 with user as described in the said Schedule

(b) at the Completion Date there having been to the reasonable satisfaction of the Purchaser no deterioration in the net assets position of the Company and the Subsidiaries from that shown in the Completion Accounts[17]

(c) Mr .... having entered into a new service contract with the Company for a term not less than .... years commencing on the Completion Date on the same terms and conditions as his existing terms and conditions save that his salary shall be not less than £ ...... per annum.

(2) The sale and purchase agreed herein is further conditional on:
(a) each of the Company and the Subsidiaries continuing to conduct its present trade until completion according to its present practice and levels of activity and in ordinary course of business and

(b) none of the Company and the Subsidiaries prior to completion entering into or suffering any transaction or event materially prejudicial to its business or to any of its assets or which may give rise to any material liability

(3) The conditions referred to in the two immediately preceding sub-clauses being for the benefit of the Purchaser the Purchaser may by notice in writing to the Vendors' said solicitors waive any of them in whole or in part

(4) The sale and purchase agreed herein is conditional upon clearances being obtained on or before the Completion Date by the Vendors under section 464 of the Act (and section 88 of the

---

[17] This sub-clause gives the purchaser an element of option and should not be readily agreed by the Vendors at least without qualification of 'deterioration' by the word 'material' suitably defined.

Capital Gains Taxes Act 1979)[18] on the basis of applications and statements of fact to be submitted to the Inland Revenue within 7 days of the date hereof in the form of the draft applications and statements annexed hereto and initialled by the parties Provided that this condition is for the benefit of the Vendors who shall be entitled to waive the same (in whole or in part) by notice in writing to the Purchaser or its solicitor.

(5) The parties hereto shall use their respective reasonable endeavours to procure satisfaction of the conditions set out in clauses 7(1)(2) and (4) hereof

(6) If any of the said conditions shall not be satisfied or waived the party entitled to the benefit of the conditions may rescind this agreement and the Purchaser shall be entitled (without prejudice to any other remedy available to it arising out of any breach of the warranties or representations herein given by the Vendors) to be paid its reasonable legal costs incurred in relation to the negotiation and preparation of this agreement and its reasonable accountancy costs incurred in relation to any investigation of the Company and the subsidiaries carried out after the date hereof.

8. (1) EACH of the Vendors undertakes to the Purchaser that for the period of ...... years after completion he will neither on his own account nor in conjunction with nor on behalf of any person firm or company

(a) carry on or be engaged concerned or interested in carrying on the business of .... within a radius of ...... miles of .... (other than as holder of shares or debentures quoted in the Official List or on the Unlisted Securities Market of The Stock Exchange) or

(b) solicit or entice away from the Company or any of the Subsidiaries any person who shall be an officer manager or servant of the Company or any of the Subsidiaries at completion or (to the knowledge of the Vendors) within ...... years thereafter

---

[18] The words in brackets should be included in the case of a share for share exchange.

(c) engage or employ or offer to engage or employ in connection with the business of .... any person who shall be at completion or (to the knowledge of the Vendors) within ...... years thereafter be an agent of or independent contractor for the Company or for any Subsidiary

(2) Each of the Vendors undertakes henceforth not to divulge any of the confidential affairs of the Company or of the Subsidiaries, and undertakes to use his best endeavours to prevent the publication or disclosure of any such confidential affairs.

9. ALL undertakings warranties representations indemnities and other obligations of whatsoever type given made or undertaken pursuant to this agreement (a) shall (except for any obligations fully performed prior to or at actual completion) continue in full force and effect notwithstanding actual completion of this agreement being effected and (b) if given made or undertaken by more than one person are given made or undertaken jointly and severally.

10. THE Vendors undertake to do execute and perform all such further acts deeds documents or things as the Purchaser may require effectively to vest beneficial ownership of the Sale Shares in the Purchaser or its nominees free from all charges liens and other adverse interests whatsoever.

11. SAVE as may be required by the rules of The Stock Exchange no party shall issue any information or statement to the press relating to the transaction herein agreed to be effected or any part of it without the prior written consent of the other parties.

12. EACH of the Vendors hereby irrevocably appoints Messrs. .... (or the firm which shall for the time being carry on its practice) to accept service of notices hereunder.

13. THE Purchaser acknowledges that it does not enter into this agreement in reliance wholly or partly on any statement or representation made by or on behalf of the Vendors save insofar as such statement or representation is expressly set out in this agreement or in the Schedule hereto.

14. NO provisions of this agreement or of any agreement or arrangement of which it forms part, by virtue of which the agreement constituted by all of the foregoing is subject to registration (if such be the case) under the Restrictive Trade Practices Act 1976 shall take effect until the day after particulars of such agreement have been furnished to the Director General of Fair Trading pursuant to the terms of Section 24 of that Act.

15. THIS agreement shall be governed by English law and the parties will submit to the non-exclusive jurisdiction of the English Courts.

16. ANY notice given pursuant to this agreement shall be in writing and may be sent by first class prepaid post to the party to whom it is addressed at his or its address as herein specified and if so sent shall be deemed to have been received two working days after the date of posting.

AS WITNESS the hands of the parties hereto or their duly authorised representatives the day and year first before written

SCHEDULE 1

Column 1 Name and address of Vendors	Column 2 No of existing £1 Ordinary Shares
Sir Francis Drake of Westward Ho, Devon	2000
Sir Walter Raleigh of The Tower, City of London	2000
Ann Hathaway of Stratford-on-Avon, Warwicks	1000

SCHEDULE 2

(Wholly owned subsidiary companies of the Company)

Column 1 Name of Company	Column 2 Authorised Capital	Column 3 Issued Capital	Column 4 Registered Shareholders
Golden Hind Tours Limited	£500	500 fully paid £1 Ordinary Shares	The Company: 499 £1 Ordinary Shares Sir Francis Drake: 1 £1 Ordinary Share
Bard Audiovisual Promotions Limited	£500	100 Fully paid £1 Ordinary Shares	The Company: 99 £1 Ordinary Shares Ann Hathaway: 1 £1 Ordinary Share

SCHEDULE 3

Directors and Secretaries of the Company and of the Subsidiaries (in this Schedule together called 'the Group Companies')

Name of Directors	Director/Secretary	Company(ies) of which he is a Director/Secretary
Sir Francis Drake	Director	The Company and Golden Hind Tours Ltd.
Sir Walter Raleigh	Director	All of the Group Companies
William Shakespeare	Director/Secretary	Director of Bard Audiovisual Promotions Limited and Secretary of all of the Group Companies

SCHEDULE 4

THIS DEED OF INDEMNITY is made the ...... day of .... One thousand nine hundred and ...... BETWEEN the persons whose names and addresses appear in the Schedule hereto (hereinafter together called 'the Vendors') of the first part and Transglobal Adventures Limited Golden Hind Tours Limited and Bard Audiovisual Promotions Limited whose registered offices are at .... (hereinafter together called 'the Companies') of the second part and Armada Hotels Limited whose registered office is at .... (hereinafter called 'the Purchaser') of the third part

NOW THIS DEED WITNESSETH AND IT IS HEREBY AGREED as follows:-

1. (1) The Vendors covenant with the Purchaser and as a separate covenant with each of the Companies that they will indemnify and at all times keep the Purchaser and each of the Companies indemnified against any diminution of the net assets of any of the Companies which results from the disallowance of relief[19] from taxation given or due to any of the Companies or from the payment by any of the Companies of any taxation assessed charged or recovered on or from any of the Companies as a result of or by reference to any event transaction action or shortfall in distribution prior to the date hereof or in respect of an accounting period or periods ending on or prior to the date hereof[20] whether alone or in conjunction with other circumstances except (i) to the extent that provision has been made for the disallowance of such relief or for such taxation in the accounts of the Companies as at .... and (ii) in respect of any matter to which reference has been made in the Disclosure Letter annexed to the Agreement dated .... One thousand nine hundred and ...... between the Vendors and the Purchaser (hereinafter called 'the said Agreement') and (iii) in respect of any disallowance of relief to any of the Companies in respect of trading losses or surplus advance corporation tax arising from a major change in the nature or conduct of a trade carried on by any of the Companies occurring [or continuing][1] after the date hereof and (iv) in respect of any matter the subject of an undertaking hereunder given by the Purchaser to the Vendors and (v) any matter the subject of a claim by the Purchaser pursuant to the warranties given by the Vendors

---

[19] Loss of tax relief will not necessarily result in an immediate reduction in the target company's net assets, i.e. where there is a reduction in loss relief available for carry forward against future profits under ICTA, s. 177(1). For an interesting discussion on this problem, and others, see Ring and Clark *Tax Warranties and Indemnities*.

[20] The deed of indemnity is intended to be executed on the date of completion.

[1] The purchaser may wish to resist the bracketed words.

in the said Agreement but only to the extent that the Vendors shall have paid the Purchaser in respect of the claim and (vi) to the extent that the Vendors shall have made a payment to the Purchaser or to any of the Companies pursuant to this deed in respect of the same disallowance of relief from or payment of taxation and (vii) any liability to tax arising by reference to any transaction undertaken by any of the Companies since [the Completion Accounts Date] in the ordinary course of business

(2) If any of the Companies shall suffer any disallowance or payment as aforesaid (or a claim relating thereto) it shall notify the Vendors in writing of such disallowance or payment (or such claim relating thereto) forthwith after it has been made and it shall permit the Vendors at the cost of the Vendors to resist any such disallowance or payment or claim in its name and have the conduct of any appeal and any incidental negotiation and neither it nor the Purchaser shall do any thing which shall or may admit or assist any such claim.

2. (1) The Purchaser hereby undertakes with the Vendors and each of them:

(a) to procure that such dividends are paid on the shares in the capital of the Company in respect of the accounting period of the Company ended on .... as to ensure that there is no excess of relevant income of the Company for such accounting period over the distributions made by it for such period for the purposes of Schedule 16 of the Finance Act 1972 and that no apportionment of the income of the Company in such accounting period is made under paragraphs 1 to 17 of the said Schedule 16[2]

(b) to hold the Vendors and each of them indemnified from and against any liability in respect of taxation whether under section 460 of the Income and Corporation Taxes Act 1970 ('the 1970 Act') or under section 34 of the Finance (No. 2) Act 1975 or otherwise assessed on or recoverable from the Vendors which would not have arisen but for:

---

[2] It is unlikely that this undertaking will be required in the case of a 'trading company' as defined by FA 1972, Sch. 16, para. 11, unless the target has substantial investment income.

(i) any winding up or cessation of the business by any of the Companies occurring after the date hereof or

(ii) the combined effect of the said Agreement and any other transaction or transactions in securities (within the meaning of section 467(1) of the 1970 Act) effected other than in the ordinary course of business after the date hereof in any of the circumstances (C) (D) (E) of section 461 of the 1970 Act concerning any of the Companies and their respective securities or assets

(c) not to permit any of the Companies after the date hereof to pay an abnormal amount by way of dividend within the meaning of the 1970 Act, section 461 in such a manner as will result in any increase in the amount of taxation payable by the Vendors over such taxation as would have been payable by them had such abnormal amount by way of dividend not been paid

(d) to hold the Vendors and each of them indemnified from and against any liability to taxation which would not have arisen but for some voluntary act or transactions done or effected either before the date hereof at the request of the Purchaser by any of the Companies or on or after the date hereof by any of the Companies or by the Purchaser or its successors in title otherwise than in the ordinary course of business

(2) The Vendors shall notify the Purchaser of any claim in respect of any of the matters mentioned in clause 2(1) hereof forthwith after it has been made and the Vendors shall permit the Purchaser at the cost of the Purchaser to resist the same in the name of the Vendors or any of them and to have the conduct of any appeal or incidental negotiation and the Vendors shall not do any act or thing which shall or shall be likely to admit or assist any such claim.

3. This indemnity shall bind and enure for the benefit of the respective successors in title of each of the Vendors and the Purchaser.

4. If any provision for taxation (not being a provision for deferred taxation) contained in the said accounts of the Companies

shall prove to be an overprovision the amount over provided shall be allowed against any liability of the Vendors hereunder.

5. (1) The obligations of the Vendors hereunder are joint and several[3].

(2) The Purchaser and the Companies may release or compromise the liability of any of the Vendors hereunder or grant time or other indulgence to any of the Vendors without affecting the liability of any other or others of the Vendors hereunder.

6. For the purpose of this indemnity 'taxation' shall without prejudice to the generality of the foregoing include income tax corporation tax advance corporation tax capital gains tax development gains tax development land tax national insurance and earnings related contributions estate duty capital transfer tax stamp duty capital duty and value added tax and shall include all costs charges interest penalties and expenses incidental and relating to the disallowance of relief and the payment of taxation the subject matter of a claim under this indemnity to the extent that the same are payable by any of the Companies[4].

IN WITNESS whereof this Deed has been entered into the day and year first above written.

THE SCHEDULE
(names and addresses of the Vendors)

SCHEDULE 5

(1) All documents required by the Companies Act or the European Communities Act 1972 to be filed with the Registrar of Companies in respect of the Company and each of the Subsidiaries have been duly filed and compliance has been made with all other legal requirements in connection with the formation of the Company and of each of the Subsidiaries and with all issues and allotments of their respective shares

---

[3] See Civil Liability (Contribution) Act 1978 for the rights and obligations of joint covenantors inter se. Any modification may be included in the present, or a separate, deed.
[4] See note 2 on p. 163.

(2) No breach of any of the provisions of the Companies Act has been committed by the Company or by any of the Subsidiaries in relation to the Company or any of the Subsidiaries.

(3) No alteration has been made to the respective Memoranda or Articles of Association of the Company or of any of the Subsidiaries which has not been disclosed in writing to the Purchaser and since the Balance Sheets Date no resolution of any kind of the Company or of any of the Subsidiaries has been passed which has not been so disclosed and pending the date of actual completion no such alteration or resolution shall be made or passed without the prior written consent of the Purchaser.

(4) Save as has been disclosed in writing to the Purchaser no loan or share capital of the Company or of any of the Subsidiaries has been created or issued or agreed to be created or issued and pending actual completion no loan or share capital will be created or issued or agreed to be created or issued.

(5) No loan or share capital of the Company or of any of the Subsidiaries has been put under option or agreed to be put under option

(6) Since the Balance Sheets Date no dividends have been declared or paid and no distribution of capital made in respect of any share capital of the Company or of any of the Subsidiaries and no loan (otherwise than in ordinary course of day to day business) or loan capital of the Company or any of the Subsidiaries has been repaid in whole or in part and before the date of actual completion no such dividends will be declared or paid and no such distributions made and no loan (otherwise than in the ordinary course of day to day business) or share or loan capital will be repaid in whole or part save with the prior written consent of the Purchaser

(7) None of the Company or the Subsidiaries has received a distribution from any company which it knows or has reasonable grounds to believe to have been made in contravention of Part VIII of the Companies Act[5].

---

[5] See Companies Act 1985, s. 277 (Consequences of unlawful distribution).

(8) No direction has been given to the Company or to any of the Subsidiaries under section 28 of the Companies Act.

(9) Neither the Company nor any of the Subsidiaries has contravened sub-sections (1) or (2) of section 4 of the Business Names Act 1985.

(10) None of the Company or of the Subsidiaries is party to any such contract as is referred to in section 169(4) of the Companies Act.

(11) All the registers and records of the Company and of the Subsidiaries contain true and accurate records of the matters purporting to be contained therein or dealt with thereby and neither the Company nor any of the Subsidiaries has received notice of any application or intended application under the provisions of the Companies Acts or otherwise for the rectification of any register or record or notice of any contention that any register or record of the Company or any of the Subsidiaries is in any respect inaccurate or improperly kept.

(12) The Balance Sheets comply with the requirements of the Companies Acts and are true and accurate in all material ressects and give a true and fair view of the financial position (including the values of the assets and the amounts of the liabilities actual or contingent and accruing or accrued whether or not quantified and whether for tax or otherwise) of the Company and of the Subsidiaries as at the Balance Sheets Date and the Balance Sheets have been prepared on a basis consistent with that adopted in previous years and in a form and manner appropriate to the respective businesses of the Company and the Subsidiaries.

(13) The Company and each of the Subsidiaries has assets the realisable value of which as calculated on the same accounting principles as adopted in preparing the Completion Accounts exceeds by a sum not less than the aggregate of the amounts

shown as 'Net Assets' in the Completion Accounts[6] the amount of all liabilities whatsoever of the Company or of the relevant Subsidiary whether actual or contingent whether quantified or not and whether disputed or not including liabilities in respect of tax whether deferred or otherwise (on the basis of the rate of tax current at the date of this agreement or if greater publicly announced as the proposed rate of taxation) for which the Company or any of the Subsidiaries is or may at any time hereafter become liable on or in respect of or by reference to the profits gains income receipts and distributions of the Company or of any of the Subsidiaries (including all amounts which under the Act or any other relevant statute are deemed to be or are to be treated as profit gains income receipts and distributions of the Company or of any of the Subsidiaries) for any period ending and in respect of any transactions or events occurring on or before the Completion Accounts Date.

(14) Proper provision has been made in the Completion Accounts for all such liabilities of the Company and of the Subsidiaries as are referred to in the immediately preceding paragraph of this Schedule[7].

(15) The financial books and records of the Company and of the Subsidiaries accurately present and reflect in accordance with generally accepted accounting principles and standards all of the transactions entered into by the Company and by the Subsidiaries or to which any of them respectively has been a party and the Company and the Subsidiaries will maintain such books and records in manner aforesaid until actual completion.

---

[6] The most recent audited accounts of the company being acquired are referred to as the Balance Sheets in Sch. 5, para. 12. The Completion Accounts will not necessarily have been audited. They will usually have been prepared shortly before exchange of contracts to fix the price and the purchaser will therefore require the vendors' warranty as to the company's net asset value by reference to the Completion Accounts rather than the last audited accounts which could be more than a year out of date.

[7] At first sight this warranty appears similar to the preceding one. However, when inadequate provision has been made for liabilities in the Completion Accounts, there will be no breach of Sch. 5, para. 13 if there happens to be a corresponding understatement in the realisable value of the company's assets. If the bulk of the company's assets are fixed assets which it would be unwilling to sell, under provision for liabilities could create cash flow difficulties.

(16) For the purposes of the Completion Accounts the stock-in-trade and work in progress of the Company and of the Subsidiaries has been valued on a basis consistent with that adopted for the purposes of the respective audited accounts of each of the Company and the Subsidiaries for each of the three years ended with the Balance Sheets Date and the with bases and policies of accounting adopted in the preparation of the said audited accounts.

(17) Neither the Company nor any of the Subsidiaries has since the Balance Sheets Date entered into any material or substantial transaction or incurred any material or substantial liability or has in any way departed from the ordinary course of its day to day business either as regards the nature or scope or manner of conducting the same.

(18) Since the Balance Sheets Date no contract or arrangement has been entered into by the Company or any of the Subsidiaries which

(i) is unusual or of a long term nature or involving or

(ii) involves or may involve obligations of a nature or magnitude calling for special mention or

(iii) involves capital expenditure exceeding in aggregate the sum of £ ... or

(iv) involves or may involve the disposal of any assets of the Company or of any of the Subsidiaries at less than the higher of book or market value or the acquisition of any asset at a price in excess of its market price or

(v) is not negotiated on an arm's length basis or differs from the ordinary contracts or arrangements necessitated by the businesses of the Company or of any of the Subsidiaries or

(vi) is restrictive of the activities of the Company or any of the Subsidiaries in the conduct of any business of the type which they respectively carry on or restrictive of the use or disclosure of any information.

Any contract or arrangement such as is referred to in this paragraph (18) is hereafter called a 'Disclosable Contract'.

(19) The Company or one of the Subsidiaries is the sole beneficial owner and has good and marketable title free from incumbrances to all of the assets included in the Completion Accounts (less any already notified in writing to the Purchaser as disposed of since then or any hereafter disposed of with the Purchaser's written consent) and to all assets acquired thereafter prior to actual completion.

(20) Subject to the Purchaser procuring the Company and the Subsidiaries to use reasonable endeavours to collect such as may be outstanding on completion all debts shown in the Completion Accounts as owing to the Company or to any of the Subsidiaries will realise their full value in the ordinary course of business and in any event within [three] months of the date hereof and there are no such debts which have arisen other than in the ordinary course of business.

(21) All charges in favour of the Company or any of the Subsidiaries have if requiring to be registered under Part XII of the Companies Act been registered in accordance with that Part XII

(22) There is set out in Schedule 6 hereto full details of the overdraft facilities available to the Company and the Subsidiaries and there is attached hereto true copies of all documents relating thereto. The Vendors are not aware of any threat to withdraw or restrict or modify any of the said facilities or of anything in this agreement or of any event or circumstance (other than an event or circumstance which is public knowledge) which may cause any of the said facilities to be withdrawn restricted or modified and pending completion the Vendors shall do nothing which may cause any of the said facilities to be withdrawn restricted or modified.

(23) There is not outstanding:

  (i) any charge lien or encumbrance on or option over the whole or any part of the undertaking property or assets of the Company or of any of the Subsidiaries or

  (ii) any contract for hire or rent hire purchase or purchase by way of credit sale or periodical payment or lease by the Company or any of the Subsidiaries in respect of personal property or any arrangements conferring a right (whether the same shall be presently exercisable or not) upon any person to take possession of any personal property of the Company or of any of the Subsidiaries or

(iii) any guarantee or contract for indemnity or for suretyship by the Company or by any of the Subsidiaries or

(iv) any factoring agreement with the Company or of its Subsidiaries or

(v) any agreement or arrangement (save in respect of the said facilities) under which any of the Company or of the Subsidiaries is jointly and/or severally liable with any other person or whereunder any other person (other than a director or employee in the normal course of the duties of a director or employee of the type in question) may commit the Company or any of the Subsidiaries to any liability

(vi) any Disclosable Contract

(24) Neither the Company nor any of the Subsidiaries is engaged in litigation (civil or criminal) or arbitration or any proceedings or enquiries before any governmental municipal or other official commission board tribunal or other administrative judicial or quasi judicial agency and having made all reasonable enquiries the Vendors do not know of any facts which are likely to give rise to the same

(25) The Vendors are not to the best of their knowledge information and belief aware of any default by any person a party to any agreement with the Company or any of the Subsidiaries which is material to any of their respective businesses

(26) (A) All licences contracts permits and agreements and the like required by the Company and by the Subsidiaries for the purpose of or in connection with owning using or dealing with their respective properties or with carrying on their respective businesses as they are now carried on (and without prejudice to the generality of the foregoing the licence specified in Schedule 7) are in full force and effect and all the terms and conditions of such licences permits and agreements and the like have been complied with and no act has been done or suffered to be done

or omitted to be done which would entitle any person or authority to cancel forfeit or modify any such licence permit agreement or the like or which would render it likely that any person or authority would do so

(27) The Purchaser's Solicitors have been supplied with a true and complete copy of the licence specified in Schedule 7

(28) Save in respect of the matters disclosed by the licence specified in Schedule 7 the Company and the Subsidiaries are respectively solely beneficially entitled to the copyright in the designs of their respective products.

(29) None of the Company or the Subsidiaries has disclosed (save in the normal course of business or to its bankers or professional advisers) or has agreed or arranged to disclose any of its know-how, trade secrets, lists of customers or suppliers or (save in the normal course of business) its price lists

(30) (A) The stock in trade fixed and loose plant and equipment and vehicles used in connection with the business of the Company and of the Subsidiaries is in good repair and condition and in satisfactory working order[8]

(31) None of the stock in trade of the Company or of the Subsidiaries is obsolete or slow moving

(32) Neither the Company nor any of the Subsidiaries has done or omitted to do anything whereby any policy of insurance effected by it including the policies details of which have been disclosed in writing to the Purchaser's Solicitors has or may become void or voidable and the Company and the Subsidiaries will keep and maintain all adequate insurance cover in respect of all their respective assets (other than the leasehold properties specified in Schedule 10).

(33) Neither the Company nor any of the Subsidiaries has nor will pending completion have any of its records systems controls

---

[8] But see Clause 6(2) of the main agreement. Caveat vendor warranty.

data or information recorded stored maintained operated or otherwise dependent upon or held by any means (including any electronic mechanical or photographic process whether computerised or not) which (including all means of access thereto and therefrom) are not under the exclusive ownership and direct control of the Company or the relevant Subsidiary The Vendors warrant that there has been no breach of any service or maintenance contract relevant to any such electronic mechanical or photographic process or equipment whereby any person or body providing services or maintenance thereunder may have the right to terminate such service or maintenance contract.

(34) There is no agreement or arrangement or practice to which the Company or any of the Subsidiaries is a party which

    (i) contravenes or is or may be subject to any reference report order or investigation under any of the provisions specified in Schedule 8 or

    (ii) is or requires to be registered under Restrictive Trade Practices Act 1976.

(35) The Company and each of the Subsidiaries:

    (i) has now made all payments due under contracts and observed and performed all the terms and conditions thereof and not done or suffered to be done or omitted to be done any acts or things whereby any rights of the Company or of any of the Subsidiaries thereunder might be prejudiced and

    (ii) is not in default of any material obligation of any nature whatsoever legally binding upon it

(36) The Company and each of the Subsidiaries has carried on business under no name other than its own

(37) The Company and each of the Subsidiaries is duly qualified as a legal person in all jurisdictions in which it transacts business requiring such qualifications and has the right to own property and transact business therein in a manner in which the business is conducted and the Company and each of the Subsidiaries has

conducted its business in accordance with all relevant laws and regulations of all such jurisdictions.

(38) No contractual arrangement to which the Company or any of the Subsidiaries is a party will be abrogated or affected by the change in ownership of the Company or by the change in ultimate control of the Subsidiaries which will result from the implementation of this Agreement

(39) Neither the Company nor any of the Subsidiaries is party to any agreement or arrangement with any other person in which any of the Vendors or any of the directors of the Company or any of the Subsidiaries is directly or indirectly interested which is material to any of the respective businesses of the Company or the Subsidiaries

(40) No substantial supplier to or customer of the Company or any of the Subsidiaries has within the period of [twelve months] prior to the date hereof ceased or (to the best of the Vendors' knowledge information and belief) is likely to cease to trade with the Company or any of the Subsidiaries.

(41) (A) The terms of employment age and length of service for the purposes of the Employment Protection (Consolidation) Act 1978 (hereinafter called 'EPCA 1978') of every director and employee of the Company and of the Subsidiaries (save those directors and employees copies of whose service agreements are annexed hereto) are those contained in Part 1 of Schedule 9 together with the conditions of employment contained in the Company's standard employment agreement a copy of which marked 'D' is annexed and pending completion the said terms and conditions will not be altered without the prior written consent of the Purchaser

(42) The copy service agreements annexed marked 'E' and 'F' contain the complete terms of employment of the persons respectively named therein whose ages and length of service for the purposes of EPCA 1978 are as stated in Part 2 of Schedule 9 and pending completion the said terms will not be altered without the prior written consent of the Purchaser save as provided in Clause 7(1)(c) hereof

(43) Pending completion neither the Company nor the Subsidiaries shall engage or offer to engage or dismiss (whether with or without notice constructively or otherwise) any director or employee without the prior written consent of the Purchaser

(44) Neither the Company nor any of the Subsidiaries is under any obligation to increase the rates of remuneration of or to pay any bonus to any of its directors or employees at any future date whether with or without retrospective effect

(45) Neither the Company nor any Subsidiary is a party to any trade union recognition agreement and no such agreement is in the course of negotiation or contemplation.

(46) There is not outstanding:

  (i) any contract of service between the Company or any of the Subsidiaries and any of their respective directors or employees which is not determinable by the Company or the Subsidiary concerned by three months' notice or less or

  (ii) any liability (other than any herein disclosed) on the part of the Company or any of the Subsidiaries to any person who is or has been one of its directors or employees and for this purpose liability includes an unenforceable obligation.

(47) All appropriate notices have been and will at actual completion have been issued under EPCA 1978 to all employees including directors of the Company and of the Subsidiaries

(48) Neither the Company nor any of the Subsidiaries nor any of their respective employees is involved in any industrial dispute and there are no facts known or which would on reasonable enquiry be known to any of the Company the Subsidiaries their respective directors or the Vendors which might suggest that there may be any industrial dispute involving the Company or any of the Subsidiaries or that the sale of the whole issued share capital of the Company may lead to such industrial dispute.

(49) None of the Company or of the Subsidiaries has any

shadow director as that expression is defined in the Companies Act Section 741(2)

(50) Save under the Transglobal Staff Pension Scheme ('the Scheme') (full particulars of which have been disclosed in writing to the Purchaser) neither the Company nor any of the Subsidiaries is paying or under any liability or contingent liability to pay or secure the payment of any pension or other benefit to any person on retirement or the attainment of a specified age or the completion of a specified number of years of service or has undertaken to make any ex gratia payment of any such nature.

(51) (A) The contributions which have been paid to the trustees of the Scheme are sufficient to fund the benefits under the Scheme attributable to any service to the date hereof which under the rules of the Scheme is liable to be taken into account in calculating benefits for any person and based on projected salaries at Normal Retirement Date (as that expression is defined in the said rules)

(B) Pending completion none of the rules of the Scheme will be altered save with the Purchaser's prior written consent

(C) The Scheme is an exempt approved Scheme within the meaning of Finance Act 1970 section 21(1) and the Vendors are not aware of any reason why the Scheme may cease to be exempt approved.

(52) None of the activities of the Company or any of the Subsidiaries is within the scope of any Order under the Industrial Training Act 1982 nor has there been any indication that any such Order is being considered or may be made.

(53) Nothing has been done in consequence of which the Company or any of the Subsidiaries has or may become liable to refund wholly or in part any employment subsidy or other grant paid under or pursuant to any Act of Parliament to the Company or any of the Subsidiaries.

(54)[9] (A) The Company is the sole beneficial owner of the Leasehold Properties short particulars of which are set out in Schedule 10 (hereinafter called 'the Properties') and the Properties subject to the rents reserved by and the covenants and conditions contained in the leases thereof are vested absolutely in the Company free from encumbrances as being properties in which the Company has an interest and are the only properties in which the Company has any right title or interest or which the Company uses or occupies

(B) The Company has vacant possession of the Properties

(C) The Company has complied with all obligations binding upon it in relation to each of the Properties including without prejudice to the generality of the foregoing the obligations under the leases thereof referred to in Schedule 10

(D) The rents specified in Schedule 10 are the annual rents currently respectively payable by the Company for the Properties and there are no rent reviews in progress in respect of the same

(E) The Company has supplied to the Purchaser a true and complete copy of the leases under which it holds the Properties and of all licences consents granted thereunder by the respective landlords

(F) The Company has no tenants or sub-tenants or licensees in respect of the Properties and the Company has not granted or entered into any agreement to grant any assignment sub-lease licence or option in respect of any part of its interest in all or any part of either of the Properties and the Company has not parted with possession of all or part of either of the Properties

(G) No notice or complaint has been received by or served upon the Company in respect of any breach or alleged breach of any such obligations as are referred to in sub-paragraph (C) hereof

---

[9] The Vendors are unlikely to agree to the inclusion both of para. 54 of Sch. 5 to and Clause 7(1)(a) of the main Agreement. Since the warranties go further than anything a purchaser's solicitor could guarantee, and since they do not preclude the usual conveyancing searches being made before exchange, in many cases they represent the better option from the purchaser's point of view.

(H) No circumstances exist which are or would on reasonable enquiry be known to the Company by virtue of which (apart from the exercise of any power subsisting in the Government or any local or public authority) the rights of the Company in relation to either of the Properties might be affected and save as disclosed in the said leases neither of the Properties is subject to any covenant whether restrictive or positive

(I) The present user of the Properties as stated in Schedule 10 is the permanent and unconditional permitted user thereof under the Town and Country Planning Acts and no development has taken place or been commenced upon the Properties in contravention of the said Acts and the said Acts have in all respects been complied with and the use and occupation of each of the Properties is in all respects lawful.

(J) No notice that may affect the Properties or the rights of the Company in relation thereto has been served by the Government or any local or public authority and no circumstances exist which are or would on reasonable enquiry be known to the Company by virtue of which the service of such notice is warranted or likely

(K) So far as the Vendors are aware or would on reasonable enquiry be aware no proposals exist or are contemplated (whether statutory or other proposals) whereby the value of the Properties or their use by the Company as stated in Schedule 10 might be prejudiced

(L) The title of the Company to the properties is properly constituted by documents of title which are in the possession or under the control of the Company and the Company has a good and marketable title to the Properties

(M) None of the Company or of the Subsidiaries has been the tenant of or a guarantor in respect of any leasehold property other than the Properties

(N) Building regulations consents have been obtained with respect to all development, alterations and improvements to the Properties

(55) (A) The Company and each of the Subsidiaries has duly made or given all returns declarations information and notices

for tax purposes which are required to have been made or given and all such returns declarations information and notices made by the Company and the Subsidiaries are up to date and correct and on a proper basis and are not any of them the subject of any dispute with the authorities.

(B) None of the Company or the Subsidiaries has received an assessment which understates its liability to tax or any payment from the authorities to which it is not entitled

(C) Every assessment to tax received by the Company or any of the Subsidiaries and not fully discharged and every statutory notice concerning tax from the authorities so received and still current has been disclosed in writing to the Purchaser

(D) Each of the Company and the Subsidiaries has paid all tax which it is respectively liable to pay and none of the Company or the Subsidiaries is liable to pay any penalty or interest in connection with any claim for tax.

(E) The Vendors have disclosed in writing to the Purchaser every notice application for clearance and election given or made to the Inland Revenue by the Company or any of the Subsidiaries (not being a notice required to be given by law) since the date of the commencement of the period of six years ending on the Balance Sheets Date

(F) None of the Company or of the Subsidiaries has outside of the United Kingdom any branch agency place of business or permanent establishment

(56) (A) All documents in the possession or under the control of the Company to which the Company or any of the Subsidiaries is a party and which are liable to be stamped have been stamped with the appropriate amount of duty or denoted not chargeable with any duty

(B) Each of the Company and the Subsidiaries has paid all capital duty for which they are respectively liable under Finance Act 1973 and none has obtained relief from capital duty under Schedule 19 paragraph 10 of that Act or relief from stamp duty under Section 55 of the Finance Act 1973 and none has obtained relief from capital duty under Schedule 19 paragraph 10 of that

Act or relief from stamp duty under section 55 of the Finance Act 1927

(C) There is no outstanding liability on the part of any of the Company or the Subsidiaries to pay any penalty in respect of stamp duty or fine in respect of capital duty nor are there any circumstances which may result in the Company or any of the Subsidiaries becoming liable to any such penalty or fine

(57) (A) In respect of all transactions occurring on or before the date hereof each of the Company and the Subsidiaries has paid all amounts of VAT for which they are respectively liable save for such amounts as are provided for in the Completion Accounts.

(B) No act or transaction has been effected whereby the Company or any of the Subsidiaries is or will be liable for any VAT calculated by reference to the supply of goods or services by any other company[10].

(C) The Company has not been required to give security for payment of VAT.

(58) (A) Each of the Company and the Subsidiaries has operated the PAYE system as required by law and has paid to the Inland Revenue all sums due to it under the PAYE system[11].

(B) Each of the Company and the Subsidiaries has paid all national insurance and graduated pension contributions for which it is liable and has kept proper books and records relating to the same.

(59) All payments by the Company and the Subsidiaries liable to be made under deduction of tax have been so made and the Company and the Subsidiaries have accounted to the Inland Revenue as required by law in respect of such payments.

(60) Neither the Company nor any of the Subsidiaries has at any time done any of the following things:

---

[10] This warranty is unnecessary where neither the target nor the subsidiaries has been a member of any other VAT group of companies.

[11] PAYE and VAT payments are always made in arrears, and this should be disclosed in the Disclosure Letter.

(i) paid or agreed to pay any sums of an income nature other than such as will be allowable in full as a deduction in computing for corporation tax the profits of the Company or of the relevant Subsidiary[12]

(ii) acquired or disposed of any asset other than at market value

(iii) since 6 April 1965 made any distribution as defined by section 233 of the Act (as modified by section 284 thereof) other than any income dividend on shares

(iv) repaid redeemed or purchased or agreed to repay redeem or purchase any of its share capital

(v) received any capital distributions to which the provisions of section 266 of the Act could apply

(vi) effected any depreciatory transaction within the meaning of section 280 of the Act on or after 6 April 1965 nor after 29 April 1969 made any distribution as described in section 281(1)(c) of the Act the effect of which is as described in section 281(1)(d) thereof

(vii) entered into any transaction to which the provisions of section 485 of the Act is applicable

(viii) been party to any transaction scheme or arrangement to which any of sections 267, 460 to 468 or 488 of the Act or sections 85 to 88 of Capital Gains Taxes Act is or may be applicable

(ix) ceased wholly or in part to use any land for industrial purposes so that a charge to tax has arisen under Development Land Taxes Act 1976, section 19 or prior to 19 March 1985 commenced a project of material development within the meaning of that Act

(x) made any claim for relief under Finance Act 1976 section 37 or Finance Act 1981 section 35[13]

---

[12] This is a widely drawn warranty.

[13] The dates referred to in this and certain subsequent warranties in this precedent are correct in relation to their relative statutory provisions, but not so in relation to the precedent as a whole since the target company was incorporated in 1984, thus suggesting use of the words 'since incorporation'.

(xi) made any claims under sections 13, 111A or 116 of the Capital Gains Taxes Act 1979, or under section 276 or 418 of the Act

(xii) issued any share capital to which the provisions of Finance (No. 2) Act section 34 could apply nor does it own any such share capital

(xiii) made during the period of five years ending on the date hereof any exempt distribution as defined by Finance Act 1980, Schedule 18, paragraph 23(1) or received a chargeable payment as defined in that Schedule

(61) The Vendors have disclosed in writing to the Purchaser the written-down values for the purposes of the Capital Allowances Act 1968 or Part III Finance Act 1971 (as the case may be) of all assets of the Company or of the Subsidiaries included in the Completion Accounts and in respect of which an entitlement to capital allowances has arisen[14].

(62)   None of the Company or the Subsidiaries is liable as lessee or agent for any Schedule A tax under section 70 of the Act or in any representative capacity for any tax under Parts VII or VIII Taxes Management Act 1970

(63) No security (within the meaning of section 237(5) of the Act) issued by the Company or the Subsidiaries and remaining at issue at the date hereof is such that the interest payable thereon falls to be treated as a distribution under section 233(2) of the Act

(64) Particulars of all elections made by the Company under section 256 of the Act have been disclosed in writing to the Purchaser and all such elections are now in force.

(65) Particulars of all arrangements and agreements relating to group relief (as defined by section 258 of the Act) to which the Company or any of the Subsidiaries is or has been party have been disclosed in writing to the Purchaser

---

[14] A balancing charge will arise on a disposal of an asset in respect of which an entitlement to capital allowances has arisen if the disposal proceeds exceed the written-down value for capital allowance purposes.

(66) Neither the Company nor any of the Subsidiaries has at any time during their financial periods ended on the Balance Sheet Date nor since that date been a subsidiary of any company (other than of the Company) or a member of a group of companies for the purposes of section 272 of the Act other than the group consisting of the Company and the Subsidiaries

(67) No tax is or will become payable by the Company or any of the Subsidiaries pursuant to section 277 of the Act in respect of any chargeable gain which has accrued or pursuant to section 278 of the Act in respect of any asset acquired by the Company or any of the Subsidiaries during the period of six years ending on the date hereof[15].

(68) Neither the Company nor the Subsidiaries have been party to any transaction to which the provisions of sections 280, 281 or 476 of the Act would apply.

(69) The Company is not liable to make any payment under sections 286 or 287A of the Act.

(70) No breach of section 482 of the Act has been committed by the Company or the Subsidiaries.

(71) There has been since 15 April 1969 no change in the ownership of the Company or any of the Subsidiaries within the meaning of section 483 of the Act or Finance Act 1972 section 101.

(72) No directions or apportionments have been made by the Commissioners of Inland Revenue under Finance Act 1972 Schedule 16 in respect of the income of the Company or the Subsidiaries for any year or period or part of any year or period.

(73) No notice or charge to surtax or higher rate tax has been served on the Company or the Subsidiaries pursuant to the provisions of the Finance Act 1972, Schedule 16.

(74) Each of the Company and of the Subsidiaries is and has at

---

[15] This warranty is unnecessary if the whole group is being sold and the holding company is, and always has been, owned by individuals.

all times since 6 April 1965 been a 'trading company' or a 'member of a trading group' as defined in Finance Act 1972, Schedule 16, paragraph 11.

(75) No such transaction as is mentioned in section 80 of the Finance Act 1972 has been effected by the Company or by the Subsidiaries

(76) Neither the Company nor any of the Subsidiaries has surrendered or claimed or agreed to surrender or claim any amount of advance corporation tax pursuant to Finance Act 1972 section 92

(77) Neither the Company nor the Subsidiaries will be under any liability to corporation tax under the Finance Act 1972, Schedule 13 or CGTA 1979, s. 40 in respect of any transaction effected on or prior to actual completion.

(78) No gain chargeable to corporation tax will accrue to the Company or any of the Subsidiaries on the disposal of a debt owing to the Company or any of the Subsidiaries not being a debt on a security.

(79) The amount deductible under Capital Gains Taxes Act 1979 section 32 plus an indexation allowance computed as though each asset of the Company or of the Subsidiaries (on the disposal of which a chargeable gain or allowable loss could arise) were disposed of on the Completion Accounts Date is not less than their respective book values as provided for in the Completion accounts

(80) Neither the Company nor the Subsidiaries have since the Balance Sheets Date made any such transfer or disposal as is referred to in Capital Gains Tax Act 1979, sections 75 or 149 nor any disposal by way of a material transaction for the purposes of Finance Act 1985 section or received any asset by way of gift as mentioned in Capital Gains Tax Act 1979 section 59 and pending completion will not make any such transfer or disposal or receive any such asset.

(81) No machinery or plant owned by the Company or any of

the Subsidiaries and used for a qualifying purpose within the meaning of Finance Act 1980, section 64(2) on the Balance Sheets Date has since ceased to be so used.

(82) In connection with the Finance Act 1981, section 48 no amount of government investment in the Company or in any of the Subsidiaries has been written off

(83) The Vendors have disclosed to the Purchaser every security held by the Company or any of the Subsidiaries after the Completion Accounts Date which is 'a deep discount security' as that term is defined in FA 1984, section 36 and every asset so held which is a material interest in an offshore fund for the purposes of Chapter VII of that Act.

(84) Neither the Company nor any of the Subsidiaries has or has had any interest in a 'controlled foreign company' (as that term is defined in FA 1984, section 82) in respect of any accounting period of such company ending on or after 6 April 1984

(85) Neither the Sale Shares nor any asset owned by the Company or any of the Subsidiaries are liable to be subject to any sale mortgage or charge pursuant to Capital Transfer Taxes Act 1984 section 212(1) nor is there outstanding any Inland Revenue charge under Capital Transfer Taxes Act 1984 section 237 over the Sale Shares or any assets of the Company or of any of the Subsidiaries.

(86) None of the Company or the Subsidiaries is liable to be assessed to capital transfer tax as transferor or transferee of value or has been a party to associated operations in relation to a transfer of value within the meaning of Capital Transfer Taxes Act 1984 section 268

(87) The Vendors have disclosed to the Purchaser all securities for the purposes of Finance Act 1985 Chapter IV held by the Company or any of the Subsidiaries on 28 February 1985 or acquired by the Company or any of the Subsidiaries after that date together with details of their respective acquisition dates and costs not being securities as aforesaid disposed of prior to the Balance Sheets Date.

(88) At actual completion the Vendors will have the right power and authority to transfer the Sale Shares free from all claims liens encumbrances and equities and the Sale Shares will have been issued in proper legal form and fully paid or credited as fully paid.

(89) The recitals to this Agreement are true.

(90)[16] All information relating to the Company and to the Subsidiaries which is known or would on reasonable enquiry be known to the Vendors which is material to be known by a purchaser of the Sale Shares has been disclosed in writing to the Purchaser and pending actual completion nothing will be done in the conduct or management of the affairs of the Company or of the Subsidiaries which would be liable to influence the judgment of such person without the knowledge and prior written approval of the Purchaser. All information which has been given to the Purchaser or to the Purchaser's solicitors or accountants in writing on or before the signing of this Agreement is true and complete and will be true and complete at actual completion.

SCHEDULE 6

[An unsecured overdraft facility for the Company of £ ... from Midminster Bank plc at 3 per cent over the said bank's base rate from time to time]

SCHEDULE 7

Licence Agreement dated .... between .... (1) and the Company (2) in respect of UK Patent Numbers ......

SCHEDULE 8

Fair Trading Act 1973
Consumer Credit Act 1974
Restrictive Trade Practices Act 1976

---

[16] This warranty is usually requested by the purchaser and just as usually resisted or modified by the vendor.

Resal Prices Act 1976
Competition Act 1980
Articles 85 and 86 of the Treaty of Rome

SCHEDULE 9

Part 1

Employee name	Job Title	Salary	Age	Statutory length of service

Part 2

Director/Employee name	Age	Statutory length of service

SCHEDULE 10

Description	Particulars of Lease and User
1.	
2.	

APPENDIX B

Enquiries before Contract on Purchase of Shares

To: Messrs............
Vendor's solicitors

Re: .... *Limited* ('*the Company*')

1. Has the Company any subsidiaries? If so, please specify.

2. Please name all companies (other than the subsidiaries of the Company) in which the Company or any of its subsidiaries owns or has agreed to subscribe for any shares or stock including loan stock. Please supply a copy of any agreement relating to such companies to which the Company or its subsidiaries is a party.

3. (a) Please supply an up-to-date copy of memorandum and articles of the Company and its subsidiaries.

(b) Have all documents required by law to be registered by the Company and its subsidiaries with the Registrar of Companies been duly registered?

4. (a) Please specify any changes in shareholdings, directors or secretary since the date to which the last annual returns have been made up in relation to the Company and its subsidiaries.

(b) Has the Company or any of the subsidiaries issued or agreed to issue any share or loan capital since the date to which their respective most recent audited accounts were made up?

(c) Has the Company or any of its subsidiaries entered into

any contract or contingent purchase contract (within the meaning of Companies Act 1985, section 165 for the purchase of its own shares?

5. With whom should we arrange to examine the statutory books of the Company and its subsidiaries?

6. Please supply a copy of the most recent Directors' Reports and audited accounts of the Company and its subsidiaries.

7. Please supply full addresses of all premises occupied or in which any interest is owned by the Company or any subsidiary.

8. (a) Please supply a copy of all leases and licences relating to premises to which the Company or any subsidiary is, or is contracted to be, a party.

(b) Please provide a plan of each property edged in red unless such a plan forms a part of any copy document supplied under Enquiry 8(a).

(c) If any premises referred to in your reply to Enquiry 7 are not occupied exclusively by the Company or a subsidiary, who does occupy them and on what terms?

(d) In relation to each of the premises referred to in your reply to Enquiry 7 please reply to the conveyancing enquiries enclosed.

(e) Are any of the premises subject to a compulsory purchase order or the subject of a resolution of a local or other authority for compulsory purchase or any proposal to make such an order?

(f) If any of the properties have been professionally valued within the last three years, please supply a copy of the valuation.

(g) Please supply the names and addresses of the solicitors who acted on the acquisition of each of the properties in which the Company or any subsidiary has an interest.

(h) Please confirm that all rents, service charges and other outgoings are paid up to date and that the last receipts will be produced on completion.

(i) Where can the title deeds be inspected?

9. In relation to the Company and its subsidiaries, please supply:

(a) An up-to-date list of staff including directors showing length of service, age, salary, notice period and position.

(b) Copies of all service agreements or of statutory particulars of employment issued to employees.

(c) Is there any liability to, or claim likely to be made by, any ex-director or ex-employee?

(d) In relation to every pension or retirement benefit scheme of the Company or its subsidiaries, please provide (i) copy trust deed and rules (ii) name, age, sex and current salary of each member (iii) list and value of assets of the scheme (iv) copy contracting-out certificate, if any, issued under Social Security Pensions Act 1975 (v) a copy of the most recent actuaries' report.

(e) Please confirm in relation to every such scheme that it is approved by the Inland Revenue and that such approval is not under threat of withdrawal.

(f) Please confirm that all employers' and employees' contributions under any such scheme have been paid up to date.

(g) Please supply a list of persons to whom employment has been offered by the Company or any subsidiary or whose contracts of employment the Company or any subsidiary will or may become obliged to take over under the Transfer of Undertakings (Protection of Employment) Regulations 1981, and in every case details of the terms of employment.

10. (a) (i) Please supply copies of all charges, debentures and guarantees given by the Company or its subsidiaries.
      (ii) Please confirm that no notice requiring repayment has been served and that there has been no breach of any covenant contained in any charge, debenture or guarantee.

(b) Except in case of trade creditors and bank overdrafts, please (i) list other creditors of the Company or any of its subsidiaries showing amount outstanding, interest rate and repayment date in each case and (ii) give details of any credit facilities negotiated or under negotiation.

(c) Please supply the name and address of all banks at which the Company or any of its subsidiaries has an account, and give details of current overdrafts and overdraft limits and state whether secured or unsecured.

11. (a) Please specify in detail the title and nature of any litigation (civil or criminal) or arbitration to which the Company or any subsidiary is a party.

(b) Is the Vendor aware of any claim made by or against the Company or any subsidiary likely to lead to litigation (civil or criminal) or arbitration?

12. Please supply a copy of all h.p., credit sale and leasing agreements entered into by the Company or its subsidiaries.

13. (a) Please supply details of all insurances effected by the Company and its subsidiaries. Please confirm that all premiums due thereon have been paid and that the Vendors are not aware of anything which could vitiate any of the policies.

(b) Please confirm that all such policies will be maintained pending completion.

(c) Is there any outstanding claim under any such policy?

14. (a) Please supply a copy of all factoring agreements, agreements for services, agency agreements, licence or distribution agreements or knowhow agreements to which the Company or any of its subsidiaries is a party.

(b) Please supply a copy of all long-term contracts and of contracts for the acquisition of any capital asset entered into other than in the ordinary course of the business of the Company or any of its subsidiaries as now carried on, or any contract containing any abnormal provisions material to a purchaser, or containing any provision whereunder the Company or any subsidiary has paid or will pay or has been or will be paid a consideration other than cash or other than market value negotiated on an arm's length basis.

15. (a) Please supply a list of debtors in excess of £... showing names, amounts and when debt becomes due.

(b) Please supply a list of debts thought to be bad or doubtful.

16. (a) Please supply in relation to the Company and each subsidiary:
   (i) address of its local Inspector of Taxes;
   (ii) the name and address of its tax advisers;
   (iii) its VAT registration number.

(b) To what date have tax returns been made?

(c) To what date have tax returns been settled?

(d) Are there any matters in dispute or under discussion with the Inland Revenue or H.M. Customs & Excise?

(e) To what date has tax deducted under P.A.Y.E./Value Added Tax been accounted for and paid over?

(f) Have any covenants for annual payments of any nature been entered into since 6 April, 1965?

(g) To what date have shortfall clearances been obtained?

(h) Has any death occurred on which a charge for capital transfer tax may arise against the Company or any of the subsidiaries or against the shares in the Company?

(i) Is the Company or any subsidiary now or has it ever been a member of a group of companies?

(j) Are there any assets in respect of which the capital gains 'cost' is different from the actual cost?

(k) Is the Company or any subsidiary now, or has it been, a 'close company'? If so, please supply details of any directions which have been made and which are outstanding. Has it received any notice of intimation that any direction will be made? If so, please supply details.

17. Please provide copies of all assessments or claims (or

notification of proposed assessment or claims) in respect of any kind of U.K. taxation (other than value added tax) received by the Company or any subsidiary since the date to which their last respective audited accounts were made up.

18. If any part of the stock-in-trade of the Company or its subsidiaries is imported, please supply details of relevant import quota restrictions. In respect of each category of goods (i) has the quota ever been exceeded? (ii) how much quota has been used in the current quota period?

19. Is any trade union recognition agreement in force, under negotiation or requested with or by any trade union or employees' association with the Company or any subsidiary? If so, please supply a copy.

20. Please list all names under which the Company or any of its subsidiaries trade.

21. Is the Company or any of its subsidiaries the registered owner or exclusive licensee of any patent, trademark or registered design (wherever registered).

22. Has the Company or any of its subsidiaries applied for registration of any patent, trademark or registered design? If so, with what result?

23. Has the Company or any subsidiary received any communication from or given any notification or made any submission to the E.E.C. Commission?

24. Please supply copies or details of any agreement or arrangement with one or more competitors (whether or not written and whether or not intended to be legally enforceable) relating to the price or conditions of sale under which any goods of the Company or any subsidiary are to be sold or any materials are to be acquired by, or any services rendered to or by the Company or any subsidiary.

25. Please supply details of any loans made by the Company or any subsidiary.

Dated ....

....

NOTE

These enquiries are not intended to be comprehensive. In any event the usual conveyancing enquiries may be submitted in appropriate cases.

APPENDIX C

Letter of Disclosure[1]

Made by the Vendor to the Purchaser and referred to in the Agreement (as hereinafter defined)

1. The terms defined in the agreement ('the Agreement') to be entered into in the form annexed hereto and marked 'A' shall have the same meanings in this Letter of Disclosure and the Schedule hereto.

2. The Purchaser's solicitors have been notified of the existence of the documents listed or referred to in the Schedule and Appendix hereto and any document referred to in the documents so disclosed and all details relating thereto shall be deemed to have been disclosed to the Purchaser prior to the date of the Agreement, whether or not such documents (or copies thereof) have been delivered to the Purchaser or its solicitors. Accordingly the Vendor shall not be and shall not be deemed to be in breach of any of the representations warranties and undertakings set out in the Agreement insofar as such representation warranty or undertaking touches or concerns any matter or document or any other information contained or referred to in this Letter the Schedule or the Appendix hereto.

3. If any inconsistency is revealed between the Agreement and

---

[1] To be effective a letter of disclosure must be delivered to the purchasers before the share purchase agreement is entered into. This obvious point is made only because one respected commentator includes the disclosure letter in his list of completion documentation.

this Letter or the Schedule hereto, this Letter and the Schedule hereto shall prevail and shall be deemed to be the relevant disclosure.

4. The disclosures herein and in the Schedule hereto are made on the basis that each matter disclosed in relation to a particular warranty is effective generally in relation to each and every warranty as may be appropriate and each such disclosure is given without prejudice to the generality and effectiveness of any other disclosure.

THE SCHEDULE

1. Memorandum and Articles of Association of .... Limited ('the Company')[2] and the copy resolutions annexed thereto enclosed with the Vendor's solicitors' letter to the Purchaser's solicitors dated ....

2. (a) The provisions of and all matters referred to in all deeds and documents (or copies thereof) relating to or in a   way affecting all or any properties owned leased or otherwise held by the Company such deeds and documents (or copies) being listed in the Appendix attached hereto and having been sent to or collected by the Purchaser's solicitors and all letters from the Vendor's solicitors, relating thereto and all written replies and statements given by the Company or the Vendor or the Vendor's solicitors, in response to enquiries raised by the Purchaser's solicitors relating to such matters up to and including the date hereof.

(b) All matters and information in relation to all properties owned leased or otherwise held by the Company which would be disclosed by searches and enquiries made with all relevant statutory and local authorities and at the Land Charges Registry and at H.M. Land Registry.

3. The information contained in all correspondence up to and including the date hereof passing from the Company, the

---

[2] If appropriate, this disclosure letter should be amended to refer to the Company's subsidiaries also.

Vendors, their solicitors or accountants to the Purchaser or its solicitors or accountants together with all enclosures attached to or enclosed therewith and all matters referred to in such enclosures.

4. All matters and information contained or referred to in all documents and papers copies of which have been supplied to one or more of the Purchaser and its solicitors and accountants by the Vendor, the Company, the Vendor's solicitors, accountants or of which copies are annexed hereto.

5. There are further disclosed the following matters:

(a) all entries and information contained or referred to in the files of the Company at the Companies Registry;

(b) all entries and information recorded or referred to in the minute books and other statutory books of the Company;

(c) the audited accounts of the Company for each of the six years up to and including .... 19... together with all tax computations for the period ending ....;

(d) the replies dated .... from the Vendor's solicitors to the enquiries dated .... from the Purchaser's solicitors.

6. PAYE payments and National Insurance contributions have been accounted for and paid up to ....

7. VAT has been accounted for and paid up to ....

8. Etc. [add disclosures as necessary].

APPENDIX D

Completion Agenda

SALE AND PURCHASE OF WHOLE ISSUED SHARE CAPITAL OF TRANS-GLOBAL ADVENTURES LIMITED ('THE COMPANY')

A. *Date:* .... 19...

Venue: ....

Parties to be present:
   (1) Sir Francis Drake: Vendor/director
   (2) Sir Walter Raleigh: Vendor/director
   (3) Ann Hathaway: Vendor
   (4) William Shakespeare: Director/secretary
   (5) on behalf of Armada Hotels Ltd ('the Purchaser')
       (i) Sir John Hawkins
       (ii) Christopher Marlowe
   (6) William Byrd on behalf of Armada Discos Ltd.
   (7) Messrs .... solicitors for the Vendors
   (8) Messrs .... solicitors for the Purchaser

B. The Vendors will table:

(1) A service contract between the Company and Mr Martin Frobisher in accordance with Clause 7(1)(c) of the Agreement.

(2) Duly executed transfers of 4999 £1 Ordinary shares in the Company in favour of the Purchaser and 1 £1 Ordinary share in favour of Sir John Hawkins and the Purchaser together with the relative share certificates.

(3) A transfer duly executed by Sir Francis Drake in favour of Sir John Hawkins of 1 £1 Ordinary share in Golden Hind Tours Ltd.

(4) A transfer duly executed by Ann Hathaway in favour of Christopher Marlowe of 1 £1 Ordinary share in Bard Audio-visual Promoters Ltd.

(5) Letters of resignation from the directors, secretary and auditors of the Company and its subsidiaries addressed to the relevant company in accordance with the draft contained in Annexure 'A', together with (in the case of the directors and secretary) ACAS forms COT3.

(6) The Deed of Indemnity referred to in Clause 5(1)(e) of the Agreement.

(7) All other documents, certificates, accounts etc. referred to in clauses 5(2)(a) to (f) inclusive of the agreement.

(8) A clearing bank draft for £10,000 payable to the Purchaser's solicitors being the deposit referred to in Clause 5(3).

C. The Purchaser will table:

(1) A clearing bank draft for £100,000 payable to the Vendors' solicitors and a clearing bank draft so payable for £... in respect of the aggregate of the amounts referred to in Clause 5(5)(d).

(2) Signed consents of its nominees to act as directors and/or secretary of the company and its subsidiaries pursuant to Companies Act 1985, s. 288(2).

(3) Duly executed counterpart of the Deed of Indemnity referred to in Clause 5(1)(e).

(4) The release referred to in Clause 5(5)(c).

D. The Vendors shall procure each of the Company and the subsidiaries to hold board meetings at which there shall be passed the resolutions set out in Annexure 'B'.

E. The Purchaser shall hand to the Vendors' solicitors, in

exchange for the items tabled under paragraph B above, the items tabled under paragraphs C(1) and (3) above and an undertaking by its solicitors within 14 days to file at the Companies Registry notification of all changes of directors, secretary, auditors and registered office occurring at completion.

F. The Meeting will close.

ANNEXURE 'A'

To: The Board of Directors
      Transglobal Adventures Ltd .... (Date)

I/We hereby resign as Director/Secretary/Auditors of the company and acknowledge that I/we have no claim whatsoever against the Company.

....
(to be executed under seal)

ANNEXURE 'B'

Minutes of a meeting of the board of directors of TRANSGLOBAL ADVENTURES LIMITED held on .... 19... at:
....

Present: Sir Francis Drake (Chairman)

       Sir Walter Raleigh
       William Shakespeare
       Sir John Hawkins ⎫   from the conclusion
       Christopher Marlowe ⎭   of Resolution No. 3

1. Sir Francis Drake and Sir Walter Raleigh declared an interest in an agreement for the sale of the whole issued share capital of the company pursuant to which they and another had undertaken to procure the passing of the following resolutions[1].

---

[1] See the Companies Act 1985, s. 317. A director interested in any contract or proposed contract with the company must declare the nature of his interest.

2. It was resolved to approve the following share transfers subject to due stamping:

Date	Transferor	Transferee	No. of £1 Ordinary Shares
......	Sir Francis Drake	Armada Hotels Ltd	2000
......	Sir Walter Raleigh	Armada Hotels Ltd	2000
......	Ann Hathaway	Armada Hotels Ltd	999
......	Ann Hathaway	Sir John Hawkins and Armada Hotels Ltd.	1

3. The following tabled their signed consents to act as directors pursuant the Companies Act, 1985, s. 288(2). It was resolved to appoint them as additional directors of the company forthwith pursuant to regulation 95 of Table A Companies Act 1948[2].

Name	Address	Occupation	Other Directorships
Sir John Hawkins			
Christopher Marlowe			

4. The said new directors took their seats on the board and requested the Secretary to note their respective interests, as follows: ....

---

[2] If the company has been incorporated after 30 June 1985 the reference will be to regulation 79 of Table A of the 1985 Regulations.

5. The resignation of the Secretary was tabled, together with ACAS form COT 3 signed by the Secretary. It was resolved to accept such resignation and to appoint Christopher Marlowe as Secretary he having signed a consent so to do in accordance with the Companies Act 1985, s. 288(2).

6. The resignation of the auditors was tabled. It was resolved to accept the same and to appoint Messrs .... of who had agreed so to act as auditors of the company.

7. It was resolved that the common seal of the company be affixed to the counterpart of a deed of indemnity in the form of the draft contained in Schedule 4 of the agreement referred to in Minute No. 1 above. An engrossment of the said counterpart being produced to the board, the company's common seal was affixed thereto in the presence of the board and attested by Mr .... and Mr ....

8. The resignation of Sir Francis Drake, Sir Walter Raleigh and William Shakespeare as directors of the company were tabled together with ACAS forms COT3 and it was resolved to accept such resignations with immediate effect.

9. It was resolved to change the company's registered office to ....

10. [Include resolution to alter the bank mandate in the form required by the company's bankers].

11. The Secretary was instructed to file the notifications as appropriate relating to the above resolutions with the Registrar of Companies.

12. There being no other business, the meeting was terminated[3].

....

Sir Francis Drake

---

[3] Where on completion the target company or one of its subsidiaries is to repay loans previously made by the vendor(s), a board resolution to the necessary effect should be added to the target company's or relevant subsidiary's completion board minutes as appropriate.

(The draft board of the Golden Hind Tours Limited and Bard Audiovisual Promotions Limited will correspond to the above save for the modification of resolution no. 1, resolution no. 2 referring only to the nominee share.

Agreement for Transfer of a Business

AGREEMENT dated .... 19...

BETWEEN

(1) SPELLBINDER LIMITED whose registered office is at 101 Nirvana Street Over-the-Rainbow Neverlandshire ('the Vendor')

(2) GULLIBLE LIMITED whose registered office is at 11 Liquidity Way Overstretched ('the Purchaser')

(3) CHARLIE MUGGINS and WENDY MUGGINS both of Dreamlands Starry Rise Neverlandshire ('the Sureties')

IT IS HEREBY AGREED as follows:

1. In this Agreement the following expressions shall have the following meanings respectively:

'the Premises'	101 Nirvana Street Over-the-Rainbow Neverland
'the Business'	the business of designers manufacturers and vendors of crystal balls now carried on by the Vendor at the Premises
'the Lease'	the Lease of the Premises dated .... and made between Wizard Insurance Limited (1) and the vendor (2)
'the Name'	Spellbinder

'the Goodwill'	the goodwill of the Business including the right to trade under the Name and the exclusive right to carry on the Business in succession to the Vendor
'the Moveable Equipment'	the plant and equipment owned by the Vendor as specified in Part I of the attached inventory marked 'A'
'the Fixed Equipment'	the plant and equipment on or about the Premises owned by the Vendor and being tenant's fixtures and fittings as specified in Part 2 of the attached inventory marked 'A'
'the Hiring Agreements'	the leasing and hire purchase agreements specified in Schedule 1 hereto
'the Industrial Property'	the patents registered trade marks registered designs and applications for any of the same and the know-how and unregistered trade marks as specified in Schedule 2 hereto and all copyrights belonging to the Vendor and used in connection with the said business
'the Stock'	the stock of completed and part completed crystal balls and raw materials for use in the manufacture of the same as at close of business on the working day prior to completion
'the Purchase Price'	Two hundred thousand pounds
'the Stock Price'	the value of the Stock as at close of business on the working day prior to the Completion date as valued at the lower of cost or net realiseable value such valuation in the default of agreement to be fixed by Messrs .... (independent valuers) as experts and

	not arbitrators (the cost of such valuation to be shared equally between the parties) and in the absence of patent error to be binding on the parties hereto
'the Deposit'	Twenty thousand pounds
'the Completion Date'[1]	the .... day of .... 19...
'the Employees'	the persons specified in Schedule 3 hereto
'banker's draft'	a banker's draft drawn on a United Kingdom branch of a clearing bank.
'the 1978 Act'	the Employment Protection (Consolidation) Act 1978
'the 1981 Regulations'	the Transfer of Undertakings (Protection of Employment) Regulations 1981
'the Directors'	Arthur and Beryl Oz both of The Cauldrons Demon Drive Neverlandshire.

2. The Vendor shall sell as beneficial owner and the Purchaser shall purchase as at and from the Completion Date the following assets and the Purchase price shall be apportioned between the said assets as follows:

2.1.1 the Lease	£80,000
2.1.2 the Moveable Equipment	£30,000
2.1.3 the Fixed Equipment	£40,000
2.1.4 the Industrial Property	£10,000
2.1.5 the Goodwill	£30,000
2.1.6 all lists of customers and all books records and documents relating exclusively to the Business	£3,000

---

[1] In this precedent certain obligations arise or terminate on 'the Completion Date' and others on 'actual completion'. Difficulties can arise where the two do not actually coincide, for example in relation to the transfer of employees under the 1981 Regulations. The vendor of a going concern will wish to keep control of the business until actual completion but will be disinclined to carry on the business beyond the contractual completion date, as a matter of obligation to the purchaser. How these problems are dealt with in any particular transaction is a matter for negotiation between the parties; how they are dealt with in the precedent is not intended to suggest a 'normal practice'.

2.1.7 the benefits of all other agreements in relation
to the Business or to any of the assets hereinbefore
agreed to be sold and all other (if any) property and
assets of the Vendor used in connection with the
Business and all rights arising from any of the same
but excluding books debts and bank accounts and
the Hiring Agreements   £7,000

3. Forthwith on the close of business on the working day prior
to the Completion Date the Vendor and the Purchaser shall
procure the Stock Price to be calculated.

4.1 The Purchaser shall pay to the Vendor's solicitors Messrs
Twinkle Twinkle Little & Star of 4 Site Way Over-the Rainbow
Neverland as stakeholders the sum of £20,000 by way of deposit.

4.2 The Lease will be sold and conveyed upon the terms hereof
and of the (National) Conditions of Sale (20th edition) so far as
the same are applicable to a sale by private treaty and subject to
the variations and conditions set out in Schedule 4 hereto. In
case of any conflict between the said (National) Conditions and
this agreement the provisions of this agreement shall prevail.

5. On completion (which shall take place on the Completion
Date):

5.1 the Vendor shall deliver to the Purchaser:

5.1.1 an assignment of the Lease in accordance with (and with
such other deeds and documents as required pursuant to) Clause
4.2. and Schedule 4 hereof

5.1.2 an assignment of the Goodwill[2] the Industrial Property
and of the assets referred to in Clause 2.1.7 hereof such assignment to be in the form of the draft annexed hereto and marked
'B' and to be executed (as the Vendor shall procure) by the
Directors as well as by the Vendor

---

[2] In this precedent the restrictive covenants are to be contained in a separate
assignment of goodwill to be executed by the vendor and the vendor's directors on completion. Where the restrictive covenants are contained in the agreement itself, the directors should be added as parties to it. Note also the
comments on the Restrictive Trade Practices Act 1976 at p. 12 above including
the advisability of an additional clause where there are more than two parties
to the agreement.

5.1.3   the Fixed Equipment the Moveable Equipment the Stock and the items referred to in Clause 2.1.6 hereof

5.1.4   a certified copy of a special resolution of the Vendor resolving to change its name to .... Limited or to another name to be approved by the Purchaser (approval to a name unconnected with the Business not to be unreasonably withheld) together with a letter from the Vendor evidencing the consent of the Vendor to the Purchaser changing its name to Spellbinder Limited

5.1.5   the written consent of any mortgagee or other person whose consent is necessary for the sale of any of the assets hereby agreed to be sold together with an appropriate release[3].

5.2   The Purchaser shall pay to the Vendor or its said solicitors by banker's draft

5.2.1   the sum of £180,000 being the balance of the Purchase Price and

5.2.2   the Stock Price and

5.2.3   (subject to Clause 13.2 hereof) value added tax at the rate in force on completion on all of the assets herein agreed to be sold other than the Lease.

5.3   the Purchaser and the Sureties shall execute and deliver to the Vendor a counterpart of the assignment referred to in Clause 5.1.1. hereof.

6.1   If completion shall not take place on the Completion Date except by reason of any default of the Vendor the Purchaser shall pay to the Vendor interest at the rate specified in paragraph 2 of Schedule 4 until actual completion on the balance of the Purchase Price and on the Stock Price.

6.2   For the avoidance of doubt it is hereby declared that the sale and purchase of each of the assets hereby agreed to be sold are inter-dependent and shall be completed simultaneously.

---

[3] I.e. when the business being sold is part of the vendor's undertaking, the remainder remaining charged.

6.3   No title to any of the assets hereby agreed to be sold shall pass to the Purchaser until actual completion.

7.1   Any book debts owing to the Vendor are excluded from the sale but shall until expiry of the period of three months after actual completion be collected by the Purchaser and paid over to the Vendor at monthly intervals debts being collected in one month being so paid over within 7 days after the end of that month.

7.2   On expiry of the said period of three months the Vendor shall be at liberty to collect any debts that may be then oustanding provided that before legal proceedings are taken by the Vendor for the recovery of any debt the Vendor shall confer thereon with the Purchaser who shall be given the option (to be excercised by payment to the Vendor of the amount of the debt within 14 days of being given the option) of purchasing the said debt.

7.3   Any payment by a debtor for the time being owing monies to both the Vendor and the Purchaser shall be allocated in reduction of the debt owing to the Vendor until the same shall have been paid in full.

8.1   The Vendor hereby undertakes:

8.1.1   to pay all debts and liabilities and to observe and perform all obligations relating to the Business or any of the assets hereby agreed to be sold incurred prior to actual completion other than at the request of the Purchaser and

8.1.2   to indemnify the Purchaser against all losses costs claims and demands arising in respect of any breach or non-performance of the foregoing covenant.

8.2   The Purchaser hereby undertakes:

8.2.1   to pay all debts and liabilities of and to observe and perform all obligations relating to the Business or any of the assets hereby agreed to be sold incurred after actual completion or incurred prior to actual completion at the request of the Purchaser and

8.2.2 to indemnify the Vendor against all losses costs claims and demands arising in respect of any breach or non-performance of the foregoing covenant.

9. The Vendor will for a period of one week following completion to the best of its ability but without incurring any liability or expense initiate the Purchaser's representatives (up to a maximum of ...... in number) into the conduct of the Business and give the Purchaser's representatives information known to the Vendor (not being information in the public domain) that may reasonably be required in connection with the carrying on of the Business and shall also after completion but without incurring any expenses or liability procure for the Purchaser the full benefit and advantage of the goodwill of the Business by recommending and introducing the Purchaser to customers and otherwise as far as practicable but without requiring any personal attendance by any representative of the Vendor after expiry of the period of one week following completion.

10.1 The Vendor has dismissed by way of redundancy those of the Employees listed in Part I of Schedule 3. In each case the Vendor has given proper notice which shall expire on or before completion[4] and has complied with all relevant statutory procedures and the Vendor shall on completion produce for the Purchaser's inspection a receipt on Form RP3 signed by each of the said Employees for the full amount of the statutory redundancy payment due. The Vendor shall indemnify the Purchaser against all liabilities costs claims and demands under or in connection with any of the respective employment contracts of the Employees listed in Part I of Schedule 3 or the termination thereof[5].

10.2 The Vendor shall not pending the Completion Date dismiss any of the Employees listed in Part II of Schedule 3

---

[4] Dismissal prior to completion will not necessarily prevent the purchaser acquiring liabilities in respect of employment contracts under the 1981 Regulations; *Apex Leisure Ltd v Barratt* [1984] ICR 452, [1984] IRLR 224, and see ch. 12 above. Hence the indemnity in this clause.

[5] The Purchaser may wish to support the Vendor's indemnity with a retention from the purchase price.

(hereinafter called 'the Transferred Employees') except with the Purchaser's consent which shall not be withheld in the case of serious misconduct.

10.3   Pending the Completion Date the Vendor shall perform and observe all its obligations[6] under and in connection with the contracts of employment of the Transferred Employees (or the obligations the Vendor would have had under and in connection with the said contracts but for the operation of the 1981 Regulations) (such obligations being deemed to include statutory obligations)[7] arising from the employment of the Transferred Employees up to the Completion Date. The Vendor shall pay to the Transferred Employees all sums to which they are entitled up to and including the Completion Date and shall indemnify the Purchaser against all liabilities costs claims and demands arising from the Vendor failing to perform and observe the said obligations.

10.4   The Purchaser shall indemnify the Vendor from all liabilities costs claims and demands arising from

10.4.1   any substantial change in the working conditions of the Transferred Employees or any of them occurring on or after the Completion Date.

10.4.2   the change of employer occurring by virtue of the 1981 Regulations and this agreement being significant and detrimental to any of the Transferred Employees including without prejudice to the generality of the foregoing any detrimental change to the vested or prospective pension rights of any of the Transferred Employees and

10.4.3   the employment by the Purchaser after completion of any of the Transferred Employees other than on terms at least as good as those set out opposite their respective names in Part

---

[6] This admittedly begs a question because if the transfer of employment is deemed to take place on exchange of contracts, the obligations will then be transferred to the Purchaser: hence the words in the first set of brackets.

[7] It is not clear whether a pre-completion breach of, say, the Health and Safety at Work etc. Act 1974 by the Vendor could be visited on the Purchaser by virtue of the 1981 Regulations. In relation to another statutory obligation of an employer, a negative answer has been given: *Angus Jowett & Co Ltd v National Union of Tailors and Garment Workers* [1985] ICR 646, [1985] IRLR 326, and see pp. 143–4 above.

II of Schedule 3 or the termination of the employment of any of them after completion.

10.5 The Purchaser assuming the outstanding obligations of the Vendor in respect of the accrued holiday entitlements and accrued holiday remuneration to completion of the Transferred Employees the Vendor will pay to the Purchaser[8] within 3 months after completion the full amount necessary to enable the Purchaser to meet the cost of providing such holiday entitlements and remuneration as at completion. Any disagreement as to the amount payable by the Vendor pursuant to this paragraph shall be settled by an independent chartered accountant to be agreed between the parties and in default of agreement to be appointed on the application of either party by the President for the time being of the Institute of Chartered Accountants. Such independent chartered accountant shall be deemed to act as an expert and not an arbitrator and his costs shall (unless he shall otherwise decide) be borne by the Vendor and Purchaser equally.

10.6 The Purchaser will so soon as may be practicable after completion at its sole expense take all such steps as may be necessary or requisite to enable the Transferred Employees to become with effect from the Completion Date members of a pension or retirements benefits and/or life assurance scheme approved by the Commissioners of the Inland Revenue and providing benefits at least equivalent to those provided for such employees who are members of the pension retirements benefit or life assurance schemes at present maintained by the Vendor (written particulars whereof have been supplied to the Purchaser)[9].

10.7 The parties hereby declare that it is their intention that the contracts of employment of the Transferred Employees shall be transferred to the Purchaser pursuant to the 1981 Regulations on actual completion hereof.

---

[8] An alternative provision would be for the purchaser to make the payments having made an appropriate retention from the purchase price.

[9] Where both vendor's and purchaser's schemes provide for benefits to be transferred to and received from another scheme respectively, this clause can be modified. The purchaser's obligation to accept transfers should be qualified since he will need the co-operation of the vendor and/or of the vendor's scheme's trustees. Actuarial advice is recommended wherever any employees of the target business are in a pension scheme.

10.8 If actual completion hereof shall take place after the Completion Date by reason of any default of the Vendor the references in Clauses 10.2, 10.3, 10.4 and 10.6 to 'the Completion Date' shall be read and construed as if they were references to 'the date of actual completion'.

11.1 The Vendor and the Purchaser shall use their respective reasonable endeavours to procure the Hiring Agreements to be transferred to the Purchaser on completion. Where such transfer is not possible then from completion the Vendor shall hold the Hiring Agreement(s) in question upon trust for the Purchaser who shall indemnify the Vendor in respect of all obligations arising thereunder after completion.

11.2.1 All contracts of the Vendor for the sale of Stock (and such other contracts relating to the Business as are not otherwise herein specifically provided for) wholly or partially uncompleted at the Completion Date shall if entered into by the Vendor on an arm's length basis and in the normal course of the Vendor's business as heretofore carried on be disclosed to the Purchaser on completion. All such contracts for the sale of stock (and such other contracts relating to the Business as the Purchaser may specify) shall subject to all necessary consents be transferred to (or where any necessary consent is not given held in trust for) and completed by and at the expense and risk and for the benefit of the Purchaser who shall indemnify the Vendor in respect thereof save for losses claims and costs attributable to acts or omissions of the Vendor prior to the Completion Date and not undertaken at the written request of the Purchaser[10].

11.2.2 The Vendor shall account to the Purchaser for all prepayments received by the Vendor in respect of all such contracts as may be transferred to the Purchaser as aforesaid whether such pre-payments shall have been received before or after the date of this agreement.

---

[10] Since the agreement provides for the Vendor to continue the business pending the Completion Date and to sell stock to the Purchaser at the lower of cost or net realisable value, the Vendor may not agree to assigning the benefit of contracts for the sale of stock without opportunity of gain. One solution may be for the Purchaser to buy that part of stock earmarked for such contracts at a price somewhere between cost and net realisable value, assuming that the latter is greater.

12. From the date hereof until the Completion Date (or until actual completion if the same shall take place after the Completion Date by reason of any default of the Vendor) the Vendor will continue the Business in substantially the same manner as heretofore for its own benefit and at its own risk and the Vendor shall not do anything which will jeopardise or diminish the goodwill of the Business or any of the assets hereby agreed to be transferred. Without prejudice to the generality of the foregoing the Vendor shall maintain the value and type of stock in trade of the Business as close as possible to the value and type at the date hereof. If the Stock Price shall be less than £...... (save because of destruction or damage by any risk against which the Stock shall for the time being be insured) the Purchaser may rescind this agreement without liability and recover its deposit and if its value as aforesaid shall exceed £...... the Purchaser shall not be required to purchase the excess and shall be entitled to determine which part of the Stock constitutes the excess for this purpose.

13.1   [11]The Purchaser undertakes to the Vendor that

13.1.1   before completion the Purchaser shall procure its registration as a taxable person for VAT purposes (if not already registered)

13.1.2   on completion the Purchaser shall produce evidence of such registration to the Vendor

13.1.3   all of the assets hereby agreed to be sold are for the use by the Purchaser for carrying on the same kind of business as that carried on by the Vendor

13.2   If the Purchaser shall comply with its obligations under clause 13.1 then (unless H.M. Customs and Excise shall have required to the contrary) the Vendor shall not require the Purchaser to pay VAT on any of the assets hereby agreed to be sold but if the Purchaser shall not so comply the Purchaser shall pay VAT on the said assets (other than the Lease) at the standard

---

[11] See generally chapter 7, Section C, above. The purchaser should not agree the undertaking in the second limb of Clause 13.1.3 without the qualification contained in Clause 13.5. The purchaser may also wish to add a proviso to Clause 13.3 to the effect that negotiations with H.M. Customs may at his option and cost be conducted by the purchaser, because penalties and interest cannot be recovered by set-off against VAT on his outputs.

rate ruling at completion or as H.M. Customs and Excise may require.

13.3   The Purchaser hereby undertakes to indemnify the Vendor in respect of all VAT which H.M. Customs and Excise shall demand in respect of the supply of any assets hereunder together with all interest and penalties payable in respect thereof

13.4   If the Purchaser shall make any payment to the Vendor under clause 13.3 hereof the Vendor shall deliver to the Purchaser an appropriate receipted VAT invoice.

13.5   The obligation of the Purchaser under Clause 13.1.3 hereof shall be by way of indemnity only in the terms of Clause 13.3.

14.   The Vendor has given to the Purchaser copies of all insurance policies maintained by the Vendor in connection with the Business. The Vendor agrees that the Purchaser shall have the benefit of any claim under any such policy (other than any such relating to the Stock) which may arise between the date hereof and the Completion Date but the Purchaser shall pay the Purchase Price in full on completion notwithstanding any damage to or destruction of any of the assets hereby agreed to be sold. The Vendor will forthwith request the insurers to note the interest of the Purchaser on the policies and will as from the date hereof maintain all such policies in full force and effect pending the Completion Date whereupon the Purchaser shall pay to the Vendor an apportioned amount of the premiums.

15.1   In this clause the following expressions shall have the following meanings respectively

'the Balance Sheet Date'   ....
'the Accounts'   the audited accounts of the Business as at the Balance Sheet Date a copy of which is annexed hereto and marked 'C' and initialled by or on behalf of the parties.

15.2   The Vendor hereby warrants to the Purchaser as follows:

15.2.1   all written information supplied by the Vendor or its professional advisers to the Purchaser or its professional advisers in regard to the Business or the Premises is true and accurate in every material particular

15.2.2.1 the contents of Schedules 1, 2 and 3 are true and complete and will be true and complete on completion save as otherwise herein provided

15.2.2.2 the terms of employment age and length of service for the purposes of the 1978 Act of the persons named in the Schedule 3 are those contained in the said Schedule together with the conditions of employment contained in the standard employment agreement a copy of which is annexed hereto and marked 'D'.

15.2.2.3 no trade union is recognised or bound to be recognised by the Vendor as representing any of the Employees

15.2.3 the Accounts give a true and fair view of the state of affairs of the Business as at the Balance Sheet Date and of the profit thereof for the year then ended

15.2.4 the Accounts make full provision for all accruing and accrued liabilities and commitments of the Vendor in relation to the Business at the Balance Sheet Date

15.2.5 since the Balance Sheet Date no unusual or abnormal contract agreement arrangement or action has been or pending completion will be entered into or undertaken without the written consent of the Purchaser

15.2.6 the assets hereby agreed to be sold comprise all the assets which are reasonably necessary to enable the Purchaser to carry on the Business substantially in the manner in which it has hitherto been carried on by the Vendor[12]

15.2.7 the Vendor has performed all obligations required to be performed by it with respect to or affecting the Business and is not knowingly in default under any laws regulating orders contracts agreements licences or obligations of whatsoever nature which affect the operations of the Business or the assets to be sold under this Agreement

15.2.8 no governmental or other approvals are necessary to permit the Vendor to enter into this Agreement and carry it into full effect

---

[12] This is not something which a vendor should normally agree to warrant since it is largely a matter of commercial judgment.

15.2.9   the current use of the Premises as [light industrial with ancillary offices] is the permanent and unconditional permitted use thereof under the Town and Country Planning Acts and no development has taken place or been commenced upon the Premises in contravention of the said Acts and the said Acts have in all respects been complied with and the use and occupation of the Premises is in all respects lawful

15.2.10   pending the Completion Date the Fixed Equipment and the Moveable Equipment will be maintained in as good repair as at the date of this Agreement fair wear and tear excepted but a breach of this warranty in relation to any of the Moveable Equipment[13] shall in no circumstances entitle the Purchaser to rescind this Agreement

15.2.11   the Vendor is not engaged in litigation arbitration or other proceedings in relation to any of the assets hereby agreed to be sold nor in relation to any of the Employees and does not know of any facts likely to give rise to the same

15.2.12   all necessary corporate action has been taken by the Vendor to authorise the execution and delivery by the Vendor of this Agreement and the sale to the Purchaser of the Business

15.2.13   save as provided by the Agreement there are not now outstanding in relation to the Business and will not be outstanding on completion:

> (i) any agreements material to the Business (other than Hiring Agreements and contracts of employment) between the Vendor and any third party which such third party shall be entitled to terminate as a result of the sale and purchase hereby agreed or of compliance with any other provision hereof or

> (ii) any contract of employment with any of the Transferred Employees expressly entitling any of the Transfered Employees to terminate the contract as a result of the sale and purchase hereby agreed or of compliance with any other provision hereof or

> (iii) any special arrangements between the Vendor and distributors or customers of the Vendor or

---

[13] This assumes that the Moveable Equipment is easily replaceable.

(iv) any agreement or arrangement entered into by the Vendor in connection with the Business otherwise than by way of bargain at arm's length

(v) any agreement for the sale of any part of the Stock which is not other than in the ordinary course of the Business as it has been heretofore carried on

15.2.14 all assets hereby agreed to be sold are the Vendor's sole unencumbered property

15.3 The Vendor acknowledges that the Purchaser has entered into this agreement in reliance on the foregoing warranties. The Vendor will forthwith disclose in writing to the Purchaser any matter which may become known to it between the date hereof and completion which is inconsistent with any of the foregoing warranties or would be inconsistent with any of the foregoing warranties were they warranted as at completion (or which is material to be known by a purchaser for value of any of the assets hereby agreed to be sold)[14].

15.4 Without prejudice to any other right or remedy of the Purchaser in respect of any breach or non-fulfilment of any of the foregoing warranties whensoever occurring any breach or non-fulfilment thereof before completion or the happening or discovery before completion of any event or circumstance which would render untrue or misleading any of these warranties shall (save as hereinbefore provided) entitle the Purchaser to rescind this agreement without liability of any kind and return of its deposit[15].

15.5 Any claim by the Purchaser arising out of breach of any of the foregoing warranties particulars of which shall not have been notified in writing to the Vendor within twelve months following actual Completion shall be deemed to have been waived, and any claim or claims which do not in aggregate exceed £... shall be waived.

16. The Vendor shall prior to the Completion Date give to the Purchaser and its advisers reasonable facilities for investigating

---

[14] The vendor should be cautious in agreeing the bracketed words. As drafted they could cover knowledge in the public domain.
[15] A harsh clause.

and verifying the Business and the assets hereby agreed to be sold. Any such investigation or verification shall not affect the warranties and indemnities herein given or hereby agreed to be given by the Vendor which shall remain in full force and effect notwithstanding completion.

17.   The books records and documents referred to in Clause 2.1.6 shall include the Vendor's value added tax returns for the six years ending on completion but shall not include those relating to the general affairs of the Vendor (other than in relation to the Business) or to any assets of the Vendor not being sold to the Purchaser provided that insofar as such excluded books and records shall relate to the assets being sold to or to the obligations being assumed by the Purchaser the Purchaser shall have the right to examine the same at all reasonable times and to make copies thereof or take extracts therefrom thereof.

18. Any notice required to be given hereunder shall be served by first class mail addressed to the registered office of the party for which it is intended and shall be deemed to have been served in the ordinary course of such mail. In proving service it shall be sufficient to show that the envelope containing the notice was duly addressed stamped and posted.

19. The Vendor will do such acts and things and execute such deeds and documents as may be necessary fully and effectively to vest in the Purchaser the assets hereby agreed to be sold and to assure to the Purchaser the rights hereby agreed to be granted.

20. No waiver by either party of any of the requirements hereof or of any of its rights hereunder shall release the other from full performance of its remaining obligations stated herein.

21. None of the parties hereto shall disclose any information regarding the existence or contents of this agreement to any third party (including the Employees) prior to the Completion Date except as may be required by the rules of The Stock Exchange or by law.

22. This agreement shall remain in full force and effect after completion in respect of any matters covenants or conditions

which shall not have been done observed or performed prior thereto and all representations warranties undertakings and obligations of the parties shall (except for any obligations fully performed on completion) continue in full force and effect notwithstanding the completion of the sale and purchase hereby agreed to be made.

23.1 The Sureties in consideration of the Vendor entering into this Agreement with the Purchaser at the request of the Sureties hereby covenant with the Vendor that the Purchaser shall pay all sums hereby agreed to be paid by the Purchaser on the days and in manner aforesaid and shall duly perform and observe all the undertakings hereinbefore contained on the part of the Purchaser and that in case of default in such payment or performance or observance of undertakings as aforesaid the Sureties will pay and make good to the Vendor on demand all loss damage costs and expenses thereby arising or incurred by the Vendor provided that any neglect or forebearance of the Vendor in endeavouring to obtain payment of the several sums hereby agreed to be paid when the same become payable or to enforce performance or observance of the several undertakings herein on the Purchaser's part contained and any time which may be given by the Vendor to the Purchaser shall not release or exonerate or in any way affect the liability of the Sureties under this Clause.

23.2 All obligations of the Sureties undertaken in this agreement are undertaken jointly and severally.

[24. It is hereby certified that the transaction hereby effected does not form part of a larger transaction or of a series of transactions in respect of which the amount or value or the aggregate amount or value of the consideration exceeds the sum of £30,000][16].

IN WITNESS whereof the parties hereto have hereunto set their hands and seals the day and year first before written

SCHEDULE 1 (The Hiring Agreements)

Date of Agreement	Parties	Equipment	Rental

---

[16] See ch. 7, section D above.

SCHEDULE 2 (The Industrial Property)

SCHEDULE 3 (The Employees)
Part I

Name	Job Title	Remuneration	Weekly/ monthly paid	Length of service for the purpose of the 1978 Act

Part II

Name	Job Title	Remuneration	Weekly/ monthly paid	Length of service for the purpose of the 1978 Act

The other terms and conditions of employment of the persons specified in this Schedule 3 are contained in standard contracts of employment a copy of which is annexed hereto and marked 'D'. In addition such persons have been customarily granted the following perquisites:

SCHEDULE 4
(Amendments to the National Conditions (20th Edition))

1. Title to the Premises shall commence with the Lease.

2. The prescribed rate of interest shall be (4) per cent over Midlays Bank plc Base Rate from time to time.

3. Vacant possession shall be given on Completion save that any tangible assets agreed to be sold by this Agreement will be left at the Premises.

4. Conditions 15(2) (3) and (4) and 21(3) shall not apply.

5. On completion the Purchaser will if requested by the landlord of the Lease enter into direct covenants with the said landlord to pay the rent reserved by and perform and observe the

covenants and conditions contained in the Lease and the Sureties will if so requested enter into direct covenants with the landlord that the Purchaser will pay the rent reserved by the Lease and perform and observe the covenants on the tenant's part therein contained. The said covenants on the part of the Purchaser and the Sureties shall be in such form and include such further provisions as the landlord may reasonably require.

6. The Purchaser and the Sureties shall execute a counterpart of the assignment of the Lease wherein the Sureties shall covenant with the Vendor that the Purchaser shall duly perform and observe the covenant on the part of the Purchaser implied therein by virtue of Section 77(1)(C) Law of Property Act 1925 and the said covenant on the part of the Sureties shall be subject to the proviso that any neglect or forbearance of the Vendor in enforcing performance or observance of the said implied covenant on the part of the Purchaser and that any time which may be given by the Vendor to the Purchaser shall not release or exonerate or in any way affect the liability of the Sureties.

DRAFT ASSIGNMENT REFERRED TO IN CLAUSE 5.1.2   'B'

THIS ASSIGNMENT made the .... day of .... 19...
BETWEEN
(1) SPELLBINDER LIMITED whose registered office is at 101 Nirvana Street Over-the-Rainbow Neverlandshire ('the Vendor')

(2) ARTHUR OZ and BERYL OZ both of The Cauldrons Demon Drive Neverlandshire ('the Directors')

(3) GULLIBLE LIMITED whose registered office is at 11 Liquidity Way Overstretched ('the Purchaser')

PURSUANT TO an Agreement between the Vendor (1) the Purchaser (2) and Charlie Muggins and Wendy Muggins (3) dated .... a copy of which is annexed hereto ('the Transfer Agreement')
WITNESSETH as follows:

1. In consideration of the sum of £47,000 (Forty-seven thousand pounds) paid by the Purchaser to the Vendor (the receipt of

which the Vendor hereby acknowledges) the Vendor as beneficial owner hereby assigns unto the Purchaser:

(i) all the goodwill of the business of designers, manufacturers
and vendors of crystal balls carried on by the Vendor at 101
Nirvana Street aforesaid including the right to the exclusion of
the Vendor to trade under the name 'Spellbinder' and the exclusive right to carry on the said business in succession to the
Vendor and

(ii) the patents registered trade marks registered designs and
applications for any of the same and the know-how and unregistered trade marks as specified in the Schedule hereto and all
copyrights belonging to the Vendor and used in connection with
the said business and

(iii) the benefit of all agreements relating to the said business
or to any of the assets agreed to be sold by the Vendor under
the Transfer Agreement and all rights arising from any of the
same (but excluding book debts bank accounts and the leasing
and hire purchase agreements specified in Schedule 1 to the
Transfer Agreement)

TO HOLD the same unto the Purchaser absolutely

2. The Vendor and each of the Directors hereby undertakes
with the Purchaser jointly and severally:

(A) for the period of .... years hereafter not whether
on its his or her own account nor in conjunction with nor on
behalf of any person firm or company

(i) to carry on or be engaged concerned or interested in de-
signing manufacturing or selling crystal balls (other than
as a holder of shares or loan stock quoted on The Stock
Exchange) within .... miles of 101 Nirvana Street
aforesaid, and

(ii) to solicit nor entice away from the Purchaser any of the
employees of the said business listed in Part II of Schedule
3 of the Transfer Agreement;

(B) to use their respective best endeavours (but without incurring any personal expense) to secure to the Purchaser the full

benefit of the assets hereby assigned to the Purchaser and not either directly or indirectly to attempt to induce the customer of the said business to deal with any other person firm or company.

(C) not without the written consent of the Purchaser to divulge (and shall use its his or her best endeavours to prevent the disclosure of) any information concerning the said business or concerning any customer or supplier of the said business

[3. Certificate of value if appropriate—see ch. 7, section D above]

IN WITNESS whereof the Vendor has hereunto affixed its common seal and the Directors have hereunto set their respective hands and seals the day and year first before written.

THE SCHEDULE (details of patents etc.)

THE COMMON SEAL etc.

Minority Shareholder's Agreement

THIS AGREEMENT is made the ...... day of .... 19... BETWEEN
.... LIMITED whose registered office is at .... (hereinafter called 'Holdings')[1] of the one part and .... LIMITED
whose registered office is situated at .... (hereinafter called
'Investments')[2] of the other part.

WHEREAS the parties are the registered holders and beneficial
owners of the entire issue share capital of .... Limited
(hereinafter called 'the Company') which was incorporated in
England under the Companies Acts 1948 and 1983 on the ......
day of .... 1984[3] and which has authorised capital of
£20,000 divided into 20,000 Ordinary Shares of £1 each of which
15,200 shares are owned beneficially by Holdings and registered
in its name and 4,800 shares are owned beneficially by Investments and registered in its name and all such shares are issued
and fully paid up.

NOW THIS DEED WITNESSETH:

1. HOLDINGS HEREBY UNDERTAKES and COVENANTS with Investments that so long as Investments remains a member of the
Company:

(1)(a) Holdings shall as and when called upon by Investments
so to do from time to time cause two nominees of Investments

---

[1] The majority shareholder.
[2] The minority shareholder.
[3] See fn 1 to Appendix A.

(who shall have given the requisite consents under the Companies Act 1985, section 288) to be appointed directors of the Company and to be removed from office as directors of the Company and to be replaced by other nominees of Investments (who shall have the requisite consents as aforesaid) and Holdings will not exercise its votes to prevent the appointment of or for the removal of the nominees of either of them for the time being of Investments (hereinafter called 'the Nominees') from office as directors of the Company except when called upon so to do by Investments.

(b) If at any general meeting of the Company any of the Nominees shall retire from office as a director of the Company then Holdings will cast its votes as a member of the Company in favour of his re-election as a director of the Company.

(c) Without prejudice to the rights of Investments under paragraphs (a) and (b) of this sub-clause in the event of Investments not appointing any nominee to be a director of the Company then Investments shall be kept fully informed as to all financial and business affairs of the Company and shall be consulted on all important policy matters (but the rights so conferred shall not be capable of operating as or conferring upon Investments the position or status of a director and shall be construed as so restricted).

(d) In addition to its other rights hereunder Investments shall be entitled to nominate a person (to be approved by Holdings such approval not to be unreasonably withheld) who shall be given access to the premises of the Company and all parts thereof during the conduct of its business and to all books of account and other records of the Company.

(e) There shall at no time be more than .... persons appointed as directors of the Company.

(2) Holdings will procure that the Company shall not without the prior written consent of Investments

(a) alter its Memorandum or Articles of Association;

(b) increase its share capital or issue any option bond or other security or unsecured loan or enter into any agreement which shall entitle the holder thereof or any third party to an allotment of shares in the Company or to vote at any general meeting of the Company or to appoint or remove any director of the Company;

(c) pass any resolution for the winding up or liquidation of the Company;

(d) form or acquire by any means any subsidiary and for the purpose of this paragraph the expression 'subsidiary' shall have the meaning ascribed to it by the Companies Act 1985, section 736;

(e) pass any resolution for the re-registration of the company as a public company;

(f)[4] pass any resolution being an authority to the directors of the Company to allot relevant securities within the meaning of Companies Act 1985, section 80;

(g) allot any equity securities within the meaning of Companies Act 1985, section 89;

(h) pass any resolution to authorise any such contract as is referred to in Companies Act 1985, section 164 or 165[5];

(i) enter into any service agreement or agreement for services or agency agreement or other long term agreement of a similar nature other than in the ordinary course of the business of the Company as it shall for the time being be carried on or except without the previous written consent of Investments being first obtained;

(j) transfer or dispose of or vest or procure the transfer or disposition or vesting of the whole or any part of the assets or undertaking of the Company whether by one transaction or a series of transactions;

(k) create or grant any debenture mortgage or charge whether fixed or floating or any other security or other than as contemplated hereby or in the normal course of business create any indebtedness;

---

[4] This and the next following paragraph are unnecessary where (i) the agreement contains a prohibition on an increase in share capital and (ii) all the authorised capital has been issued.

[5] I.e. a contract or contingent purchase contract for the purchase by a company of its own shares.

(l) create or grant any leases tenancies or licences of whatsoever nature in respect of its property;

(m) except to customers of the Company in the normal course of business lend or advance monies to or guarantee the indebtedness of any person firm or corporation;

(n) acquire any new capital asset or undertaking or enter into any material or long term contract or significant capital commitment or investment save in respect of office machinery and equipment reasonably required in the ordinary course of the business of the Company;[6]

(o) change the nature or scope of its business or undertake any business other than ....

(p) pay any remuneration to its directors;

(q) at any time enter into any contract or transaction

  (i) except in the ordinary course of its business and upon an arm's length basis or
  (ii) whereby any person would or might receive remuneration calculated by reference to the income or profits of the Company or whereby its business or any part of its business would be controlled otherwise than by its board of directors;

(r)[7] have as its accounting period any period other than a period of twelve months and have as the date of the end of any accounting period any date other than ....;

(s) have as its auditors any firm other than Messrs. ....;

(t) delay in rendering accounts to its customers or ordering goods and services required in the ordinary course of the business of the Company;

(u) alter the accounting policies heretofore adopted by the

---

[6] This paragraph will need modification if company cars are to be exempt.
[7] When the agreement contains an obligation on the majority shareholder to buy the minority shareholding at a valuation related to the Company's profits, this and the following three paragraphs of Clause 1(2) are designed to inhibit 'creative accounting'.

Company save as required by law or save in accordance with a general accounting practice hereafter adopted;

(v) in respect of any financial year of the Company pay or distribute any amount to its shareholders in any capacity by way of dividend bonus or other distribution of a similar kind including any management fee directors' fees salaries or remuneration and bonuses or other payments unless such amount shall be divided in the same proportions in all respects as the respective shareholdings of Holdings and Investments bear to the total share issued to the shareholders;

(w) (i) surrender the whole or part of any trading losses or other amounts eligible for relief from corporation tax pursuant to the provisions of the Income and Corporation Tax Act 1970 ('the Act'), section 258

(ii) surrender the benefit of the whole or any part of any surplus advance corporation tax paid by the Company in respect of any accounting period.

(3) None of the paragraphs of sub-clause (2) thereof shall be limited or restricted by reference to or inference from the terms of any other of those paragraphs.

(4) Holdings shall procure that in respect of the matters or things specified in the proceeding sub-clauses hereof which are (or but for this Agreement would be) within the competence of the board of directors of the Company no power or authority shall be delegated by the said board to any managing director committee or directors or other person or body of persons.

(5) Holdings shall indemnify the Company in respect of any tax payable by it or restriction of relief made to it in respect of that part of any capital gain accrued or deemed to have accrued to the Company and not received by the Company for its own use and benefit absolutely and Holdings shall not make against the Company in respect of such part of any capital gain any such claim as is contemplated by section 277(2) of the Act.

(6) Holdings shall procure that there shall be distributed as soon as practicably possible as dividends to the shareholders of the Company in respect of each accounting period not less than ... per cent of the lesser of its profits available for distribution within the meaning of Companies Act 1985, Part VIII and of its

net distributable profit (as hereinafter defined) of that accounting period. 'Net distributable profit' in relation to any accounting period means the net profit as shown by the audited statutory accounts for that period after making the following adjustments (if not already made) namely deducting all trading expenses and provision for corporation tax in respect of the profits of the period (after allowing for any reliefs or allowances) and extraordinary expenses and after deducting losses brought forward from previous accounting periods.

2. Holdings undertakes that as from and including the date of this Agreement and for so long as Investments is a member of the Company Holdings will provide interest free or procure the provision interest free of sufficient working capital for the Company to enable the business of the Company to be maintained at a level not lower than currently undertaken and without prejudice to the generality of the foregoing Holdings undertakes to provide interest free or procure the provision interest free of working capital facilities of £ .... For the purposes of this sub-clause the expression 'working capital' means capital exclusively available to fund the day-to-day trading of the Company and no part of which shall or may be required to fund any liabilities of the Company on capital account whether existing at the date hereof or not and whether or not quantified and whether or not contingent.

3. Investments shall have the right ('the Put Option') to require Holdings to purchase all the shares registered in the name of Investments and representing 24 per cent of the equity share capital of the Company[8] on the following terms:

(i) The Put Option shall be exercisable by notice in writing to Holdings during the [three] months immediately following the expiry of the period of [five] years commencing on the date of this Agreement.

(ii) The price at which the shares shall be purchased by Holdings (the 'Put Option price') shall be 24 per cent of [five] times

---

[8] As this clause is drafted the put option will be exercisable only if the minority shareholder maintains its stake at 24 per cent. Clause 1(2) will prevent the share stake of the minority shareholder being diluted so that only the voluntary acquisition or disposal of share by the minority shareholder will disentitle it from exercising its option.

the average of the pre-tax audited profits of the Company (or where the accounts for any accounting year have not yet been audited the pre-tax profits of the Company for that year after charging all proper and reasonable expenses) for the three accounting years of the Company preceding the exercise of the Put Option.

4. In the event of the exercise of the Put Option

(i) the Put Option price under Clause 3(ii) hereof shall be agreed between the auditors of the Company and accountants nominated by Investments (such accountants to have the right to examine the books and records of the Company during normal office hours on reasonable notice) and in default of agreement shall be fixed by an accountant nominated by the President for the time being of the Institute of Chartered Accountants acting as an expert and not an arbitrator whose decisions shall be final and binding on the parties hereto and

(ii) the sale of the shares to which the option relates shall be completed on the expiration of one month following the determination of the Put Option price. On completion the Put Option price shall be paid by banker's draft in exchange for duly executed transfers and the relative share certificates and the resignation of the Nominees incorporating in each case an acknowledgment that he has no claim against the Company.

5. Holdings undertakes to Investments that it will indemnify Investments against any tax payable by it or disallowance to it of any relief from tax under the provisions of section 460 of the Act in consequence of the circumstances set out in paragraph (c) of section 461 of the Act as a result of anything done by Holdings after it acquires the shares of Investments and in particular (but without prejudice to the generality of the foregoing) as a result of the Company paying an abnormal amount by way of dividend within section 467(3) of the Act.

6. (1) Save to give effect to the Put Option neither Investments nor Holdings shall transfer any of their respective shares in the Company or any beneficial interest in such shares without the consent of the other which consent unless otherwise expressly provided by its terms shall be deemed to be a consent to a

transfer subject to the pre-emption provisions contained in the following sub-clauses of this Clause.

(2) If a consent shall be given under sub-clause (1) hereof whichever Investments or Holdings desires to transfer its shares ('the Intending Transferor') shall before transferring any share in the Company give notice (a 'Purchase Notice') in writing to the other ('the Purchaser') of such desire stating the number of shares it desires to transfer and the sum which it fixes as the fair value per share.

(3) If within the period of one month after a Purchase Notice has been given the Purchaser shall not have notified the Intending Transferor in writing that it wishes to purchase the said shares at the price stated in the Purchase Notice the Intending Transferor shall at any time within three months after the expiration of the said one month be at liberty to sell the shares specified in the Notice to any person at a price being not less than that specified in the Purchase Notice provided that if Holdings shall be the Intending Transferor and the Purchase Notice shall have been in respect of a controlling interest in the shares of the Company Holdings shall not be at liberty to sell the shares as aforesaid unless it shall procure that Investments shall be given the identical opportunity similarly to dispose of the whole of its shareholding at the same price per share payable at the same time.

(4) If the Purchaser notifies the Intending Transferor that it wishes to purchase the said Shares then the Intending Transferor shall be bound upon payment of the price specified in the Purchase Notice to transfer the said shares to the Purchaser and completion shall take place one month after such notification.

7. In the event of a breach of any of the terms hereof by Holdings Investments shall be entitled (without prejudice to any other rights or remedies available to it whether under this Agreement or otherwise) within six months of the said breach coming to the knowledge of Investments by notice in writing to require Holdings to purchase within three months of the service of such notice the entire shareholding of Investments in the Company at a price per share calculated on the basis that the whole of the issued share capital of the Company is valued at an amount

equivalent to the fair value of the whole undertaking of the Company at the date of the breach as a going concern taking into account the value of its goodwill but without taking into account any reduction in the value of the goodwill or of its other assets caused or likely to be caused by the breach.

The price payable for each share shall equal the valuation of the whole of the issued share capital of the Company multiplied by the fraction where the numerator equals one and the denominator equals the number of shares in the Company issued and fully paid[9].

8. Holdings and Investments agree that they will each procure that the transferees or other successors in title of any shares held by them shall enter into an agreement with the other party hereto to the effect that any such transferee will observe and be bound by the undertakings and covenants herein contained so far as they affect the transferor of such shares and further to the effect that the transferee shall procure an agreement on the part of the transferee of any of the said shares from it in similar terms.

9. In this agreement any reference to a statutory provision shall be deemed to include a reference to that provision as statutorily amended or re-enacted.

10. Any notice to be given hereunder shall be sent by recorded delivery post to the registered office of the party to whom it is addressed and any such notice shall be deemed to have been served at the expiration of 48 hours after the same was posted.

IN WITNESS etc.

---

[9] If the company has issued shares of different classes, this clause will require modification.

Index